Shakespeare
New Dimensions

By the same author

G.K. Chesterton: A Critical Study

From Correction to Grammar and Stylistics

Shakespeare

New Dimensions

K. DWARAKANATH

PRESTIGE

Published by
PRESTIGE BOOKS
3/28, East Patel Nagar
New Delhi 110 008

2000

ISBN: 81-7551-072-2

Composed by Pivot Computers, Delhi 110 006
Printed by Dhawan Industries Offset, New Delhi 110 028

Contents

The Great Tragedies

Influence Studies

Language and Style

The Tragedy of Hamlet's Character

Hamlet is by nature pensive and thoughtful and hence, he does not act; he acts only when he is provoked and excited. When he acts, he does so rashly. Hamlet is obsessed with the second marriage of his mother, which, he thought, was hasty and incestuous. Hamlet also thought that Claudius was a very unworthy successor to his father, the late king of Denmark whom he had idealized. But Hamlet can do nothing about it and he goes on brooding over it for weeks.

Does Hamlet not act at all? He does, but only when he is provoked and excited. At other times, he can only express his emotions in his soliloquies. There are eleven exclamations and interjections in the first thirty-one lines of his first soliloquy. This statement itself needs an exclamation mark! At the end of this soliloquy, he gives expression to his feeling of isolation. He exclaims:

> But break my heart, for I must hold my tongue. (I.ii.59)

It is the same Hamlet who reacts fiercely and threatens to create another ghost by killing anyone who obstructs him from meeting the ghost of his father on the ramparts of the fort. Horatio and Marcellus doubt the intentions of the ghost and they try to hold the prince back. They only wanted to save Hamlet from what they regarded as a possible disaster. The prince is all but physically prevented from going with the ghost. But Hamlet loses his temper, becomes emotional and gives them a piece of his mind.

> Unhand me, gentlemen.
> By heaven, I'll make a ghost of him that lets me. (I.iii.84-85)

Hamlet is occasionally subjected to attacks of ungovernable temper. These are Hamlet's behavioural responses when he encounters the objects of his emotions. This is by no means sufficient reason to see a streak of madness in Hamlet's character. He is in full control of his mind and senses when he is not excited. Unlike a madman, he is not only painfully aware of his own weakness, but he can switch back to his normal conduct from his pretension as a madman whenever we wants to. When he is free from temper, his sensibility is characterized by wit, humour, courtesy, judicious comments and philosophical insight.

The readers expect Hamlet's parents to sympathize with and caution him. And they are not disappointed. Hamlet's father was well aware of his son's impulsive nature and when he denounces his brother Claudius, he calls upon his son to be careful in handling his mother, though she has married Claudius. The late king has come out of his grave to exhort his son to take revenge against Claudius, but not against Gertrude.

> Let not the royal bed of Denmark be
> A couch for luxury and damned incest.
> But howsoever thou pursue this act,
> Taint not thy mind, nor let thy soul contrive
> Against thy mother aught; (I.v.82-86)

The Alexander Shakespeare edited by B. Davies for the publishers, Collins, regards the word "taint" as a caution against endangering Hamlet's 'sanity.' The Cambridge edition of *Hamlet* of which John Dover Wilson is the editor regards it as an 'ominous injunction.' In both these editions, the ghost fears a rift in the lute of Hamlet's mind.

What exactly does the ghost of Hamlet's father mean by the word "taint"? Let us see what the word means in the other plays of Shakespeare before we turn to the Oxford English Dictionary. In *Twelfth Night*, Maria says to Olivia (IV.iii.13) that Malvolio is "tainted in's wits." Maria, Sir Toby and the Fool have worked out a plot to give the impression that the censorious and self-important steward is insane.

The use of the word "taint" does not lead to the same meaning in *Macbeth*, another masterpiece by Shakespeare. In this tragedy, Macbeth says with confidence, though he is in despair, 'I cannot taint with fear,' till Birnam Wood would come to Dunsinane. (V.iii.3) This sentence should be treated as passive voice as the Macmillan edition of the play rightly puts it, and its meaning is

'I cannot be tainted with fear.' Evidently, Macbeth himself cannot speak of his brain cracking. The usurper means only that his mind cannot be affected with fear or stained with the dishonourable thing called fear.

In *Hamlet*,the verb is a part of active voice and this fact makes a lot of difference. Secondly, in *Twelfth Night*, the verb is followed by the adverbial phrase "in's wits." Here in *Hamlet*, it has the noun "mind" as its object. It is a Transitive verb and, according to Oxford English Dictionary, the word "taint" as a VT means (1) weaken, (2) stain one's honour, (3) to affect with weakness, (4) to imbibe with some undesirable quality, (5) to hurt, to influence and the like. Therefore, it is not correct to assume that the ghost warned Hamlet against the onset of insanity. The supernatural visitor advises the prince not to allow his mind to be imbued with bias, animus or hatred against his own mother. The ghost is truly chivalrous! The more precise conclusion would be that moral lapses of this kind had better be left to the judgement of the heaven.

Hamlet's mind can become emotional very rapidly. But it needs provocation. The revelation that Claudius was not only adulterous but was also a murderer rouses the emotions of the Prince. As the ghost fades away, Hamlet trembles with emotion and swears to avenge his father's murder. In this soliloquy of seventeen lines, there are seven exclamations. This emotion, however, is not matched by action at all. Hamlet acts only when he is provoked, provided he encounters the object of his emotion immediately.

Hamlet's frivolity subsequent to his meeting with the ghost has invited comments from scholars and critics. This frivolity borders on irreverence and Hamlet uses even the idioms of magicians who performed magic on the stage. Is Hamlet's mind unhinged? Are his wits tainted? Our answer should be a clear "no." Hamlet had a deep aversion to Claudius who had married his widowed mother, though he was, according to him, far inferior to his dead father. Hamlet had no option but to bottle up his feelings as they were related to his mother's marriage only. Now another truth is revealed to him that Claudius who is sitting on the throne of Denmark, is a murderer. This is not just a moral lapse to be judged by God as was Gertrude's marriage, but a cognisable offence publicly condemnable. The discovery enables Hamlet to convert his bottled up feelings into public action. Hamlet experiences a feeling of triumph and that is the reason for his frivolity in imitating the voice of

Marcellus and alluding to the ghost in the language of magicians of his day. Moreover, by resorting to frivolity which is the opposite of solemnity prompted by the ghost, Hamlet can keep off the subject of his revelation and talk wild and whirling words, as Horatio puts it. But his wits are by no means tainted. The only thing in his character that worries the readers is his obsession with his mother's remarriage and his ungovernable temper. The transition between the magician's rite in the lines

> Well said, old mole! canst work i' th' earth so fast?
> A worthy pioneer! Once more remove, good friends.
> (I.v.162-64)

and Hamlet's announcement to Horatio and Marcellus that he would "put an antic disposition on" is quite smooth and, as desired by Hamlet, succeeds in bafling them. That Hamlet disliked acting to carry out the mission of revenge entrusted to him by his father's ghost is quite clear from the concluding lines of the scene. When he was excited by the traumatic discovery of the truth, he resolved to sweep to his revenge. But as the excitement and the accompanying emotion of triumph caused by the discovery of the crime of Claudius waned, his resolution weakened proportionately. The brooding and pensive Hamlet overshadows the rash and excitable Hamlet.

> The time is out of joint, O cursed spite,
> That ever I was born to set it right! (I.v.188-89)

Something external is always required to prompt Hamlet to act. Two months pass after the meeting with the ghost. The arrival of a company of actors stimulates him to action. Hecuba's theatrical grief in particular prompts Hamlet to take his plan forward.

The prince is subjected to emotion and excitement again. There are eight exclamations in the first forty lines of his second soliloquy in which he sees a stark contrast between himself and the actor's role. In fact, the soliloquy begins with an emotional self-condemnation. There are six references to passion in the play and two of them are found in this soliloquy:

> Ay, so Good bye to you! Now I am alone.

O, what a rogue and peasant slave am I!
Is it not monstrous that this player here,
But in a fiction, in a dream of passion,
Could force his soul so to his own conceit (II.ii.545-49)

The player's emotion is imaginary, but the prince has a cause for real passion. In fact, the cause itself can rouse passion in him. The actor is only enacting the role of Hecuba and in contrast, Hamlet's situation is a fact of life. He imagines what the actor of Hecuba's role would have done, if he were in Hamlet's position.

What's Hecuba to him and he to Hecuba,
That he should weep for her? What would he do,
Had he the motive and the cue for passion
That I have? He would drown the stage with tears,
And cleave the general air with horrid speech!
Make mad the guilty . . . (II.ii.555-60)

Hamlet condemns himself for being a man of words and not a man of action. He is no better, he goes on to say, than a drab who is known for squandering her feelings in words.

No doubt, Hamlet allows his brain to cool and plans the play to verify the guilt of Claudius. But this plan of action is only a means of obtaining the proof. The play is the thing wherein he would catch the conscience of the king.

The third soliloquy of Hamlet is the most famous stage soliloquy in the world. Hamlet realizes that in his case, there is a big gap between thinking and action. In fact, Hamlet is his own critic. It is true that there is no visible sign of emotion in this soliloquy of thirty four lines. There is just one exclamation which is uttered when Hamlet describes Ophelia whose sight interrupts his meditation.

Does this absence of interjection mean that Hamlet has at last ceased to be emotional? It would be a failure of perception, if we think so. By nature, Hamlet is excessively emotional, more emotional than what the occasion can sustain and in that state of emotion only, he acts and acts only rashly. That is the tragic flaw of his character. At other times, he is cool. Hamlet is certainly giving expression to emotion even in the soliloquy, 'to be or not to be,' though the number of exclamations is insignificant.

To perceive emotion, we need not always turn to outward signs. Remember Hamlet leaping into the grave of Ophelia in a fit of excitement to challenge Laertes's claim. We need not always turn either, to physiological states like heart-beat or colouring of the cheek. According to psychology, there are three aspects of emotion. "The first is *behavioural* i.e., the kind of activity in which the emotional person engages. This is generally easily detected and is of the waving-arms-around variety. The second is *physiological* which consists of considerably more discreet behavioural signs, not always obvious to the observer, but which may be detected by suitably sensitive instruments. The third is *psychological* or introspective and this refers to the 'state of mind' of the individual when he is angry or whatever." (*Pears Cyclopaedia*, 94th edition, p. Q 25) The psychological variety cannot be directly sensed by the other individuals. To what type then does Hamlet belong? Hamlet's emotion when he leaps into the grave of Ophelia can be easily detected. The second variety of emotion analysed above cannot be profitably discussed here, since it involves the presence of the person before us and the sensitive instruments with which we can detect the emotions. Coming to the third variety, it is easy to see that Hamlet belongs to this last variety also, since he is by nature introspective. Hamlet does not belong to just one type but fits into two types.

That a young and full-blooded prince who is an heir to the throne of Denmark should think of suicide to avoid life's ills and misfortunes is sufficient indication that he is in an emotional state of mind. Such a state is not normal.

> For who would bear the whips and scorn of time,
> Th' oppressor's wrong, the proud man's contumely,
> The pangs of despis'd love, the law's delay
> The insolence of office, and the spurns
> That patient merit of th' unworthy takes,
> When he himself might his quietus make
> with a bare bodkin? (III.i.70-76)

In the first soliloquy too, Hamlet had considered suicide and had given up that thought, because it was forbidden by God, but he had elaborated a reason for such a thought, namely, his mother's hasty and incestuous marriage with Claudius. In contrast, this soliloquy mentions no personal reason for the contemplation of suicide and the misfortunes he mentions are general. It is quite possible that Shakespeare had read the works of thinkers like Montaigne and picked up the material for this soliloquy from their writings.

This soliloquy is important from another point of view. For the first time, Hamlet gives expression to the view he has taken of his own character, though characteristically he has generalized it as though it is common to all human minds:

> Thus conscience does make cowards of us all;
> And the native hue of resolution
> Is sicklied over with the pale cast of thought,
> And enterprises of great pitch and moment
> With this regard, turn their currents awry
> And lose the name of action. (III.i.83-88)

A detailed contemplation of the proposed action and its pros and cons weakens the resolution to act, till it loses the name of action. This chapter on Hamlet's character began with the statement that Hamlet does not act when he is pensive and thoughtful which he generally is and that he acts rashly when he is excited. However, this frailty of Hamlet is not the frailty of all. In the play itself, Laertes and Fortinbras are strong contrasts with Hamlet.

Hamlet employs images of sickness to describe his weakness. Thinking too much, Hamlet does allow his resolution to become pale just as sickness robs a man's face of his natural healthy colour. When Hamlet suddenly sees Ophelia who, he thought, had jilted him, Hamlet attacks her with the barbs of his sarcasm, pushes her away and walks out of the place. This is the only scene in the play where Hamlet is alone with Ophelia. Action even by an emotional person depends upon the degree of offence given to the victim. For the more dramatic behavioural response of Hamlet's emotion, we must wait till he meets his mother alone in her bed room when she sends word to him in order to rebuke him.

Horatio is Hamlet's best friend and rouses his admiration. Hamlet's praise of Horatio has no secret motive and he does not have to flatter his friend for getting his co-operation in obtaining the proof of his uncle's guilt. Horatio is a man of equanimity and philosophical detachment. Hamlet knows that his friend is

A man that fortune's buffets and rewards
Hast ta'en with equal thanks; and blest are those
Whose blood and judgement are so well comeddled
That they are not a pipe for fortune's finger
To sound what stop she please. (III.ii.68-72)

Hamlet admires those traits in Horatio's character which he himself lacks. He has no axe to grind when he praises Horatio profusely. Hamlet was in the world of courtiers whose common characteristic was to flatter those who had power and money. Horatio is the odd man out in this world. Hamlet becomes emotional and embraces Horatio—there is no stage direction for this gesture—when he concludes his full-throated praise with the words

Give me that man
That is not passion's slave, and I will wear him
In my heart's core, ay, in my heart of hearts,
As I do thee. (III.ii.72-75)

Hamlet thinks that unlike Horatio, he is a passion's slave and that he is swayed by emotions. He is, undoubtedly, right. Admiration is a positive emotion and when the object of this emotion is encountered, even the optimum response takes the form of a gesture like embrace. But the emotion of hostility is a different matter and it needs a different kind of response. Sitting beside Ophelia at the commencement of the play, he hurts her with the barbs of his caustic comments. He rebukes Rosencrantz and Guildenstern by giving them a piece of his mind.

On way to his mother's room, he sees Claudius. Hamlet is in a triumphant mood as a result of the success of his plan. The prayer of Claudius and what Hamlet construed as confession and repentance prevent him from acting. The scene reminds Hamlet of the complaint of his father's ghost that Claudius murdered him when he was relaxing, without giving him time for confession, repentance and absolution. Hamlet feels that Claudius will go to heaven if he is stabbed to death while he is praying and repenting.

The first major behavioural response of Hamlet can be seen in the closet scene. He is alone with his mother for the first time in the play. The meeting is more an encounter and takes place at the initiative of Gertrude herself. Gertrude rebukes Hamlet but

Hamlet strongly feels in every nerve of his body that it was she who should be rebuked for what he considered to be her moral infirmities.

> *Queen*: Hamlet, thou hast thy father much offended.
> *Hamlet*: Mother, you have my father much offended.
> (III.iv.9-10)

Gertrude's rebuke boomerangs; Hamlet pays a Roland for an Oliver, using the same sentence structure as his mother had used with devastating effect. Hamlet at that moment was gloating over his success in obtaining the proof of the crime of Claudius and he had come to meet Gertrude, riding the crest of the wave of triumph. He is provoked by this reference to Claudius and all the bottled up feelings are let out with a vengeanee.

Provocation comes from another source also. Polonius raises a cry when Hamlet treats his mother rudely. Fools rush in where angels fear to tread. Hamlet mistakes him for Claudius and kills him. This is the first death resulting from Hamlet's action. But Hamlet's mind is so dominated by the emotion related to his mother's character and actions that when it finds an outlet, there is no room in it for the feeling of remorse at this ghastly mistake. There is in his mind no regret or fear of consequences. Hamlet has found the target of emotions and he embarks upon the course of freeing his emotions which he had restrained for nearly four months. He gives his mother a piece of his mind. Hamlet's feelings find their match in action, but he does not go beyond pushing her on to her couch so that she has no alternative but to listen to his charges. His feelings are related to her moral lapse only. Hamlet becomes a moral prosecuter and his mother the accused against whom he lists several charges till he is emotionally exhausted. Even his father's ghost does not succeed in restraining him. What stands out prominently is Hamlet's obsession with the physical side of his mother's remarriage with Claudius who was an unworthy man even without the charge of murder. Hamlet's prosecution is thorough, because he has waxed eloquently as a prosecutor and judge. After this traumatic experience, Hamlet calms down and his relations with his mother become normal. He experiences a calm of mind, all passion spent, because Gertrude has realised her folly.

Vehemence is totally absent in Hamlet's fourth soliloquy occasioned by the contrast between himself and Fortinbras, the prince of Norway. It is significant to note that Hamlet has not met the foreign prince whom he admires, but has only heard about his military plans. In the soliloquy prompted by the actor's recitation of Hecuba's role, there are eleven exclamations in a passage of forty one lines. But in the present soliloquy, there are only three exclamations in a passage of thirty three lines, though in both the soliloquies, Hamlet criticizes himself for not taking prompt action.

That Hamlet's action is the behavioural response of his emotion can be illustrated by his confrontation with Laertes. This action was precipitated by excitement which seized the prince during Ophelia's funeral. Laertes's action at a particular place and at a particular time provokes Hamlet and subjects him to ungovernable temper. Laertes's leaping into his sister's grave to demonstrate his love and grief precipitates Hamlet's feelings and excitement. This leads to Hamlet's behavioural response in the form of his leaping into Ophelia's grave himself to challenge Laertes on what he calls the theme of their love for Ophelia:

> I lov'd Ophelia; forty thousand brothers
> Could not, with all their quantity of love
> Make up my sum. What will thou do for her? (V.ii.263-65)

It is not the character of Laertes as such that rouses Hamlet's emotion and its behavioural response, but only a particular action at a particular moment. That is why this emotion does not last long. As a matter of fact, Hamlet feels sorry when emotion is followed by cool thought. He expresses his regret when he later talks to Horatio, his confidant.

> But I am sorry, good Horatio;
> That to Laertes I forgot myself;
> For by the image of my cause I see
> The portraiture of his. I'll court his favours,
> But sure the bravery of his grief did put me
> Into a towering passion. (V.ii.75-80)

It was the demonstration, the theatricality of Laertes's grief that provoked him. Their emotions were the same, but Hamlet had to match the behavioural response of the son of Polonius because he was also guided by emotion. In his confrontation with Ophelia's brother, he warns him:

> I prithee take thy fingers from my throat;
> For, though I am not splenitive and rash
> Yet have I in me something dangerous,
> Which let thy wiseness fear. Hold off thy hand. (V.i.252-55)

Hamlet is aware that only normally, he is not irascible and rash, and that at times, he is.

Gertrude herself whom it is easy to misunderstand reveals a rare understanding of Hamlet's strength and weakness, when she tries to save her son:

> This is mere madness;
> And thus awhile the fit will work on him;
> Anon, as patient as a female dove
> When her golden couplets are disclosed,
> His silence will sit drooping. (V.i.278-82)

A mother ought to know her son's character. But Gertrude's insight does not go deep enough. Hamlet does not lose his temper by fits and starts. He is, without doubt, an introvert, an emotional person. The rashness of his action is due to the provocation. Such a situation is transformed by him into a visible behavioural response.

Hamlet uses the word "rash" in two succeeding scenes. In the first of them, he uses it to warn Laertes. Later, in his talk with Horatio about his experiences on board the ship, Hamlet dwells on the benefits of rashness. As a result of his rash intrusion into his courtiers' cabin Hamlet discovers that they are carrying with them what is virtually his death warrant.

> And prais'd be rashness for it—let us know
> Our indiscretion sometimes serves us well,
> When our deep plots do pall; (V.ii.6-9)

The Adverb of Manner, "rashly" is a part of the sentence that Hamlet speaks later, immediately after Horatio's affirmative response. Hamlet praises rashness and goes on to say that rashly he groped in the dark for the cabin of Rosencrantz and Guildenstern and stole the sealed papers that were addressed to the king of England. He opened the letter and read it. The contents of the letter made him realize that the end justified the means. Stealing and reading the letter addressed to someone else was, no doubt, unethical, but the contents of the letter gave him a shock. Provoked by his uncle's perfidy, Hamlet changed the contents of the letter so that the carriers of the letter would be his substitutes for the English excecutioner's axe. Even the grim comment of Horatio,

> So Rosencrantz and guildenstern go to't. (V.ii.56)

does not unsettle Hamlet's sense of certainty that the two courtiers were aware of the contents of the commission they were carrying. Hamlet is relaxed after what he calls his rashness has saved him. He is shocked into the belief that

> There's a divinity that shapes our ends
> Rough-hew them how we will. (V.ii.10-11)

Hamlet thus shifts a part of the burden of responsibility to the invisible providence.

The discovery of his uncle's perfidy proves to be an impetus to his promised revenge. After the invitation to play the fencing match with Laetrtes, there is no distance between plan and action. Hamlet is drawn into the vortex of action and driven towards his mission. He is allowed no time to brood over what he has not done and what he should do.

There is no choice from now on between psychological response and behavioural response; no choice between the possibility of suffering the slings and arrows of outrageous fortune and taking up arms to oppose them. Action follows swiftly: provocations and excitement are followed by the encounter with the objects of emotion. The tumultous scene involving four killings begins on a note of courtesy and conciliation. Hamlet seeks pardon from Laertes and explains to him his rudeness during Ophelia's burial.

> Give me your pardon, Sir, I have done you wrong;
> But pardon't, as you are a gentleman.
> This presence knows,
> And you must needs have heard how I am punish'd

> With a sore distraction. (V.ii.217-21)

Dr. Samuel Johnson says in his criticism of the play that Hamlet was dishonest in his explanation to Laertes. I do not think that Johnson is right. By the words "sore distraction," the prince does not mean any mental disturbance, but his susceptibility to excitement which would be sometimes ungovernable. No doubt, he calls it madness twice in the same speech, but it should be taken only in the metaphorical sense. It is true that Hamlet causes suffering to others by overreacting when he is provoked, but the pity of his situation is that he is not his normal self at such moments. That is his tragic flaw, the flaw that causes his tragedy.

Revenge had become Hamlet's sole mission in his life after the explosive revelation by the ghost. The use of poison both in the drink and the sword was the immediate provocation that spurred Hamlet's action of revenge. Here the emotion of intense hostility found the object of that emotion not only immediately, but within reach. Therefore, we find the optimum behavioural response in the form of stabbing Claudius.

For once Hamlet becomes a man of action. The emotion and excitement generated by the treachery of his uncle find their counterpart in Hamlet's action which is his response. The word "poison" or "venom" catapults him into a commanding position.

> O villainy! Ho! Let the door be locked.
> Treachery! Seek it out. (V.ii.303-4)

Hamlet acts as a man of royal blood. Taking control of the situation, he not only acts, but commands others. For a while, the readers are taken aback by the sudden emergence of a man of action. They see an astonishing transformation. As yet, Hamlet does not know the source of treachery, and as the repentant Laertes reveals it, Hamlet leaps like a panther on to the platform and stabs the king.

> The point envenom'd too!
> Then venom, to thy work. (V.ii.313-14)

While stabbing Claudius and forcing him to drink poison, Hamlet swears furiously, "thou incestuous, murderous, damned Dane.' What spurs Hamlet is not the realization of the danger to his own life, but the 'incest' and the murder committed by Claudius. The situation allows no time for thinking too precisely on the event. As in case of the cry of Polonius for help from behind the curtains, there is no time for 'conscience' to make Hamlet a 'coward.' This is the reason of the success of Hamlet's mission. The emergency does not allow merely physiological or psychological response, but maximum behavioural response. "The rest is silence."

No other play of Shakespeare has attracted as much critical attention as Hamlet. Even the lay readers turn to this tragedy again and again, perplexed and fascinated. No other play has been produced on the stage as many times as the tragedy of the prince of Denmark. But some problems remain. They are: (1) Hamlet's obsession with his mother's second marriage (2) his dwelling on the physical side of the married life of his mother during his confrontation with her in her room (3) Hamlet's callousness and possible error in sending Rosencrantz and Guildenstern to their death (4) Hamlet's self-dramatization at the time of his death and (5) Hamlet's choice of Fortinbras as his successor to the throne of Denmark.

It is not so much the death of Hamlet's father as his mother's remarriage that casts the pall of gloom on Hamlet's life. In his highly emotional soliloquy with its numerous exclamations, the prince deplores Gertrude's hasty remarriage. He questions the wisdom of his mother in marrying a person who was a very unworthy successor to the late king of Denmark. But at the heart of all these disapprovals, we find the notion that Gertrude was voluptuous and it was her sensuality that led her to her second marriage in total disregard to her middle age, forbidden relation and unworthiness of Claudius. But how long should Hamlet go on lamenting this development?

The entire state of Denmark is reconciled to the queen's remarriage and the accession of Claudius to the throne. But Hamlet does not, at least to the former. Hamlet who is disgusted with Gertrude's second marriage is a full-blooded young man considered by Ophelia to be a model for courtiers, soldiers and scholars.

> O, what a mind is here o'erthrown!
> The courtier's, soldier's, scholar's eye, tongue, sword;
> Th' expectancy, and rose of the fair state,
> The glass of fashion and mould of form,
> Th' observ'd of all observers—quite, quite down!
>
> (III.i.151-55)

True, Hamlet is a student of philosophy. But he is also a young man in love with Ophelia. How can a man in the full blossom of his youth and pink of health become so pessimistic and gloomy over the second marriage of his mother? Hamlet's emotion over this fact does not seem normal.

It is one thing to feel disgusted by the queen's re-marriage, but quite another to let his life be clouded by gloom, pessimism and prejudice against women. Hamlet goes to the extent of exclaiming that he would have preferred to be a dead man, if the everlasting had not fixed his canon against self-slaughter. What we see here is not a momentary feeling; it colours his whole life. Is his emotion not excessive, the reader is left wondering.

Hamlet is a keen observer and his range of observation includes the manifestations of his mother's sensuality. He regards even her love of her first husband as nothing more than an appetite.

> Why, she would hang on him
> As if increase of appetite had grown
> By what it fed on; (I.ii.143-45)

Hamlet allows this feeling to become an obsession with him at the expense of all good things of life that are enjoyed by young men of his age. He pursues this matter with a vengeance during his meeting with his mother, after his successful production of Gonzago's play. He describes to her face her love in terms which any other young man would have found too delicate to mention.

> Have you eyes?
> Could you on this fair mountain leave to feed
> And batten on this moor? Ha! Have you eyes?
> You cannot call it love; for at your age
> The hey-day in the blood is tame, it's humble,
> And waits upon judgement; and what judgement
> Would step from this to this? (III.iv.66-72)

Again, the imagery is that of eating and appetite. Hamlet takes his mother to task and the charge against her is her sensual love. The question that arises here is whether a young man would subject his own mother to this kind of questioning. Hamlet compares her mother's voluptious relations with her two husbands. In fact, he goes on to prescribe a remedy for her enslavement by sensuality.

What right has Hamlet to condemn his mother's sensual love which is, after all, a personal matter? A young man who can write love letters to Ophelia in a sensuous language expresses disgust at his mother's love as if Claudius and Gertrude are pigs.

> Nay, but to live
> In the rank sweat of an enseamed bed,
> Stew'd in corruption, honeying and making love
> Over the nasty stye! (III.iv.93-96)

Even the intervention by the ghost of Gertrude's first husband does not calm the storm in Hamlet's mind.

> Mother, for love of grace,
> Lay not that flattering unction to your soul,
> That not your trespass, but my madness speaks;
> It will but skin and film the ulcerous place,
> Whiles rank corruption, mining all within
> Infects unseen. (III.iv.146-51)

Hamlet's disgust and anger at his mother's sensuality find an outlet in the images of skin diseases. The son goes on in the same emotional state to advise her to desist from going to her husband's bed and if such an abstinence is difficult, practise it step by step and day by day! Hamlet's emotions and consequent eloquence need here in their sweep the vocabulary of a saint, priest, physician and psychiatrist. The ghost of his father whom he had idealised intervenes and tries to restrain him. Thankfully, Hamlet's emotional tirade against his mother proves to be an eye-opener to her.

> O, Hamlet, speak no more!
> Thou turn'st my eyes into my very soul;
> There I see such black and grained spots
> As will not leave their tinct. (III.iv.89-92)

Hamlet's regret at the killing of Polonius by mistake is rather perfunctory: there is no feeling of remorse. Polonius had, like a detective, tried to pry into Hamlet's strategy of antic disposition which he had put on. As a result of the courtier's intervention,

Hamlet had lost the love of Ophelia and as for his strategy, he had found Polonius a frustrating factor. The prince is a hypersensitive soul and his callousness matches the extreme degree of his sensitiveness.

> Thou wretched, rash, intruding fool, farewell!
> I took thee for thy better. Take thy fortune!
> Thou find'st to be too busy is some danger. (III.iv.33-35)

The angry young man is without doubt callous in reprimanding the dead man; this is the price Polonius pays for his meddlesome nature. The more sensitive a man is, the more callous he will be towards the victim of his emotion. The emotion of hostility that dominates Hamlet's mind has allowed no room for any other feeling.

A similar explanation can be given for Hamlet's callousness in his dealing with Rosencrantz and Guildenstern. He sends them to the executioner's axe without batting an eye lid under the impression that they were a party to the conspiracy against him, though he has no unquestionable proof. In fact, he had already sealed their fate on the day of his meeting with his mother and he told her that he enjoys paying them back in their own coin.

> They bear the mandate; they must sweep my way
> And marshal me to knavery. Let it work;
> For 'tis the sport to have the engineer
> Hoist with his own petard; (III.iv.206-9)

Horatio's grim remark, after Hamlet tells him what he has done, does not disturb his conscience. Evidently, this is due to the frustrations of an extremely sensitive man. As long as the issues to which an emotional man is sensitive are not resolved, he is likely to be callous in proportion to his frustration towards the party that created those issues.

Hamlet is frustrated even in his revenge against Claudius. He does kill Claudius to avenge his father's murder, but a victim of the poisoned sword of Laertes, he is not able to explain to the world the reason for slaying Claudius and causing the deaths of several others. This frustration cannot, however, justify Hamlet's self-dramatization at the moment of his death.

The prince is concerned only with what he calls his wounded name which he wants to be cleared by Horatio who should continue to live in this 'harsh world.' But he has enough breath to express his support to the possible claim of Fortinbras to the throne of Denmark. Though Fortinbras is not a Dane, Hamlet supports the election of the Norwegian prince as the king of Denmark which is bereaved with the death of Hamlet and Claudius.

Hamlet who had delayed action for a long time—he is himself painfully conscious of this delay—finds a minor provocation even in the last moments of his life. When Horatio in an uncharacteristic mood tries to take his own life in the Roman style, the prince acts swiftly, seizes the cup of poison and exhorts his friend to draw his breath in pain in this harsh world to explain to the world the mystery of Hamlet.

The prince of Denmark acts only under the stress of emotion and provocation. At other times, he only thinks and does not act.

Conflict of Generations in *King Lear*

Is it not possible to view the tragedy of *King Lear* from the angle of the conflict of two generations, the older and the younger? The play begins with a brief account of the birth of Edmund: in other words, with the comment made by Gloucester, a member of the older generation on Edmund, his younger son. The play ends literally with a comment by Edgar, a member of the younger generation on King Lear and the Earl of Gloucester, the most important members of the older generation. The significance of this structure should not be lost sight of.

The theme which I am trying to locate in the play should not be mistaken for what under the same is suggested nowadays. Today, we do talk of generation gap and the conflict between the values held dear by the older generation and the revolt against them by the men and women of the younger generation. The leftist cause, religion, class, tradition, monarchy—these are some of the values that have divided the two generations in the post world-war era.

In *King Lear*, there are no ideologies or causes of a very general nature dividing the two generations. But there is a conflict caused by other things. Rebellion is there, but not of the kind which we notice today in the conflict between the two generations. Rebellion in *King Lear* does not have a broad, philosophical basis, though some rationalization is attempted by the younger characters. Even in this drama, the elders cannot absolve themselves of the responsibility of giving cause for the revolt of the younger sort. Maybe, some law, institution, or custom is to blame: maybe, it is ancient. Nevertheless, the older generation may not have given any thought to it, nor found it necessary to change it, let alone abolish it. The result is that the older generation gets identified with what the younger generation regards as unjust or moribund and this situation is naturally the breeding ground of revolt. Custom, conservatism, restraint and old age become in a way interchangeable terms, while revolt, demand for change and subjective emotion are the characteristics of the younger sort.

When the two generations do not see eye to eye with each other, conflicts become inevitable. This is true even when no ideology or tradition offers itself as the spur for kicking the sides of conflict. But there is also in some cases the resolution of the conflict through realisation of error and forgiveness. This realisation may extract a heavy price and the conflict may be resolved only after a violent upheaval. Even in such cases, it is not difficult to see the nature of revolt.

The cynicism and callousness underlines Gloucester's remark on his natural son in the opening scene. In fact, the play begins with the appearance of the characters of the sub-plot first, a little while before the crisis of the main plot unfolds itself. The old man's comment is worth quoting. Admitting that Edmund is his illegitimate son, he says that he no longer blushes to acknowledge him. He adds further in his dialogue with Kent that Edmund is dearer to him than even Edgar who is not only his legitimate son, but also older than Edmund,

> But I have a son, sir, by order of law, some years elder than this, who yet is no dearer to me in my account. Though this knave came something saucily to the world before he was sent for, yet his mother was fair; there was good sport at his making, and the whoreson should be acknowledged.
>
> (I.i.18-23)

Gloucester is an earl, not a working class man, but he talks crudely about the pregnancy of Edmund's mother. In the passage quoted above, he gloats over the fun he had, resulting in the birth of Edmund. All this he says to Kent right in the presence of Edmund himself. The old man does not realize that what was fun or sport for him might be a stigma for his natural son. He does not realize what effect it will have upon Edmund. Even the Earl of Kent who is a bold and sensible man does not try to restrain Gloucester who is sowing the wind to reap the whirlwind. Gloucester's indecorous remarks continue, piling stigma on stigma. Gloucester casually adds that Edmund was out for nine years and he would be out again. It may be noted that Kent who even defies King Lear when he ill-treats his daughter, Cordelia, finds no reason to advise Gloucester to be more cautious in his remarks on his illegitimate son.

Kent's comment on the birth of Edmund gives the impression that he regarded fornication as some forgivable fun. Gloucester and Kent do not seem to realise their responsibilities as members of an older generation. Gloucester does not apparently subscribe to the Biblical saying that if parents eat sour grapes, their children's teeth will be set on edge.

The older generation can, it must be conceded, show signs of constructive and positive attitude towards the next generation. Lear's initial plan of divesting himself of his responsibilities as a ruler and placing them on the shoulders of the youngsters is certainly commendbale. At least it is sound in principle. It is only natural, therefore, that rights and responsibilities should be transferred to the younger people and that the older generation should retire and take rest. Lear announces his plans with the best of intentions along those lines.

> Give me the map there. Know that we have divided
> In three our kingdom; and 'tis our fast intent
> To shake all cares and business from our age, while we
> Unburdened crawl towards death. (I.i.36-40)

The younger generation represented by his three daughters including Cordelia is not surprised by the decision taken by their father. They are prepared to shoulder new responsibilities. By accepting its new rights and duties, the younger generation will allow King Lear his well deserved rest. Each generation has its sphere earmarked for it and it is graceful and natural on the part of the king to shed his authority in a formal sense and ask the younger generation to bear new responsibilities. The old king would like to grow older gracefully without worries and cares.

In the play, as it happens, what goes wrong is not the plan itself, but the basis on which it is executed. It is logical that the youngsters accept both rights and responsibilities while the old men live a retired life and give advice only when it is solicited. In principle, the king's plan is guided by wisdom. If the plan does not yield the expected result, the king can blame nobody but himself. The king's love for flattery, self-will and obduracy frustrates his plans. It is a different matter that Lear suffers more than what he deserves.

Cordelia represents the younger generation as much as her sisters do, and she does so better. At the outset, it may appear strange, if not absurd, to describe her as a rebel. But she is a rebel in the true and best sense of the word. A hypocrite cannot be a rebel and Cordelia is no hypocrite. How can the persons who always try to find out who has the power and, therefore, try to please him be accepted as rebels? Against whom are they rebelling? Cordelia is no such flatterer. She revolts against the criterion adopted by the king and by his daughters for different reasons. This revolt of the younger generation requires immense courage and capacity for suffering to say

> Haply, when I shall wed,
> That lord whose hand must take my plight shall carry
> Half my love with him, half my care and duty.
> Surely, I shall not marry like my sisters,
> To love my father all. (I.i.99-103)

Courage of conviction and capacity to suffer without hesitation are the hallmarks of a true rebel and Cordelia has these traits in plenty. She does come between the dragon and his wrath, and she does not make from the shaft when the bow is bent and drawn. The youngest princess has another essential quality of a rebel and that is to sacrifice anything for the cause of truth. Cordelia leaves her country with only the imprecations of her father and with no share in her father's kingdom. She is a true rebel and sticks to truth irrespective of the consequences. She is courageous, though not clever.

Even the devil can quote the Bible. Goneril and Regan say that it is right and natural that the old man should transfer his kingdom to the younger generation when he is becoming senile due to old age. The elder sisters even talk of virtue that has been disregarded by Cordelia, according to their view. When Cordelia takes leave of them, this is what Goneril says to her, speaking on behalf of Regan and herself.

> You have obedience scanted,
> And well worth the want that you have wanted. (I.i.277-78)

Goneril and Regan are aware that Lear loved Cordelia most and they justify their own action by seeing signs of senility in his treatment of their youngest sister. Goneril is right when she observes:

> He always loved our sister most, and with what poor judgement he hath now cast her off appears too grossly.
> (I.i.287-89)

While making an attempt to escape from the reality of what their own conscience tells them, they stumble upon the exact truth. But unlike the Earl of Kent, they do not spring to the defence of their sister, nor do they protest like him. They are not rebels in the true sense of the term. What they want is only gain.

The remarks of Goneril and Regan immediately after the departure of their sister can be put in the mouth of any sensible young man who is wary of the infirmities of the older generation. I am not referring to Regan's remark only, but Goneril's which is more elaborate.

> The best and soundest of his time have been but rash: then must we look from his age to receive not alone the imperfections of long engrafted condition, but wherewithal the unruly waywardness that infirm and choleric years bring with them.
> (I.i.292-93)

These are the younger generation's remarks on the weaknesses of the older generation. If they are taken out of context, these words appear quite appropriate in any public debate on the need to retire old people and put younger people in their place. But as I said earlier, even the devil can quote the scriptures.

Edmund also can convert his self-seeking into a cause. Law, custom, older generation—these three collocate easily. The older generation has grown with traditions, customs and laws and it has neither the determination nor the motivation to change them. What was good for me is good enough for the young people—this is the typical attitude of the older generation.

Edmund, the younger son of the Earl of Gloucester, finds the prevailing law and custom galling. Why should the estate of his father be inherited only by Edgar, his half-brother, and why should the younger son be deprived of it? Edgar was born a few months earlier and can that be enough reason?

> Wherefore should I
> Stand in the plague of custom, and permit
> The curiosity of nations to deprive me,
> For that I am twelve or fourteen moonshines
> Lag of a brother? (I.ii.2-6)

Even if Edmund were a legitimate son, he would not have inherited the estate of his father according to the custom of primogeniture. In the time of King Lear it was a custom with the force of law. "Curiosity" in the above soliloquy means the scrupulousness in observing the custom. The young man rebels against this plague of custom and he cannot understand how the older generation can tolerate it. This custom makes a lot of difference to him, because it prevents him from inheriting the estate of his father on the ground that he is not the first-born. Evidently, the people who have grown old with this custom have never thought of changing this custom.

Just as Cordelia rebels against her father's concept of love based on monopoly, Edmund, the younger brother, rebels against the concept of inheritance, which confers monopoly on his elder brother. There is, of course, a difference. Cordelia, the youngest daughter, does not target her father. Rather, she has sympathy for him. But Edmund makes his father his target and he goes to any length to hurt him to gain what he wants. If he had campaigned for a change of custom, he would have been a true rebel and champion of the younger generation. But he chooses a different path.

There is another custom of which he is a victim. Custom attaches a social stigma to the birth of an illegitimate child and the victim has to carry this stigma throughout his life. Like the younger issue, the illegitimate son is deprived of the right to inherit his father's estate. But Edmund does not skulk and his banner of revolt flutters as breezily for the bastards as for the younger issues. He champions the cause of the children born on the wrong side of the bed and his rhetoric reminds us of the eloquence of Shylock who champions the cause of persecuted race. One wonders whether Shakespeare intended to raise a laugh in the theatre by giving a cheeky liveliness to Edmund's rhetoric.

Sometimes, Shakespeare puts the words of the devil in the mouth of a good man. The principle that prompts the revolt of the young against the old can be found in the forged letter supposed to have been written by Edgar.

> This policy and reverence of age makes the world bitter to the best of our times, keeps our fortunes from us till our oldness cannot relish them. I begin to find an idle and fond bondage in the oppression of aged tyranny, who sways, not as it hath power, but as it is suffered. (I.ii.47-52)

Notwithstanding the presence of figures of speech, particularly, Hendiadys, it is not difficult to see the theme of the conflict of generations even in this forged letter. Reverence, oldness, aged tyranny, best of our times, idle and fond bondage, oppression—these are the key words, the notes in the orchestration of the revolt of the younger men against the older. The younger generation has no patience to wait. The older generation seems oppressive and tyrannical, with the result that the younger sort revolt against it.

The theme of the conflict between the interests of the two generations is present in the veneer of logic laid on the advice supposed to have been given by Edgar. How long should the young wait? Should they wait till it is too late to enjoy what is, after all, their due? Are not the old oppressive and tyranical? Is not the traditional reverence shown to customs and old people detrimental to the young? We begin to hear the voice of the Angry Young Man as we start understanding the implications of the forged letter and the reader is tempted to think that the conflict between the two generations is the theme of the play.

Edmund who has drafted the letter which he attributed to his elder half-brother can also quote him in the absence of the latter. Edmund goes on to quote Edgar in his reply to a question by his credulous father.

> Never my lord. But I have heard him oft maintain it to be fit that, sons at perfect age, and fathers declined, they should be as ward to the son, and the son manage the revenue. (I.ii.73-74)

The statement brings into focus once again the mutual obligations of the older and the younger generation. The old cannot go on enjoying the family revenue endlessly, exercising supervision, if not control, not only over revenue but also over the children who have grown up. The young have their own life to live and, therefore, they must have their own revenue. In other words, the older and the younger generations should exchange places.

Ideology alone cannot and does not shape the course of events. The individual characters also have a role to play. Edmund is an unprincipled man and he knows it; but what is astonishing is that such characters also indulge in rationalization. Goneril does not have to acquire what she desires. She has already been given this, unsolicited. But she is young: Lear is old and also authoritarian and, no wonder, Goneril is cross with him. The old man has not become wise, though he has advanced in age. Goneril, like Edmund, rationalizes the conflict between the old and the young.

> Idle old man,
> That still would manage those authorities
> That he hath given away! Now by my life,
> Old fools are babes again, and must be used
> With checks as flatteries, when they are seen abused.
> (I.iii.17-21)

Notice again the theme of the conflict between the older and the younger generations. The old man has not retired and he is not living a life of religious devotion and meditation. He is still a man of the world and he exercises his authority which he has given away. He continues to be self-willed and authoritarian. Lear's imperfections bring him into conflict with the youngsters who have ambition, strength and youth that can take on responsibilities. The latter are, therefore, critical of the oldsters who have none of these assets any more.

In *King Lear*, the wicked characters belong to the younger generation: they always emphasise their rights and never their duties. In contrast, the older generation emphasises the duties of the youngsters who ought to be guided by values like gratitude and reverence for age. Such an argument is not by itself unreasonable, provided it is restrained by a sense of obligation to the old. The wicked young characters seize this argument and exploit it fully for promoting their own material advancement bereft of moral values.

To Goneril, the king, her father, is only a foolish old man who has given away his kingdom to the youngsters at the right time, but who continues to exercise his royal authority without any responsibility. She thinks that the old need rebukes now as frequently as they received flatteries when they had power. The princess places truth upside down and she takes full advantage of her father's self-will and obduracy. For the sake of the defence of her action and for the sake of appearance, she erects a theory which looks rational and which can be applied by the younger generation in similar situations and in different places:

> As you are old and reverend, should be wise. (I.iv.240)

Goneril has a long list of complaints against the king and his knights whom she charges with noisy and disorderly conduct and even with lust which turns her mansion into a brothel. For all we know, she might have been grossly exaggerating the foibles of her father and his entourage. After all, offence is the best way of defence!

Fortunately, the play does not mislead the readers, for there can be in a play more than one view of the same issue. Even the court jester accuses the king of foolishness, but as it happens, it requires wisdom to understand the Fool. When the Fool says,

> Thou shouldst not have been old till thou hadst been wise. (I.v.43)

he is not echoing what Goneril had said a few lines earlier. There is an apparent contradiction, no doubt, but the contradiction is resolved when the ironical remark makes it known that what is wisdom in Goneril's remark is foolishness in the jester's remark.

One of the dimensions of the relation of the older generation with the younger generation is the child-father relation. This is an inviolable bond regarded as sacred by all religious faiths. Even the villain who is ready to violate it for his own personal gain can illustrate this religious commandment provided he is hypocritical. Edmund's plot against his half-brother can take him to the farthest limit of hypocrisy:

> But that I told him the revenging gods
> 'gainst parricide did the thunder bend,
> Spoke with how manifold and strong a bond
> The child was bound to th' father— (II.i.45-48)

If irony is the instrument of the Fool, hypocrisy is the instrument of the illegitimate offspring of Gloucester when either of them dwells on the offspring-parent relationship. Goneril and Regan, however, do not have to resort to either irony or hypocrisy, because they are now in possession of what they wanted. They can afford to talk bluntly, but they also generalize about old age and young age. Regan is no less 'rational' than her sister and they are birds of the same feather. When Regan hears Lear's complaints against Goneril, she springs to Goneril's defence, because ostensibly Lear is old and senile and should be ruled by the younger people. Regan talks about old age and its infirmities.

> O, Sir, you are old;
> Nature in you stands on the very verge
> Of confine. You should be ruled and led
> By some discretion that discerns your state
> Better than you yourself. (II.iv.143-47)

Once again we can see that the two sisters are quite adept in theorizing about the older and the younger generation in order to defend their treatment of their father. In old age, nature stands on the very limits of its confine and, therefore, Lear should be led by the younger generation represented by her and Goneril. The two sisters who are young have the normal physical and mental faculty which enables them to see Lear's mind better than Lear himself. The old man's fault is not the division of the kingdom, but his old age. After all, he gave away his kingdom at the right time and that was a wise decision!

The general remarks made by one sister can be attributed easily to the other, because their attitude of filial ingratitude is the same. Goneril defends herself in a language which can be used by Regan quite appropriately.

> How have I offended?
> All is not offence that indiscretion finds
> And dotage terms so. (II.iv.191-93)

Goneril drives home the point that the king, their father, is mentally feeble due to old age and, therefore, he is not capable of discretion. The conflict between the two generations reaches the climax. Lear turns to God who is the only strength of the weak.

> You heavens, give me patience—patience I need!
> You see me here, you gods, a poor old man,
> As full of grief as age, wretched in both. (II.iv.267-69)

The father is conscious of the inescapable fact that he is old and he bemoans that his grief is as great as his age. In the conflict between the two generations, he wants the heavens to side the old because they are ill-treated by the younger generation. Lear realizes that old age is wretched and that he cannot secure even his true needs, let alone luxuries.

That Lear is painfully conscious of his old age is not surprising, for he is more than eighty years of age. When in his tirades against the storm in the heath, he describes himself as 'a poor, infirm, weak and despised old man' he is not thinking of what his daughters regard as dotage and mental feebleness. Lear has in mind his physical frailty resulting from extreme old age. The reason for his plight is nothing other than filial ingratitude, according to his thinking. He does not look upon himself as a party in the conflict between the older and the younger generations. This concept is the creation of Goneril, Regan and Edmund.

Edmund is convinced that the young have no chance at all, unless the older generation moves out. He is waiting for the latter event which he tries to bring about.

> This seems fair deserving, and must draw me
> That which my father loses—no less than all.
> The younger rises when the old doth fall. (III.iii.22-24)

All is grist that comes to his mill. A machiavellian by nature, he does not hesitate to exploit the secret of the invasion by France imparted to him by Gloucester, to bring about the downfall of Gloucester, his father. This treachery is given the veneer of the theory that the young cannot have a life of their own, unless the old fall. If Gloucester does not fall, his son will make him fall.

Goneril and Regan have risen without any effort on their part, unless sleek hypocrisy is regarded as an effort. But Edmund, a bird of the same feather has not yet, and hence he sacrifices every principle for the sake of supplanting the old.

I will persevere in my course of loyalty, though the conflict
be sore between that and my blood. (II.v.24-25)

This is the assurance he gives to the Duke of Cornwall. Edmund is prepared to be an informer and betray his own father in order to supplant him. Unlike Goneril and Regan, Edmund does not theorize about dotage and infirmities of old age, only because no man who is old has become a burden upon him. But he must rise, he cannot wait indefinitely till the natural causes remove his father and elder brother.

It is noteworthy that Lear and Gloucester do not rationalize the reversal of the situation resulting from the treatment meted to the fathers by their children. Gloucester wants winged vengeance to overtake the ungrateful and monstrous children (Refer to III.vii.65) but he formulates no theories about the young.

Edgar stands apart and is a class by himself in the group of the younger characters in the play. The machinations of his younger brother and the credulousness of his father drive him into the disguise of a destitute, but he never becomes cynical, neither does he seek solace in fulminating against the older generation even after he sees his own situation placed upside down in the life of King Lear. Even in the most wretched condition as poor Tom, he can voice the Biblical commandments including 'obey thy parents.' What is significant, the play concludes with his homage to the older generation in a language that bears repetition in similar situations in all ages to come.

The oldest hath borne most: we that are young
Shall never see so much, nor live so long. (V.iii.325-26)

This he says notwithstanding the tragic mistakes made by the older men. Patience, tolerance and humility breathe from every word in this speech. What is important from the point of view of this essay can be glimpsed in these concluding lines of the play. This theme is subsumed in the larger theme of the absurd and Godless universe which is unresponsive to the needs of the decent people whose suffering is out of all proportion to their mistakes of judgement.

Othello: Points without Counterpoints

Is *Othello* a play of unproved accusations and claims? When an accusation is made, we expect it to be either denied or established. In *King Lear, Hamlet* and *Macbeth*, the charges are proved or denied in one sense or the other. Moreover, they are made openly, in broad day-light. But in *Othello*, there are complaints and accusations, innuendoes and insinuations that do not lead to denials or proofs. Iago complains that in the army, he has been superseded by Cassio who was selected by Othello for the post of the lieutenant and, therefore, he has no reason for liking the general. Who is Cassio, he asks derisively. Cassio was a non-combatant, an arithmetician, a calculator who had not seen a single battlefield. He supercedes Iago, an ensign already in the service of the army.

> And what was he?
> Forsooth, a great arithmetician,
> A fellow almost damned in a fair wife;
> That never set a squadron in the field,
> Nor the division of a battle knows
> More than a spinster; (I.i.18-24)

Iago has seen action in many a battle, at Rhodes and Cyprus, but he, though a combatant, has been superceded by a debitor and creditor. In his next speech, Iago accuses Othello of overlooking his seniority, what he calls gradation and goes on to charge Othello with graft and favouritism. He puts it so effectively that today an official can quote Iago's words in his complaint that the time honoured seniority has been overlooked and that he has been passed over, since promotion is effected by graft and favouritism.

The question that is relevant here is whether the accusation against Othello is refuted or not. Let us grant that seniority alone is not the criterion at the time of promotion to certain types of posts. But what were the compelling reasons for appointing Michael Cassio who was not a combatant, but only an accountant? What were the virtues of this comparatively junior man whom Iago calls a debitor and creditor? Nowhere in the play an attempt is made by any character who has no axe to grind, least of all, by Othello, to explain and justify the choice of Michael Cassio. In the other tragedies of Shakespeare, we have both points and counterpoints but the same cannot be said of *Othello*.

There is also a charge within a charge. Not content with downgrading Cassio, the superceded ancient describes Cassio as "a fellow almost damn'd in a fair wife." This comment too is not refuted anywhere in the play and Cassio's wife, granted that she is beautiful, has no defender. If Cassio is cuckolded, where is the proof? At any rate, what is the basis for the gossip? The play leaves the question unanswered.

When I say that the accusations and claims remain without being proved or rebutted in the play, I am not referring to comments that are belied by the events that take place later. Brabantio's bitter remark is one such example. Though resigned to his daughter's marriage with Othello, he cautions the moor that Desdemona who deceived her father may deceive her husband also. This is an unromantic view and a possibility, but we know that the subsequent events speak volumes for Desdemona's rectitude and devotion to Othello. In a similar way, another generalization that covers Desdemona and others is also belied by the events which follow. Desdemona is white and young: Othello is not so young and he is a moor. Iago propounds his theory that such a marriage will not succeed. His realism tells him that Desdemona should change for youth. After the initial excitement ends and the peacock glow of romance fades, Desdemona will turn to men of her own race and to men younger than Othello. This is another realistic, if not cynical, view and we know that it is also proved wrong in the exceptional case of Desdemona whose love for Othello does not diminish.

> She must change for youth: when she is sated with his body, she will find the error of her choice: she must have change, she must. (I.i.356-57)

What Iago does not realize is that there are splendid exceptions to his theory and that a marriage of true minds is an over-fixed mark that looks on tempests and is never shaken.

After making the general observation quoted above, Iago says in the same breath

> If sanctimony and a frail vow betwixt an erring barbarian and super-subtle Venetian be not too hard for my wits and all the tribes of hell, thou shalt enjoy her; therefore make money.
> (I.iii.353-56)

Here Iago is not making a general comment on Venetian women. On the contrary, it is a reference to Desdemona whom he describes as a super-subtle Venetian. In fact, he pairs Othello and Desdemona, speaking of them as "an erring barbarian and super-subtle Venetian." It is not clear from the play why Iago thinks of her as super-subtle. The entire play unfolds only her noble and gracious character with a mind as clear as a mountain stream. The view presented by Iago is neither corroborated nor denied.

Iago has no reason to think ill of Desdemona, since his grudge is only against the moor who has appointed Michael Cassio as his lieutenant, passing over Iago. He may talk about her caustically later in a language of innuendoes, but now there is no motivation. In her speech in which she defends her elopement with Othello before an audience of the Duke and the senators including her father, Desdemona does speak of the separation of her duty towards her father from her duty towards her lover and husband. But her speech is as sentimental as it is logical. In fact, it is her genuine feelings and not so much the logic that convince us of the rightness of her stand. Desdemona says no less and no more than what Cordelia says while addressing her father at the time of the division of the kingdom. That is why it is surprising to hear Iago paying her a left-handed compliment.

One of the gravest insinuations made by Iago again goes without confirmation or refutation. As a villain, Iago gives reasons in his soliloquy for the hatred he is harbouring in his mind.

> I hate the moor;
> And it is thought abroad that 'twixt my sheets
> He's done my office. I know not if't be true; (I.iii.384-86)

Iago himself admits that his charge of Othello's fornication is based on rumour. But the accusation is so grave and goes so much against the grain of Othello's character that we expect to hear views both for and against it. But we are disappointed. What matters is not so much the suspicion as the gravity of the charge made against Othello, but he does not seem to be aware of this hearsay at all. To say that Shakespeare wanted to present the non-romantic aspect of human character side by side with the romanticization of Othello does not dispel the cloud of doubt, in spite of Emilia's vehement refutation later on. She is a person involved and not a third party and therefore, her refutation does not help us draw any conclusion.

The readers of the play should be careful, lest they take Iago's statements at their face value. Assuring Roderigo of his continued support in his attempt to win Desdemona, Iago says:

> Mark me with what violence she first loved the moor but for bragging and telling her fantastical lies. And will she love him for still prating? (II.i.219-21)

When Othello described the background of Desdemona's love for him at a meeting of the Duke and the senators, he could not help describing what he had said in reply to Brabantio's enquiry.

> Her father loved me; oft invited me;
> Still questioned me the story of my life,
> From year to year, the battles, the seiges, fortunes
> That I have pass'd
> I ran it through, even from my boyish days,
> To the very moment that he bade me tell it; (II.i.128-33)

In response to Brabantio's request, Othello was prompted to run through his own past from his boyhood to his immediate past and he could not help describing the battles and seiges, escapades and adventures in which he had a part and in which his courage and heroism had been called into play. It was his hair-raising adventures that inspired Desdemona's love for him and if Othello was a typical braggart, the Duke and the senators would not have totally relied on Othello for the defence of Cyprus from the Turkish invasion. We have evidence here to suggest that Othello was not indulging in self-praise, but was speaking the truth. In contrast, Iago's dismissal, cynical as it is, that all those battles and adventures are fantastical lies is not followed by any evidence. Othello does lead the Italian navy to Cyprus to ward off the Turkish invasion and he remains a hero in the eyes of the readers. What Iago says cannot be regarded even a partial truth.

The villain's comments and insinuations are mostly found in his soliloquies and that fact itself is proof that what he is saying is not intended to please or provoke anybody. It is in one such soliloquy that Iago states:

> That Cassio loves her, I do well believe't. (II.i.280)

What the cad is saying is not a conjecture but a statement made on the basis of his belief. But where is the evidence for it? Earlier, before the arrival of Othello, when Iago, Desdemona, Cassio, Emilia and others are relaxing and waiting for the arrival of Othello in the Cyprus harbour, Cassio makes a chivalrous gesture by holding the palm of Desdemona and smiling upon her, but even Iago had not taken this gesture as proof of Cassio's love for his "captain's captain." In fact, Iago describes these gestures as 'tricks' and 'courtesy.'

> If such tricks as these strip you out of your lieutenantry, it had been better you had not kissed your three fingers so oft which now again you are most apt to play the sir in.
> (II.i.171-74)

The villain knows that what Cassio had done was only a gesture of courtesy, a chivalrous gesture, but the same Iago now says in his soliloquy that Cassio loves Desdemona and that he does well believe it. This comment is not made to mislead anybody, because it is made in his soliloquy and Iago says that he believes it. This is another instance to show that Iago makes observations and comments for which there is no basis.

In the same soliloquy Iago returns to the suspicion that casts a slur on the personal character of Othello. Iago claims that he too loves Desdemona, though not for the sake of sex, but

> Partly led to diet my revenge
> For that I do suspect the lusty Moor

Hath leaped into my seat, the thought thereof
Doth like a poisonous mineral gnaw me inwards;
And nothing can or shall content my soul
Till I am evened with him, wife for wife; (II.i.288-93)

Tooth for tooth, eye for eye, wife for wife! But as I said earlier in a similar context, this highly damaging remark is not either supported or denounced in the play by any objective observer. Iago's comment is very defamatory but the author of the play does not extend it beyond a mere suspicion in the mind of Iago. There is no doubt, however, that Iago feels it very strongly, so strongly that he is continuously tormented by this suspicion which even goads him to revenge. In fact, if we take his speech at face value, the main action of rousing Othello's jealousy which leads to his tragedy is only an alternative to his proposed plan to commit adultery with Desdemona as revenge. Still no proof is provided in the play either to support or deny this grave charge made by Iago against the moor. Emilia, no doubt, denies the charge and condemns it, but Othello himself remains unaware of the charge.

This particular soliloquy from which the above quotations are taken and discussed makes me wonder whether Iago is going mad. See how in the very next remark, he states his suspicion that Michael Cassio too might have fornicated with Emilia, Iago's wife.

I'll have our Michael Cassio on the hip,
Abuse him to the Moor in the rank garb—
for I fear Cassio with my night cap too— (II.i.299-301)

The reader feels like pitying Iago whose wife, Iago suspects, has committed adultery with not only Othello, but also with Cassio: with Iago's boss and with the younger man who superceded Iago in promotion. Again, nowhere in the play is there a shred of evidence to point the accusing finger at Michael Cassio, let alone Othello. But Iago states his suspicion breezily and if Cassio also suffers as a result of Iago's plan to make Othello jealous, so much the better, since it would be double revenge, killing two birds with a single stone. Iago is not brash, but dead earnest: still there is no evidence either to support or repudiate his comments, though Cassio is no saint, as far as sex is concerned. Iago's boast that he would

Put the Moor
At least into a jealousy so strong
That judgement cannot cure (II.i.294-96)

should be taken with a grain of salt. Is jealousy the right word for the discomfort and agitation in the mind of Othello when his mind is poisoned by Iago with the tale that his wife Desdemona and his lieutenant Michael Cassio are on intimate terms? The answer depends partly upon the definition of the word, jealousy, and partly on the answer to the question whether Othello was certain that Desdemona was unfaithful to him.

We have not yet exhausted all the comments and slanders of Iago that are not subsequently supported or denied by a third party. In the first Act of Iago's plot against Othello to bring about discord between Othello and Cassio, there is a scene of drunkenness in which Cassio has been involved. When Montano asks Iago whether Cassio is often under the influence of wine, Iago answers.

'Tis evermore the prologue to his sleep;
He'll watch the horologue a double set,
If drink rock not his cradle. (II.iii.129-31)

This is canard, there is no doubt. Only a few lines earlier, we ourselves read that Cassio was most reluctant to drink again because he had already 'drunk' a cup and in a subsequent scene, we find him bitterly regretting his drunkenness in the citadel during the watch. Iago has his own way of besmirching the characters of people. He praises without reservation the positive aspect of a person's character first and pretending to hesitate, he starts insinuating till his insinuation ends in a slander. For, has he not himself said a minute earlier that Cassio is a "soldier fit to stand by Caesar and give directions"? What a splendid tribute! In fact, this is only one of the many examples of beauty, splendour and nobility, both moral and physical, that we notice in the images of *Othello* which is so unlike *Macbeth, King Lear* and *Hamlet* in this respect. But this aspect of the play needs to be elaborated in a separate paper.

Othello himself does not have any occasion to defend or justify his appointment of Cassio at the cost of the supercession of Iago. The suspicion that Othello had fornicated with Emilia, Iago's wife, is never challenged by anybody and we have to depend upon what we know about the moor's nobility to dismiss the ancient's suspicion and accusation.

The villain has assured Roderigo that he could have Desdemona, if only Iago's cunning is able to break the frail vow between what he calls an erring barbarian and a super-subtle Venetian. A day later, after making sure that Othello is willing to hear any disparagement of Desdemona, Iago makes a sweeping generalization about Venetian women to drive home the point that Desdemona is not the faithful wife:

> I know our country's disposition well;
> In Venice, they do let heaven see the pranks
> They dare not show their husbands; their best conscience
> Is not to leave't undone, but keep't unknown. (III.iii.203-6)

Once Iago realizes that Othello is turning a willing ear to hear the criticism of Desdemona, he presses further with this generalization presenting an uncomplimentary picture of Venetian women of whom the senator's daughter is one. This is slander against a nation and Othello can believe it, since Iago, as he puts it, is a Venetian and he knows the national characteristics of the Venetian men and women, whereas Othello is an alien, a non-white and a moor. Iago needs this damaging generalization because he is slandering Desdemona, a fellow Venetian and Othello has no reservation in accepting it, since it suits the mood in which he finds himself.

One of the pawns in Iago's strategy is the formulation of the theory that Othello's marriage with Desdemona is incompatible and, therefore, it would not last. Even this view of the general's marriage is neither supported nor contradicted by anybody in the play. How can a young and good-looking European lady be matched with a dark African of advanced age? According to Iago's theory, Desdemona's choice of Othello is not natural in any sense.

> Ay, there's the point: as—to be bold with you—
> Not to affect many propos'd matches
> Of her own clime, complexion and degree
> Whereto we see in all things nature tends—
> For, one may smell, in such, a will most rank,
> Foul disproportion, thought unnatural. (III.iii.229-34)

This is a theory and generalization which appears to be quite convincing, but nobody rebuts it on the ground that love is blind and that Desdemona is an exception who sees beauty in this thick-lipped moor. In all other plays of Shakespeare, a cynical view of this kind meets with its counterpoint in the observations of some other characters in the same play. But in *Othello*, there are no counterpoints to the points made by Iago and only the events that follow contradict what he generalizes. After learning that the Turkish fleet did not reach Cyprus and that there was no imminent war, the Duke of Venice asks Othello to return to Venice. This is what we learn from Othello himself.

> Sir, I obey the mandate,
> And will return to Venice. (IV.i.260-61)

But Iago, in one of his last schemes which he hatches to ward off the danger to his life and limb from Roderigo, tells him that Othello is proceeding towards Mauritania.

> O, no; he goes into Mauritania . . . (IV.ii.225)

Mauritania is in Africa, but according to Othello, who had read the letter from the Duke, he is returning to Venice. In the play, there is no confirmation or refutation of what Iago says by an observer, other than Iago or Othello. The latter's statement has greater authority since he makes that statement to Lodovico after reading the letter brought by him to Cyprus.

In one of the scenes in Othello's lodging, when Desdemona is preparing to go to bed, Emilia does talk a bit but flippantly about adultery in reply to a question by Desdemona, after she has crooned a sentimental song about a young woman betrayed and deserted by her lover. But can we take this seriously? Emilia is a woman with her feet placed firmly on the earth. She is a realist, while Desdemona is a romantic. But she is only trying to cheer up Desdemona as the latter is very despondent. Emilia may not be a romantic; nobody expects Iago's wife to be one. But her defence of a woman who is prepared to commit adultery for the sake of the world, that is, if the world is offered in exchange, should be taken only as a joke and as a possible conduct outside the romantic and idealistic vision. In a later scene when all lies stand exposed, Emilia herself denounces that gossip.

It is significant to note that at least one remark of Iago is confirmed by a third party who can be expected to be objective. In the beginning while revealing the genesis of the hatred for Othello, the ancient had contrasted himself with Michael Cassio with a view to denigrating the latter. Iago had seen action in the battlefields, whereas Cassio was, according to Iago, a mere calculator and certainly a non-combatant. Towards the end of the play, when tragedy begins to unfold itself gradually, we find Lodovico saying that the ancient is "a very valiant fellow."

Iago himself is cornered after the murder of Desdemona is disclosed and he neither contradicts nor stands by what he had said on earlier occasions. When Othello asks

> Why he hath thus ensnared my body and soul? (V.ii.344)

Iago gives no reasons for his wicked actions.

> Demand me nothing: what you know you know.
> From this time forth I never will speak a word.

Let us not ask him questions, so that he will tell no lies. The utterances of Iago we have considered so far include statements, observations and even a resolve. The affirmative accusations of Iago are all lies and the readers would have no hesitation in agreeing with Samuel Johnson that Iago is a blatant liar.

It is true that there is no third party or observer who dismisses Iago's statement as false. It is only the events and the characters who unfold themselves as the play gets under way that show how false Iago's statements are. But there are some utterances of Iago in the form of predictions and judgements that deserve the reader's attention a little more.

Some of the predictions and even a resolve of the villain are based on his reading of the situations and, therefore, the logic of arguing that they are false does not present itself. One such thing is his confident prediction that the marriage of the moor and the Italian damsel would not last long. A psychologist who has written on literature regards such statements as half truths. Granting that psychology is a great branch of learning, can we accept the existence of half truth, besides the two opposites, namely, truth and falsehood? Maud Bodkin observes in her study of literature that the plot of *Othello* is built not merely on falsehood but also on partial truths besides untruths. Maud Bodkin's statement is a classic example of mistaking the trees for the wood. Shakespeare's play includes the multiple vision in which there is more than one possibility, while the play revolves round one such possibility only.

In *As You Like It* also, a possibility outside the romantic vision is projected, though humorously, but the play remains essentially a romantic comedy. When Orlando states that he would die for love, Rosalind, herself a romantic, remarks: "men have died from time to time, and worms have eaten them, but not for love." (IV.i.86-87)

Maud Bodkin gives the example of Desdemona's romantic elopement with Othello and her quick marriage with him and she bases her illustration on Iago's comment that Desdemona is a super-subtle Venetian and that Othello's account of his battles and adventures is a tissue of fantastic lies. It is true that there are a number of incompatible factors in the marriage like age, race and colour but then true love is blind, as Jessica says in *The Merchant of Venice*. I think Shakespeare was concerned with particular characters like Othello and Desdemona and the non-romantic possibilities in the play are only possibilities but not probabilities. What Desdemona would have done in the subsequent months if she had not been murdered is only a matter of speculation and that would not be the tragedy of Othello as Shakespeare had conceived it. Such a possibility lies outside the scope of his play. Here we are concerned only with Shakespeare's *Othello*.

Before concluding this essay, I would like to add that it is not clear from the play whether Othello's own tragic error was caused by jealousy, a sense of honour or jurisprudence. In some circumstances, he does act like any jealous husband.

The male jealousy of Othello shares some common features with the male jealousy in *The Winter's Tale*. In both it is the paddling of palms of the other man that is taken as the unimpeachable evidence of the physical intimacy of the wife with the other man. King Leontes expresses his discomfort at the sight of what he regards as the intimacy of Hermione and King Polixenes, the king of Bohemia who was his guest. He does not mind his queen's success in persuading the royal guest to prolong his stay, though king Leontes himself had failed earlier in his persuasion.

This entertainment
May a free face put on, derive a liberty
From heartiness, from bounty, fertile bosom,
And well become the agent; it may, I grant:
But to be paddling palms, and pinching fingers,
As they now rare, and making practis'd smiles,
As in a looking glass, and then to sigh, as 'twere
The mort of the deer—, that is entertainment
My bosom likes not, nor my brows. (I.ii.111-19)

This reaction can be compared to Othello's declaration

'tis not to make jealous
To say my wife is fair, loves company,
Is free of speech, sings, and dances well; (III.iii.185-87)

The gesture of physical intimacy was taken as the proof of infidelity. The talents of an artistic kind or her fairness would not make Othello jealous. In an earlier scene, to drive home the point that Desdemona is becoming too friendly with Cassio, Iago asks Roderigo:

Did thou not see her paddle with the palm of his hand?
(I.ii.251)

The act of paddling with the palm of the hand of the other man cannot be a mere coincidence if we compare the jealousy of Leontes with the jealousy of Othello. In both the cases, it is the first act of misunderstanding which is changed into jealousy.

Secondly, as in *The Winter's Tale*, in *Othello* also the attempt made by another character to disabuse the mind of the jealous man succeeds in making the jealous man angrier and adds fuel to the fire. Camillo's earnest efforts to disabuse the mind of Leontes fail. The king of Sicily goes to the extent of accusing Camillo of lying. In *Othello*, the moor dismisses the advocacy of Desdemona with contempt.

In another circumstance, he stresses the cause which means in the context the offence which a court can take notice of. If Desdemona is not punished with death, she would betray more men and, therefore, a preventive action like that which is conceived by a judicial mind is needed. In some other circumstances, the moor speaks of the sense of honour that drove him to murder. Desdemona herself has given away her honour by giving away—Othello thought that she did—the fabulous handkerchief he had presented to his wife. Othello himself is not certain which factor motivated his tragic action. He seems to be certain that he was overwrought and, as a result, he was perplexed in the extreme. He wants the beholders of the murder and his own suicide to speak of Othello as a person

> not easily jealous, but being wrought
> Perplexed in the extreme. (V.ii.47-48)

Othello has not ruled out jealousy but his state of mind is quite complex. His mind had been continuously wrought and over-wrought by Iago's clever insinuations and, at the same time, he could not help submitting to the commanding idealization of Desdemona. Othello was also certain that he was sacrificing Desdemona on the altar of honour.

He did not hate Desdemona at all, he believes. When asked earlier what should be said of him, he answers:

> Why, anything:
> An honourable murderer, if you will;
> For nought but did I in hate, but all in honour. (V.ii.296-98)

Othello, according to this justification, killed Desdemona in defence of the character which a married woman should have. He believes that Desdemona had given away the handkerchief to Cassio, an adulterer, who in turn had given it as a gift to a prostitute whom he had been visiting. Is that not a dishonorable thing, he could ask himself. But the moor also acts as a prosecutor, judge and executioner at once.

> It is the cause, it is the cause, my soul.
> Let me not name it to you, you chaste stars!
> It is the cause. Yet I'll not shed her blood,
> Nor scar that whiter skin of hers than snow
> And smooth as monumental alabaster—
> Yet she must die, else she'll betray more men. (V.ii.1-6)

Othello is judging an offence and while he does not name it, the implication in the second sentence is clear. It is, as he believes, the compromise of her chastity. The judge should act in time, lest she should betray more men. Othello is a reputed army general to whom honour is of utmost importance. When he is disarmed by Montano and his sword is given away to Gratiano, the general resigns himself to the loss of honour.

Jealousy is a mean and petty emotion and it is reflected in the images and rhythms of the language spoken by the person affected by it. Othello is a magnificent warrior of commanding personality and traces his lineage to noble families. His love of Desdemona whom he romanticizes needs for its expression a language of majesty and sensuous images. He would not like to shed her blood. Yet she should die because if she continues to live, she will betray more men including the man who was her partner in adultery. Othello may put out the light of the candle in Desdemona's bed room, but he will always be able to light it again, when he wants it. But if he puts out the light of her life, he needs nothing less than the "Promethean heat" to reilluminate the candle of her life.

If Desdemona had not been guilty—she is not, but he thinks she is—Othello would not exchange her for the whole world; not even for a world—"of one entire and perfect chrysolite." At his journey's end, after he has realized the magititude of his error, he likes the world to speak of him as

> One whose hand,
> Like the base Indian, threw a pearl away
> Richer than his tribe; (V.ii.347-49)

The purity, the sensuous beauty and the splendour of these images of Othello's language when he idealizes Desdemona should be contrasted with the images and rhythms of his language a few hours earlier than the murder of Desdemona. The moor who thinks that Desdemona is so gentle and noble that she can "sing the savageness out of a bear" has recourse to images like devil, monster, cuckold and the like when he is stung by the poison of jealousy. In just a couple of scenes, he uses the word devil five times and other hell-related words also five times, while the words monster and cuckold serve his purpose four times and twice respectively. Words like strumpet, whore and bawd are strewn across the web of his emotional language and when sexual jealousy seizes him, he can speak even a crude language. Othello's expression splutters when under an emotional stress caused by Iago's direct charge against Cassio, he exclaims.

> Lie with her! lie on her—we say lie on her when they belie
> her.—Lie with her! 'Zounds, ther's fulsome! (IV.i.38-39)

This splutter is in stark contrast with the smooth sailing of Othello's poetic language studded with lovely, sensuous and majestic images when he is idealizing Desdemona. The jealous Othello who had earlier found the language of poetry to match his sensuous romanticization of Desdemona's person exclaims now whether he should continue to

> keep it as a cistern for foul toads
> To knot and gender in. (IV.ii.62-63)

Who can deny after reading this passage that the noble moor was not seized by jealousy? We must, of course, concede the fact that Othello does not belong to the average breed of jealous husbands. He idealizes Desdemona and is not jealous of her talents and gifts. He will not live a life of suspicion and uneasiness, eavesdropping and prying day after day. He is a man of decisive action and acts promptly to get rid of either jealousy or the woman. It is difficult to agree with Coleridge when he argues that "Othello does not kill Desdemona in jealousy, but in a conviction forced upon him by the almost superhuman art of Iago, such a conviction as anyone would and must have entertained who had believed Iago's honesty as Othello did." Jealousy is one of the driving forces behind the moor's action, but not the only one. Othello was also actuated by his concept of 'cause' and his equally important cause of 'honour.' This makes his motives highly complex and apparently mutually contradictory. In judging Othello's motives, the readers of Shakespeare's play are as much 'perplexed in the extreme' as Othello himself.

Heaven and Hell in *Macbeth*

The events in Shakespeare's *Macbeth* ostensibly occurred in the middle of the eleventh century which is an important transition period in the history of Europe including Scotland. The Dark Ages were drawing to a close, yielding place to the Middle Ages which were less dark, but not enlightened yet like the seventeenth century. Therefore, it is not unreasonable to seek in Macbeth words and phrases of religion concerning blessing and judgement escaping from the lips of the characters who committed the basic crime and those other characters who were ranged against the criminals.

Macbeth became the king of Scotland in the year 1040 and was killed in the year 1057. Evidently, the Scottish thane and king belonged to the Christian era. Christianity in those days was Roman Catholicism. Aversion to sin. belief in the judgement by God and repentance are some of the basic features of religion in general and Christianity in particular. It is these very features that are conspicuously absent in the lines attributed to Macbeth after the murder of King Duncan. In the pre-murder career of Macbeth, these words of religion related to the life after death make their appearance once. Gratitude to God which is another cardinal feature of Christianity is absent in the utterances of Macbeth. The practical demonstration of the truth of one of the prophecies of the weird sisters very soon after its utterance has a traumatic effect on Macbeth's early career, but it does not make him exclaim to thank God even perfunctorily.

The first of the three notes of welcome that were spoken by the witches was the practical demonstration of their clairvoyance, but the second was the first of the two real prophecies that shape Macbeth's future which proves to be tragic. The fulfilment of this prophecy within a few minutes of its unsolicited utterance can be expected to have a far-reaching effect on the career of Macbeth, a very ambitious man. A great honour has been conferred upon the valiant general, without his seeking it. But what is his immediate reaction? Macbeth does not thank king Duncan, let alone thank God. Not even an involuntary exclamation of that kind escapes his lips. His first reaction is an aside;

> Glamis, and Thane of Cawdor:
> The greatest is behind. (I.iii.117-18)

Macbeth does thank Rosse and Angus; there is no doubt about it, but he does so only mechanically and his turning to Banquo shows that he has switched over to his ambition which he has been nursing all the while. A Christian of the Middle Ages that he is, he does not have a word to thank God for the unsolicited but well-deserved honour.

In his soliloquy, Macbeth mentally conceives the shortcut to the throne of Scotland. Neither the supernatural soliciting of the instruments of darkness nor the unethical nature of the murder bring to Macbeth thoughts about God, the fountainhead of morality. On the contrary, the playwright employs his poetic powers to present the images of the physical sensations of the evil of parricide, the treasonable murder of one's own king.

> If good, why do I yield to that suggestion
> Whose horrid image doth unfix my hair,
> And make my seated heart knock at my ribs,
> Against the use of nature? (I.iii.134-37)

The dethroning of the king who symbolises order and hierarchy is transformed into the image of the seated heart knocking against the ribs of the would-be murderer. In the medieval notion, the king is appointed by God Himself and, therefore, it is astonishing that this medieval thane does not at this stage for once mention God who will not forgive the offence of regicide.

What Macbeth is going to achieve in future becomes dominant in his mind and, therefore, the present loses its importance. What is not is what is, to put it in the words of the thane himself. There is nobody to excel Shakespeare in the art of presenting our fears and anxieties in terms of physical sensations and paradoxes. There is no doubt that Macbeth wonders in one of his numerous asides whether he could not become the king without bestirring himself.

If fate has ordained that he should become the king of Scotland, the crown might reach his head without his determined and conscious effort.

> If chance will have me king, why, chance may crown me
> Without my stir. (I.iii.143-44)

Even here Macbeth is thinking of only fate or chance, but not God's will. The most common reaction is to speak of the will of God, but Macbeth's language has no place for it.

The announcement by King Duncan that his eldest son would be crowned the prince of Cumberland and that he would be the successor to the throne of Scotland appears to clinch the mind of Macbeth who decides on hearing this announcement to seize the crown by unfair means. The Thane of Cawdor appeals to the stars to quench their fires so that there may not be light to see the black deed which he would perform.

> Stars, hide your fires!
> Let not light see my black and deep desires;
> The eye wink at the hand; yet let that be,
> Which the eye fears, when it is done, to see. (I.iv.50-53)

So far, Macbeth does not seem to have thought of the existence of God who presides over the moral order of the world. He does not ask himself whether God would forgive him if he commits the crime of murdering a blameless and graceful king. His appeal is only to the stars so that the world may be covered with darkness. He wants his eye to wink at the hand, but he wants the action to be performed, though the eye may fear to see it done.

We can justify the reference to the stars by assuming that Macbeth had thought of the night as the best time for murder. Macbeth was aware of the blackness of his ambition and the planned murder to realize it, but he does not appeal to God to save him from temptation, as a Christian normally does.

Macbeth murders King Duncan who is his king, for the sake of realizing his ambition. In the Middle Ages, this was considered to be regicide, the murder of one's own king anointed by God Himself. In the Middle Ages, people had no doubt about it and, therefore, we can expect in the play many words and phrases that either mean "heaven" and "hell" or collocate with those words. King Duncan was a gentleman to his finger tips and he even expresses his gratitude to the general by conferring the earldom of Cawdor on him. This graceful, grateful, God's anointed king is murdered soon afterwards by the very recipient of that new honour.

The Age of Macbeth was also the Age of Faith. The courtiers were not, therefore, perplexed. They were just horrified and religious faith prompted them to place Macbeth on the side of Devil and hell. In fact, the speeches of all the principal characters including the Macbeths illustrate the clear-cut distinction between heaven and hell, between God and Devil with no middle ground between the two contraries. Nothing challenged their minds: they were neither confused or perplexed. Religion made it easy for them to range themselves on the side of either God and heaven or Devil and hell.

The distribution of these words and phrases drawn from faith among the speeches of the various characters makes an interesting reading. After all, they were necessary lexical items for condemnation, exclamation and even plain description. The following table illustrates the distribution of such words and their percentage in the speeches of various characters in the play.

Word	*Number of times employed*
Heaven	4
Hell	3
Devil/fiend	2
The great doom	1
Blaspheme	1
Lord's anointed temple	1
Angel	1
Damned	1
Sainted	1

Macbeth is the protagonist of the tragedy and as expected, he speaks the largest number of lines in the play. In extreme contrast, we have minor characters like the gentlewomen-in-waiting, the old man and the doctor who speak very few lines. Macbeth, the hero/villain of the play, speaks about six hundred and ninety eight lines, but the words of religion or after-life are hardly one and a half per cent. Even this insignificant occurrence is concentrated in the first half of the play: in the second half, the occurrence of such words is literally nil.

As it happens, the percentage of the distribution of words and phrases of religion and after-life is the lowest in the lines spoken by Macbeth, the perpetrator of the crimes and in the lines spoken by Lady Macbeth, his ardent instigator and supporter. The actual figures are 1.3 and 1.7 respectively. Again, the percentage is the highest in the lines spoken by Malcolm and Macduff, the most important characters among those who want to avenge Macbeth's crimes and re-establish the normal order in Scotland. It is 8.2 in the speeches of Macduff and 9.1 in the speeches of Malcolm, Duncan's heir. They speak 139 and 183 lines respectively, the highest after Macbeth and his wife. I have not taken into account the lines spoken by the doctor and the old man whose roles are those of passive and pious observers. The percentage is, of course, the highest in the speech of the porter with a staggering 33%, but then he takes the place of a jester with caustic and symbolic comments. He is the porter of the hell-gate in both comic and symbolic sense, because while imagining that he is the keeper of the hell-gate, he is really guarding the gate of Macbeth's castle turned into a hell by Macbeth and Lady Macbeth. There is a repeated knock on the gate and the process of the return of normalcy and its reassertion begins symbolically. The violent disruption of the normal world-order cannot be permanent. Let us return to the villains and anti-villains of whom Macbeth occupies the centrestage.

Macbeth, the hero and villain speaks hardly nine words related to heaven and hell, but there are other related words, namely, "angel," "church," "soul," "devil," and "God," though Macbeth may not literally use these words, since he can also speak a metaphorical language. Some of these phrases are so evocative that they release vibrations which make them more effective than mere arithmetical number and percentage. Of these nine words, "church" is only a part of the incantation used by Macbeth to conjure the witches to answer his questions. The remaining eight words are directly connected with heaven and hell. The crime and its condemnation are both basic and simple. Those who support the crime and the criminals are on the side of hell and devil: those who are fighting the perpetrators of the crime are on the side of God, heaven and angels.

Macbeth himself is sensitive to the proposed crime and he employs words of religious connotation to oppose it; he knows the price he has to pay for it. King Duncan's

virtues
Will plead like angels, trumpet-tongued, against
The deep damnation of his taking-off. (I.vii.18-20)

The phrase "deep damnation" indicates that Macbeth is aware that the murder of his king and guest is a sin leading to eternal condemnation in hell. Macbeth is contemplating the crime, but the first one-third of his soliloquy has no place for anxieties about the next world. This part of the soliloquy is dominated by the images of the judiciary: even-handed justice, instruction and judgement. Macbeth is more concerned with the consequences in this world than the judgement after his death in the next world.

Words of religious connotation are found in the central part of the soliloquy. But even in this part of his speech, the words, "angel," "deep damnation" and "cherubim" do not retain their hold on his mind. He does not linger on in those thoughts and expand and elaborate them. Incidentally, Macbeth himself doubts whether the first image of a naked new-born baby striding the blast is satisfactory. That is why he selects an alternative by adding the conjunction "or" and replaces the newborn baby with the cherubim suggested by the image of the baby. The cherubim is not a new-born baby but an angel. "Deep damnation," "angel," "trumpet," "cherubim"—the collocation is complete. But after reaching the climax in the phrase, "deep damnation," Macbeth returns to the consequences in this world.

And pity, like a naked new-born baby,
Striding the blast, or heaven's cherubim, horsed
upon the sightless couriers in the air,
Shall blow the horrid deed in every eye,
That tears shall drown the wind. (I.vii.21-27)

Macbeth is more concerned with the pity and sympathy for Duncan that would be roused in the minds of the people in this world itself than with the unforgivable nature of the sin of this proposed action and its consequences in the next world. In fact, Macbeth returns to non-religious imagery in the last part of the soliloquy. His imagery of horsemanship in the third part of the soliloquy shows that

Macbeth is lamenting that he has no spurs to prick the sides of his purpose, the purpose of usurping the throne of Scotland. But the central image of Duncan's virtues pleading like angels against the deep damnation of his taking off continues to linger on in our minds.

The soliloquy which he utters just before he commits the primary crime shows him in a tense and frantic state of mind and it has no place for images of after-life. The imagery in the first half of his speech is purely psychological and the second half of this soliloquy is all about the darkness of the night suitable for witchcraft, wicked dreams, murder and the like. The background of such a night, Lady Macbeth's provocative comment and instigation, not to speak of the bell which she has arranged, reinforce each other and push him finally across the line dividing the crime from passiveness.

There is an allusion to heaven and hell in this soliloquy. The bell is intended as the knell for Duncan and the reference to heaven and hell here is only an euphemism for Duncan's death to be caused by Macbeth. The allusion to the prating of the stones may sound Biblical (St. Luke, XIX, 40) but the allusion is not related to the context, because in the Bible there is no reference to secrecy.

Macbeth never addresses God, but when describing his state of mind after the regicide, he refers to the brief prayers of the sleeping sons of Duncan. One of them mumbles in his sleep "God bless us" and the other mumbles "Amen." It is this sacred word that could not be uttered by Macbeth and in his report to his wife, he bemoans that the word stuck in his throat.

> But wherefore could not I pronounce 'Amen'?
> I had most need of blessing, and 'Amen'
> Stuck in my throat. (II.ii. 31-33)

This moral inability to say "amen" brings us back to what Macbeth has described as the deep damnation of murdering Duncan, his king and guest. We thus see that though Macbeth utters hardly nine words of religious connotation, barely 1.3% of the total number of lines he speaks in the play, a few of them are so evocative that they make good the smallness of number. Till this point, the thane is not able to free himself from the thought of deep damnation, though he is also struggling to concentrate on the practical consequences of murder in this world. But some time after the murder, a change takes place. Insecurity, disillusionment, frustration and the resulting despair occupy his mind and Macbeth is driven inexhorably from crime to crime.

Even after the initial and basic crime, Macbeth is not able to shake off the thoughts of after-life entirely. Words of religious and spiritual connotation are not entirely absent from his utterances. For example, the following famous lines that touch the chords of our hearts:

> If't be so,
> For Banquo's issue have I defiled my mind,
> For them the gracious Duncan have I murder'd
> Put rancours in the vessel of my peace
> Only for them, and mine eternal jewel
> Given to the common Enemy of man, (III.i.64-69)

Macbeth speaks of soul and Satan, the common enemy of man. Bitterly complaining that Banquo's children would be his successors, Macbeth expresses his horror at the thought that for them he has sold his eternal soul to the devil. Underlying this complaint, there is the admission that he is now a damned man and that he is spiritually finished. The first part of this speech is all about this world and only a part of the speech is about the next world. Macbeth is as much concerned with his own state of mind as with that of Duncan. He has murdered his gracious king and at the same time, put bitterness in the vessel of his peace to achieve only a barren crown for himself. Till this point, Macbeth harps upon his own state of mind as much as on the price he has paid. From now on, Macbeth is so desperate for survival, that he concentrates on his own state of mind and the words of after-life have no use for him. Macbeth's moral consciousness reaches its meridian in his rueful statement that he has sold his eternal jewel to the devil, and in his subsequent utterances we find no room for words like "God" and "soul," "heaven" and "hell." The word "churches" he utters is only a part of the rhetoric to threaten the witches.

Macbeth has no use for religious faith even when Banquo's ghost appears at the party he gives to the courtiers. He does not pray to God and his spontaneous exclamations do not include words of that category. On the other hand, he resorts to self-dramatization and even goes to the extent of envying Duncan who has now peace which has eluded Macbeth.

> Better be with the deed,
> Whom we to gain our peace, have sent to peace,
> Than on the torture of the mind to lie
> In restless ecstasy. (III.ii.19-22)

It is nothing but the evasion of truth on the part of Macbeth to say as he does in the second line above, that in order to gain his and Lady Macbeth's peace of mind, he sent Duncan to peace. He is evidently evading the reality of murdering Duncan and denying the succession to his children in order to realize his own ambition of gaining the throne of Scotland. Here, we do not find any thought about the crime of murdering one's king and guest, but the dramatization of his own mental torment. Macbeth has no thought about the brutality of murdering the king and his grooms, nor does he think about Malcolm and Donalbin who have been falsely implicated in the crime. The emphasis is on his own state of being.

A change comes over Macbeth. As his crimes increase his suffering, he indulges more and more in self-dramatization. Religious faith offers an objective yardstick to judge one's own actions. It did so particularly in the Middle Ages when Europe was Christian and Catholic—but words of religious connotation are conspicuously absent in his speeches after the significant admission that he has sold his soul to the devil. Macbeth is driven into a corner when the hostility to the rule of the usurper assumes the form of rebellion and invasion from outside. War is at his doorstep and he finds that he has won only curses from his people. This is how he describes the situation:

> I have liv'd long enough; my way of life
> Is fall'n into the sere, the yellow leaf;
> As honour, love, obedience, troops of friends,
> I must not look to have, but in their stead
> Curses, not loud, but deep, mouth honour, breath
> Which the poor heart would fain deny, and dare not.
> (V.iii.22-27)

Macbeth has sown the wind and reaped the whirlwind. As civil war and destruction close in from all sides, he laments that in his old age, he cannot look forward to have honour, love and obedience but only curses and lip-sympathy. In this speech, there isn't a single word about what he had himself earlier described as the deep damnation nor about denying succession to Duncan's sons. There is some degree of self-pity and self-dramatization but no self-condemnation. Macbeth's speech gives the impression that he is the victim of what he has done, but the real victim is Duncan.

The news of the death of Macbeth's wife should have called forth exclamations in words of religious import or words related to after-life. But the response to the message—"The queen, my lord, is dead"—has no room for words like "God," "heaven" and "forgiveness," because Macbeth erects an absurdist and existential philosophy by generalizing his own personal experience. The only expression of sympathy for Lady Macbeth is his very enigmatic comment: "She should have died hereafter," by which he means that a less turbulent times would have been more appropriate for her death. The subject of death does not lead to prayers and wishes for the dead in this famous response of Macbeth.

Macbeth says that all men are fools and the grave is nothing but dust into which the body is turned eventually. Life is brief and insubstantial at the same time. The concept of immortality which is central to religious faith is totally absent in this speech. The world is a stage where life which is insubstantial like a shadow struts and frets for a while and is gone. Life is absurd, if not idiotic. It is not designed by God but is a tale told by an idiot. This view of life is an absurdist and existential view according to which life is meaningless and man is living alone in a Godless universe. After having admitted once in the past that he had sold his soul to the devil to purchase the crown, Macbeth ceases to think of after-life, God and devil, heaven and hell.

The false favours bestowed upon Macbeth by the weird sisters who spoke with a forked tongue encourage him to displace in his mind the thoughts about God and heaven, devil and hell with the deceptive certainties offered by the witches. Retribution closes in from all sides and the usurper dies.

Macbeth betrays the weakness of dramatizing his own state of mind and the situation in which he finds himself. When he says mournfully that in his old age he cannot expect to receive honour, love and obedience but only curses, he is pitying himself, but he does not think of the suffering he has caused to others including the Macduff family. He has turned Scotland into a hell for all those people who have placed loyalty and law above personal ambition. The self-dramatization of the sufferings of Macbeth includes the implied warning that however heroic you are, you reap only what you have sown.

Lady Macbeth is Macbeth's collaborator and instigator. She is the only person who is on the side of Macbeth. After Macbeth becomes the king of Scotland, the initiative passes into his hands and Lady Macbeth recedes into the background. She fades away gradually into the murky candle-lit nights of her sleep-walking scenes. She speaks about two hundred and twenty lines and she speaks words of after-life only four times.

The percentage of words of after-life is 1.7 compared to Macbeth's 1.3. Lady Macbeth's words related to after-life throw clear light on her character. Three of these four words she utters are hell-related words! She needs such words, because without her urging and instigation, Macbeth would not have resorted to murdering Duncan. She needs the invocation to the spirits of hell to turn her into a monster by unsexing her and charging her with characteristics that are anything but feminine and human. She needs the support of the "murdering ministers" of hell to turn her life-giving and nourishing breast milk into gall! At this stage, Lady Macbeth is planning to commit the murder personally instead of prompting Macbeth to do so. Hell is the company most suited to her.

Come, thick night
And pall thee in the dunnest smoke of hell,
That my keen knife see not the wound it makes,
Not Heaven peep through the blanket of the dark,
To cry, "hold, hold!" (I.v.50-54)

The words "spirits" and "murdering ministers" are hell-related words. Lady Macbeth utters such words three times in a single speech of sixteen lines. She does speak the opposite and life-creating word "heaven" once, but only in the negative sense. Lady Macbeth's prayer to night is that it should cover itself with the thickest smoke of hell so that even heaven may not be able to see what she plans to do and ask her to stop.

The monstrosity which Lady Macbeth invites is unnatural. It

is an aberration and her human nature asserts itself after the murder of Duncan, though not immediately afterwards. Unlike Macbeth's mind which has all the masculine drive and energy, Lady Macbeth's mind breaks down under the strain of the realization of her guilt and inability to confess publicly. "Night," "murky" and "hell" are the words that collocate again in her last utterances in the sleep-walking scene. Among the words denoting after-life spoken by her, the word "hell" is dominant.

Of all the adversaries of Macbeth and his wife, the most active and prominent are Macduff and Malcolm, the son of Duncan and the heir to the throne of Scotland. In the beginning, Macduff is taken in by Macbeth's hypocrisy, but not for long. The thane flees to England and urges the heir of Duncan to start the military campaign to oust Macbeth. His flight results in the slaughter of his wife and son. He has, therefore, an additional motive to challenge and kill Macbeth in a hand-to-hand fight. Malcolm's speech of strategic self-denigration is a bit tedious and risky, and Macduff in this dialogue with Malcolm and in a few short but meaningful sentences later, speaks about one hundred and thirty nine lines in all and there are in them about sixteen religious terms, accounting for not less than 9.1%, very much higher than the percentage of their occurrence in the speeches of Macbeth and Lady Macbeth. In Macbeth's case, the figure is only about 1.3. The following table explains the number of times these words occur and their nature too.

Character	*No. of Lines*	*Words of After Life*	*Percentage*
Macbeth	698	9	1.3
Lady Macbeth	221	4	1.7
Macduff	139	11	8.2
Malcolm	103	17	9.1
Duncan	73	2	2.7
Banquo	61	4	6.5
Old Man	11	1	9.1
Ross	23	1	4.3
Doctor	30	3	10
Porter	22	7	33

Of these, the words "heaven" and "hell" account for 81%. Since the crime committed by Macbeth is atrocious deserving eternal damnation, the occurrence of these words is frequent. Macbeth and his wife are on the side of hell: Duncan and his late queen are on the side of heaven. Macduff's judgement leaves no room for doubt. In the Age of Faith when people believed quite literally in the existence of heaven and hell, this clear-cut division is natural.

> Not in the legions
> Of horrid hell can come a devil more damn'd
> In evils to top Macbeth. (IV.iii.56-58)

According to this categorical denunciation, Macbeth's evil cannot be equalled even by the most wicked devil coming from hell. There is no room for doubt and complexity.

According to Macduff, Malcolm's father was a sainted king and his mother, the queen, lived her life in such a way that it was a preparation for the next world, bringing up her son more on her knees (she prayed frequently) than on her feet. Macduff may in a fit of despair ask whether heaven could look on the butchery of his family like a mute spectator. But this blaspheme is only momentary. The Thane of Fife, like a pious Christian, regards himself as a sinful man who has paid for his sin in the form of the slaughter of his wife and children. On hearing the news of the tragedy, he prays for the peace of their souls.

> Heaven rest them now! (IV.iii.227)

We can contrast this prayer with the response of Macbeth who, like Macduff, hears the news of the death of his wife. On hearing the message that the queen is dead, Macbeth does not pray for the rest of her soul, but remarks only that she should have died later, that is, after the normal times had returned. Driven from crime to crime, Macbeth gives expression to an atheistic and pessimistic view of life, whereas Macduff prays to heaven for the peaceful rest of the souls of the dead in his family.

Macduff's grief not only leads him to prayer for the peace of the souls of his wife and children, but also acts as a spur to decisive action against Macbeth. Macduff prays what he calls gentle heavens to bring him quickly face to face with Macbeth in the battlefield and even expresses the wish that heavens should forgive Macbeth if he escapes Macduff's encounter and challenge.

From front to front
Bring thou this fiend of Scotland and myself;
Within my sword's length set him; if he escape,
Heaven forgive him too! (IV.iii. 32-35)

We can easily see how frequently Macduff uses the words of after-life: "fiend," "heaven," "hell" and the like. But Macduff does not really invoke heaven's forgiveness for Macbeth, for he is certain that Macbeth would not be able to escape alive from his encounter. When the final hand-to-hand fighting takes place, the most apt phrase in Macduff's vocabulary to describe Macbeth is "hell-hound." It is interesting to note that the swear word "hell" is uttered in the play nearly as frequently as the word "heaven." After all, the crime committed by Macbeth is heinous and the Age of Macbeth was also the Middle Ages, the Age of Faith.

These words denoting rewards in after-life, namely, "heaven" and "hell," besides "God's anointed temple," "blaspheme," "sainted" king and the "great doom" indicate clearly Macduff's concept of kingship and loyalty. The basic contraries are heaven/hell and angel/fiend which are characteristic of the Age of Faith. In fact, of all the epithets spoken by Macduff concerning after-life, "heaven" and "hell" are the most frequent. Among the rest, the most frequently spoken words are "angel" and "devil" that collocate with the former contraries. Murder and holiness, treason and loyalty, virtues and vices were seen by the characters in clear-cut divisions.

Malcolm, the other chief antagonist ranged against Macbeth can be bracketed with Macduff. Scion of the royal family and heir to the throne of Scotland, he has, like Macduff, reason to be extremely hostile to Macbeth. Words of religious belief like "God" and "devil," "heaven" and "hell" are uttered by him as frequently as by Macduff. Malcolm speaks about one hundred and eighty three lines and words of after-life are spoken seventeen times: nearly nine per cent. He is the only character in the play to address God directly;

Devilish Macbeth
By many of these trains hath sought to win me
Into his power, and modest wisdom plucks me
From overcredulous haste: but God above

Deal between you and me! (IV.iii.117-21)

Like most of the characters hostile to the usurper, Malcolm finds it apt to regard Macbeth as a devil. In the final scene of the play, Lady Macbeth is described as Macbeth's fiend-like queen. This attributive adjective fits into the simple beliefs of the people in the Middle Ages. Malcolm does not spend much of his breath in denouncing Macbeth. Being the heir-designate to the throne of Scotland, he is more interested in the coming war against Macbeth and the inevitable restoration of law and order which meant punishing the wicked and rewarding the virtuous. The role of the prince is charged with responsibility and he is on the side of God whose blessings he needs. In fact, nearly ten words of after-life spoken by him are related to heaven and God.

Malcolm prays to God to remove all the means that make the Scottish loyalists strangers. He is the only character in the play to think of Christendom. The Middle Ages saw Christianity giving the people of Europe a sense of unity and purpose. Thanking England for giving military support, Malcolm pays a generous tribute to Siward.

Gracious England hath
Lent us good Siward, and ten thousand men;
An older, and a better soldier, none
That Christendom gives out. (IV.iii.189-92)

Life was not secular during the Age of Faith. A king, however absolute his power, could not transgress the commandments of religion.

The frequency of the occurrence of the words of after-life and Christian belief in Malcolm's speech is partly due to the fact that Malcolm, a royal guest in England, describes to Macduff the miraculous powers which the king of England possessed as per the beliefs of the people. This belief leads to an implied contrast between the life-denying Macbeth of Scotland and the life-affirming king of England. There are five heaven-related words in Malcolm's speech of thirteen lines in response to a query by the curious Macduff.

Malcolm's way of testing the loyalty of Macduff is rather tedious, though the dialogue lists the qualities of a wicked king and those of a virtuous king. But when victory is in sight at the end of the war against Macbeth, Malcolm shows that he is a man of action and a good organizer. He does refer to Macbeth as a butcher and Lady Macbeth as a fiend. The rest of the speech is devoted to the cause of the restoration of order. But like Macduff he too needs the words related to after-life many times: "God" and "heaven," "devil" and "hell" and the words that collocate with them appear seventeen times in Malcolm's speeches.

We have so far considered the speeches of the principal characters of the two groups: those who abetted and committed the crime and those who reacted to it by fighting against them. Now we turn to the speeches of those characters who cannot be so neatly labelled. There is, for instance, the father of Malcolm. King Duncan is an early victim of Macbeth's treason; he speaks seventy three lines before he is murdered. In them, words of religious belief are only two: sin and God. The percentage of such words in the lines spoken by Duncan is 2.7 which is not much higher than the percentage in the lines spoken by Macbeth and Lady Macbeth. This statistics is interesting because while King Duncan is a saintly and blameless character, the Macbeths are perpetrators of evil. The former's character is heavenly while the latter two have consciously embraced evil itself.

The word "sin" is uttered by King Duncan in a self-deprecatory tone and not for condemning any action associated with hell. It is his modesty that prompts him to say to Macbeth

> The sin of my ingratitude even now
> Was heavy upon me. (I.iv.15-16)

What the King says is more an expression of piety than a description of an action that leads a man to hell. The other word, "God" is used by the king indirectly in a rather involved sentence.

> Herein I teach you,
> How you shall bid God yield us for your pains
> And thank us for your trouble. (I.v.12-14)

King Duncan does not address God here. He asks Lady Macbeth to request God to make him her guest so that she might take a lot of pains to play the hostess and thank the king for her trouble.

Banquo is another character who can be considered in this context, because like Duncan he is also victim of Macbeth's treachery and he too cannot be regarded as belonging to any group. He speaks about sixty one lines and his words related to after-life are only four in number. Of these four words, only one is related to hell, that is, "devil." Unlike Malcolm and Macduff, he does not utter this epithet to describe Macbeth, but only to link the witches with devil.

> What! can the devil speak true? (I.iii.108)

Banquo is not without personal desire, but he has no hesitation in describing the witches as the instruments of darkness. He does not beg their favour, neither does he fear their hate. At the same time, he is curious about his prospects.

The three other words categorized above are related to God. It is not Duncan, but Banquo who observes on arrival at Macbeth's castle:

> This guest of summer
> The temple-haunting martlet does approve
> By his loved mansionry, that the heaven's breath
> Smells wooingly here: (I.vi.3-6)

Granting that the phrase "heaven's breath" means only the wind, the very fact that Banquo chooses to describe it that way and his choice of the word "temple" indicate that he is not a renegade like Macbeth who has deserted God and gone over to the devil. This view is reinforced by the speech of Banquo a little before the murder of Macbeth in the latter's castle.

> merciful powers!
> Restrain in me the cursed thoughts that nature
> Gives way in repose! (II.i.7-9)

Banquo does not want to sleep, though he is drowsy lest he should have dreams induced by wicked thoughts. Banquo appeals to the powers of heaven to save him. He has not yet seen a thing which could be compared to hell or seen anybody who could be called devil. He prays to heaven to save him in contrast with Macbeth who sells his soul to Satan.

There is no mention of hell or devil in the language of Banquo even after the murder of King Duncan is discovered, because his suspicions are vague.

> Fears and scruples shake us:
> In the great hand of God I stand; and thence
> Against the undivulg'd pretence I fight
> Of treasonable malice. (II.iii.129-32)

There are fears but there are also scruples. The major prophecy of the witches is nearer fulfilment. But then there are values and scruples which confront his own hope. Banquo is a good man who would not violate the law of the land. He turns once again to heavens. His vocabulary has no use yet for hell and the devil. Banquo plays his cards carefully; but he is neither a villain nor a saint.

The gentlewoman who takes care of Lady Macbeth is like the doctor on the periphery of the world of the two Macbeths. She knows nothing definitely about the public life of the country. Crimes have been committed by her own aristocratic employers, but she is innocent of them. Therefore, in the lines spoken by her there is no room for the words like hell and devil. A gentle and warm-hearted lady, she speaks hardly twenty one lines in which there is room for heaven and God so far as the words of after-life are concerned. Lady Macbeth's sleep-walking scenes, her actions and words puzzle her as she does not know Lady Macbeth's role in the primary crime. All that she can say is;

> She has spoke what she should not, I am sure of that:
> Heaven knows what she has known. (V.i.116-17)

There is a hint that Lady Macbeth knows some secret of dreadful nature. Loyal to her mistress, this warm-hearted lady-in-waiting does not let her mind be seized by impatience. When the doctor exclaims "Well, well, well," she takes the exclamation literally and requests him:

> Pray God it be, sir. (V.i.46)

The doctor too can think of God only and not of hell or the devil.

Lady Macbeth's problem is psychological and not physical, but the doctor knows also the cases of those who have died 'holily' in their beds, after prayers and last rites. The case of Lady Macbeth is different and the doctor does not know what the patient has known. His medical knowledge stops here and he concedes modestly:

> More needs she the divine than the physician—
> God, God forgive us all! (V.i.71-72)

The doctor speaks nearly thirty lines and he takes the name of God three times. Both the gentlewoman and the doctor mention only heaven and God, because they are more observers than participants in the story of heinous crime. The criminal record of Macbeth and his wife is a closed book to them.

The old man is another minor character in the play who deplores the crime but does not know definitely who the criminal is. Like the gentlewoman and the doctor, he is a pious and God-fearing character who speaks only eleven lines. When he bids farewell to Rosse, he invokes God's blessings.

> God's benision go with you and with those
> That would make good of bad, and friends of foes!
> (II.ii.40-41)

The old man is a peripheral character who condemns evil but makes no attempt to find out the criminal. If we go by the proportion of after-life words to the number of lines spoken by him, the figure that emerges is nine percent. The old man is introduced by the playwright to add to the play some sensational omens. The gentlewoman, the doctor and the old man do not influence the course of events in the drama. They are gentle God-fearing people who do not know who committed the crime. They have only vague fears and indulge in vague speculation. Their role in the play is choric in character.

There is one unusual character whose grim and humorous monologue of about twenty two lines is dominated by the word "hell" and five other words that collocate with it: "hell-gate," "Beelzebub," "other devil," "devil porter" and "ever lasting bonfire." The word "heaven" is also in the same speech, no doubt, but only to emphasize the road going in the opposite direction. The priest's equivocation to heaven itself will take him to the opposite region. For a moment, the porter in Macbeth's castle becomes the porter of hell. He imagines that he is the porter at the hell-gate without his knowing that he is in the figurative sense guarding the gate of the hell of Macbeth and Lady Macbeth. The equivocation of the priest who is involved in the gun plot is in tune with the equivocation of the weird sisters that leads Macbeth to hell.

At the beginning of the Middle Ages, people believed in the existence of heaven and hell. Their condemnations, statements, exclamations and wishes are dominated by the pairs of contraries, God/devil and heaven/hell. The regicide and other crimes of Macbeth roused some basic emotions and in the age of faith, piety and simplicity, these two pairs of contraries expressed those emotions.

The Influence of Shakespeare on Melville's *Moby Dick*

The impress of William Shakespeare on *Moby Dick*, a great American work of fiction, can be seen not only in the rhetoric of the novel, but also in certain other important aspects which unfold themselves as we go through the novel carefully. A study of the life of Herman Melville, the author, reveals the fact that he was a keen student of Shakespeare's plays. The rhetoric employed by the author can be found in the passages that look like soliloquies. The first person narrator of the story is Ishmael. He joins a whale-hunting expedition in a ship called *Pequod* which had anchored in Nantucket. He finds it necessary in the early part of the novel to defend and champion the class of whale-hunters who, he believes, are treated with derision by the public. The eloquence he employs to defend the profession reminds us of Shylock who defends and champions the cause of the persecuted Jewish community to which he belongs. A part of Ishmael's tirade in the chapter appropriately called "The Advocates" begins with a series of wh-questions.

> Why did the Dutch in De Witt's time have admirals of their whaling fleets? Why did Louis XVI of France, at his own personal expense, fit out whaling ships from Dunkirk, and politely invite to that town some score or two of families from our own island of Nantucket? Why did Britain between the years 1750 and 1788 pay to her whalemen in bounties upwards of £ 1,000,000? And lastly, how comes it that we whaleman of America now outnumber all the rest of the banded whalemen in the world; sail a navy of upwards of seven hundred vessels manned by eight thousand men; yearly consuming 4,000,000 thousand dollars; the ships worth, at the time of sailing £ 20,000,000; and every year importing into

> our harbours a well reaped harvest of £ 7,000,000? How comes all this, if there be not something puissant in whaling?
> (Chap. 24, p. 76)

Ishmael's defence of the whaling industry is quite convincing. The style of the passage is characterised by some very striking features: 1. Eloquence 2. Rhetorical questions coming in rapid succession 3. A "wh" word, "why" and "how" at the beginning of each question 4. Similarity of sentence structure marked by "wh" word + (past tense + do) + Noun/Subject.

When Solanio and Salerio, each a follower of Antonio, tease and taunt Shylock about his daughter's flight, they succeed only in provoking Shylock's eloquent advocacy of his race.

> Hath not a Jew eyes? Hath not a jew hands, organs, dimensions, senses, affections, passions? Fed with the same food, hurt with the same weapons subject to the same diseases, healed with the same means, warmed and cooled by the same winter and summer as a Christian is? If you prick us, do we not bleed? If you tickle us do we not laugh? If you poison us, do we not die? (*The Merchant of Venice*, III.i.61-68)

This part of Shylock's speech is marked by 1. eloquence 2. a succession of rhetorical questions 3. the questions beginning with the auxiliary, "hath," a form of "have," and questions beginning with the conjunction, "if" and 4. repetition of the same sentence structure, aux (hath) + not + noun phrase + noun. This structure can be seen in the first two questions. The next two questions also have similar structures: conjunction (if) + Noun Phrase/Subject + Transitive Verb + Noun Phrase/object. These four features of the style and eloquent plea on behalf of a much maligned community can be found in Ishmael's rhetoric in *Moby Dick* when he champions the whaling profession.

Ishmael takes a cue from William Shakespeare's *Julius Caesar* for his distrust of lean and hungry people. He cautions the owners of whale-hunting ships against employing such men for manning the mast heads of the ships: "Beware of enlisting in your vigilant fisheries any lad with lean brow and hollow eyes; given to unseasonable meditativeness." (Chap. 35, pp. 139-40) The advice reminds one of Julius Caesar's suspicion of men like Cassius.

Let me have men about me that are fat:
Sleek-headed men and such as sleep o'nights:
Yond Cassius has a lean and hungry look;
He thinks too much: such men are dangerous. (I.ii.191-94)

Leanness of the person, hollow eyes (hungry-looking), meditativeness (thinks too much) all these are the qualities that are shared by men whom Ishmael and Julius Ceaser find unreliable. Jobs and situations are different, but the disqualifications are the same. The characteristics of men placed in positions of trust are also the same. One cannot help tracing the influence of Shakespeare here.

Even so commonplace a thing as comparison to which Herman Melville resorts in order to illustrate a point he is making breathes the influence of his reading a play of Shakespeare. When asked by Peruvian sailors what the word "canallers" meant, Ishmael replies that they are American boatmen. Their experience is limited to inland navigation which fits them to the adventure of whale-fishery on the high seas. The caller—this word is not found in the Oxford English Dictionary—lived a wild life and Steelkilt goes on to say:

> Freely depicted in his own vocation, gentlemen, the canaller would make a fine dramatic hero, so abundantly and picturesquely wicked is he. Like Mark Antony, for days and days along his green-turfed, flowery Nile, he indolently floats, openly toying with his red-cheeked Cleopatra, ripening his apricot thigh upon the sunny deck. (Chap. 54, p. 221)

The phrase, "dramatic hero," and the description of Antony's romance with Cleopatra on the river Nile constitute another tell-tale evidence of Shakespeare's influence. The fact that even this all-male story of a whale-hunting adventure can accommodate an allusion to Mark Antony's sensuous life with Cleopatra is sufficient indication of Herman Melville's submission to the attraction of Shakespeare's Roman play.

There is a more direct reference to Shakespeare in the novel. One of the striking features of Richard III is his own description of his physical deformity.

I, that am rudely stamp'd, and want love's majesty
To strut before a wanton ambling nymph;

> I, that am curtail'd of this fair proportion,
> Cheated of feature by dissembling nature,
> Deform'd, unfinish'd, sent before time
> Into this breathing world, scarce half made up,
> And that so lamely and unfashionable
> That dogs bark at me, as I halt by them; (I.i.16-23)

To Herman Melville this hunch-backed Richard III becomes an adjective to describe the unauthentic and monstrous depiction of whales in the signs over the shops of the oil dealers. A detailed description of the whale is a favourite topic in *Moby Dick* and the author is keen that any description of a whale should be authentic, whether literary or pictorial. The author devotes a whole chapter to what he regards as the monstrous pictures of whales and after dismissing several representations of this animal, asks:

> As for the sign-painter's whales seen in the streets, hanging over the shops of oil dealers, what shall be said of them? They are generally Richard III whales with dromedary humps, and savage. (Chap. 55, p. 234)

The hypothesis that Shakespeare's influence is seen in *Moby Dick* is only strengthened by another direct reference to Shakespeare in the novel.

> Few are the foreheads which like Shakespeare's or Melancthon's rise so high, and descend so low, that the eyes themselves seem clear, eternal, tideless mountain lakes: and all above them in the forehead's wrinkles, you seem to track the antlered thoughts descending there to drink, even as highland hunters track the snow prints of the deer. (Chap. 79, p. 307)

That Herman Melville can think of Shakespeare in the most unlikely place speaks volumes for the pervasive influence of the Elizabethan playwright on the novel. The American author is only describing in detail the anatomy of the sperm whale, particularly its head and he cannot help thinking of Shakespeare's forehead rising high and descending low and comparing his eyes to the clear, everlasting and tideless mountain lakes. Evidently he had seen a portrait of Shakespeare drawn by his contemporary. I cannot recall any British writer paying homage to Shakespeare's portrait which is well known. In the next sentence not quoted here, the author of the novel speaks of the god-like dignity inherent in the kind of brows which the bard of Avon had.

Melville does not find it incongruous to turn to the pages of Shakespeare's *Antony and Cleopatra*, when he wants to describe the flight of the whales.

> Towards the noon whales were raised; but so soon as the ship sailed down to them they turned and fled with swift precipitancy; a disordered flight, as of Cleopatra's barges from Actium. (Chap. 84, p. 325)

The description of this infamous retreat of the frightened Egyptian queen and her ships in the naval engagement with the forces of Octavius Caeser can be quoted in full here to justify the relevance of the comparison.

> On our side, like the token'd pestilence,
> Where death is sure, yond rebaudred nag of Egypt—
> Whom leprosy o'ertake;—i' the midst o' the flight,
> When vantage like a pair or twins appear
> Both as the same or ours the elder—
> The breeze upon her, like a cow in June,
> Hoists sail, and flies. (III.viii.8-14)

The flight of Cleopatra's naval vessels proved to be a turning point in the war between Egypt and Rome and it is certainly a historic event described in poetic terms by Shakespeare. Herman Melville is so much ensnared by the British dramatist that he uses a comparison between Cleopatra's retreat and the flight of the whales when the ship *Pequod* approaches them.

The fact that even in the most unlikely place in the novel there is a veiled allusion to Shakespeare is sufficient evidence to show that the author of *Moby Dick* was familiar with his plays. A historical play of Shakespeare centring around Henry VI and the tranquil cruising in the nineteenth century have ostensibly little in common. While pursuing the white whale called Moby Dick, the sailors reach the calm pacific ocean after several months of sailing. Describing this phase of their adventure, the narrator adds:

> At such times, under abated sun; afloat all day upon smooth, slow-heaving swells; seated in his boat, light as a birch canoe; and so sociably mixing with soft waves themselves, that like the hearth-stone cats they purr against the gunwhale; these are the times of dreamy quietude, while holding the tranquil beauty and brilliancy of ocean's skin, one forgets the tiger heart that pants beneath it; and would not willingly remember that this violet paw but conceals a remorseless fang.
>
> (Chap. 114)

Here is a veiled allusion to *Henry VI*, part III. The Duke of York who is imprisoned, insulted and mocked by queen Margaret rebukes her with the words, "O tiger's heart wrapp'd in a woman's hide!" (I.iv.137) This line became famous during Shakespeare's time itself and his envious contemporary and fellow playwright, Robert Greene made the line even more famous by his transparent allusion to it in his famous attack on Shakespeare. Melville uses the key words of the line "tiger's heart" and "hide" to describe the gentle calmness of the sea beneath the surface of which lingered the ferocious whales. The fact that the author of *Moby Dick* uses the word "skin" instead of "hide" does not dilute the force of our argument. The images in Shakespeare's plays are so dominant in the novelist's mind that he turns to Shakespeare's plays for a metaphor.

As stated above, the impress of Shakespeare in *Moby-Dick* is not confined to actual speeches. Here is an example of this impress seen in the attitude and the action of the sailors. Captain Ahab puts down the quadrant and tramples upon it in a mood of anger and resignation till it goes to pieces. "Aye, thus I trample on these, thou paltry thing that feebly points on high; thus I split and destroy thee." (Chap. 18) This action preceded by the soliloquy reminds the reader of Richard II's action of dashing a looking glass to pieces in a mood of anger and resignation, when he is asked by Bolingbroke to surrender his crown (IV.i).

The angry and spirited captain of the ship, the storm that engulfed it, the lightning and the thunder, the soliloquy of the defiant captain addressed to the storm—all these prompt the reader to recall the storm scenes in *King Lear*. The parsee kneeling before the captain reminds the reader of the frail and young Fool in the storm scene in the play. Ahab resembles Lear in the sense that both are angry old men defying the piercing lightning and tumultous storm in their soliloqies. Visibility in *Pequod* had been reduced considerably and apprehending someone walking on the deck, Starbuck shouts "Who is there?" This question is similar to Kent's question "who's there besides the foul weather?" The gentleman's response in the play "one minded like the other most unquietly" suits captain Ahab's condition perfectly.

Both Ahab and Lear share a tone of defiance while addressing Nature in their soliloquies. However, Ahab's soliloquy ends more like the conclusion of Shelley's "Ode to the West Wind."

In some chapters in *Moby Dick*, the narrative method is replaced by the dramatic method. We have stage directions besides dialogues in them. Chapters 120, 121 and 122 can be cited as examples.

While proceeding to the state cabin of Captain Ahab, the temptation to kill the captain seizes Starbuck's mind. Ahab is asleep and the situation bears a close resemblance to the approach of Macbeth towards the bed chamber of King Duncan with a view to killing him. What is even more important is the soliloquy and the anguish underlying the soliloquy about the ethical aspect of what the sailor in *Moby Dick* and the general in *Macbeth* propose and plan. In *Moby Dick* too Starbuck is "wrestling with an angel" (chap. 123, p. 452) and in *Macbeth*, it is cherubin, an angel who tries to dissuade Macbeth from committing the murder of his king, the captain of the state. After the image of cherubin makes its appearance, Macbeth who is in great anguish says to his wife: "we will proceed no further in this business." The sailor in the American novel is saved by his angel, whereas Macbeth submits to the taunting and goading by his wife, and commits the murder.

As in Shakespeare's plays, soliloquies abound in *Moby Dick* though it is a prose novel. When a life buoy is to be cobbled out of a coffin, the ship's carpenter is called. He does not like this particular job, and delivers a long soliloquy that ends chapter 126. Again like some of Shakespeare's soliloquies, it is partly humorous and somewhat cheeky, if not entertaining.

Captain Ahab's dialogue with the carpenter who is converting a coffin into a life buoy echoes Hamlet's and the gravedigger's style. There is a direct allusion to Shakespeare's play when Ahab says to the carpenter who is at work: "and the gravedigger in the play sings, spade in hand. Dost thou never?"

Just as the prince of Denmark goes on asking questions and gets answers from the gravedigger, the captain of *Pequod* goes on putting questions to the carpenter who answers them all wittily like the gravedigger. The only contrast is that the sexton in *Hamlet* is preparing the grave for the dead, and the carpenter goes on preparing a life buoy for the living.

Allusions to Shakespeare's plays crop up in the most unexpected places in *Moby Dick*. The entire novel is the long story of revengeful Ahab who wants to hunt and kill the white whale. For a long time during the voyage, the captain is not able to locate the white whale. The other vessels which had gone whale-hunting are also not able to give him any information. Moby Dick has escaped their darts and harpoons. The author adds

> and now that all his successive meetings with various ships contrastingly concurred to show the demonic indifference with which the white whale tore his hunters, whether sinning or sinned against. (Chap. 130)

Lear's agonising realisation that he is partly to blame for his suffering and his simultaneous conviction that his epic suffering is out of all proportion to his sin express themselves in a highly condensed statement which Melville finds appropriate to describe the whale's ferocious attack on the hunters who go to the distant seas to hunt and kill him with their darts and lances. Is the white whale not more sinned against than sinning?

At a critical moment when Ahab and his shipmates are fighting a heroic battle against the white whale in the stormy ocean, Stub, one of the sailors, finds death staring him in the face. He does not want to die in the whale-hunting adventure of his captain who is monomaniac and in his soliloquy, he addresses Nature as Lear does in *King Lear*:

> Look ye, sun, moon and stars! I call you assassins of as good a fellow as ever spouted up his ghost. (Chap. 135, p. 501)

The expression reminds us of the storm scenes in *King Lear* in which the king in the course of his tirade against the storm, rain, thunder and lightning calls them servile ministers. After calling upon them to let fall their horrible pleasure on him and after an expression of self-pity, the old man adds:

> But yet I call you servile ministers
> That with two pernicious daughters join
> Your high engendered battles 'gainst a head
> So old as this. (III.ii.21-24)

What is similar is not the theme. Stub is no Lear. But it is the critical moment, apostrophe to the elements of Nature, the accusation and the expression 'I call you' resulting from it that are common. Elements of Nature are charged with being hostile and the expressions begin with the same words.

Melville was continuously aware of the vision and technique of Shakespeare, while writing *Moby Dick*. Narrating the history of the problem of the blacksmith's foot, the author observes: "Out of this revelation, part by part, at last came out the four acts of gladness, and the one long, and as yet the uncatastrophied fifth act of the grief of his life's drama." (Chap. 112, p. 427) The author refers to the early and happy years of the blacksmith's life and the latter part characterised by suffering. The four acts, the fifth act and catastorophe are the key words.

In the course of the novel, Ishmael alludes to the epicure who eats a calf's head (the flesh within the skull). Expressing his sympathy for the calf, the narrator adds:

> And that is the reason why a young buck with an intelligent looking calf's head before him, is somehow one of the saddest sights you can see. The head looks a sort of reproachfully at him, with an 'et tu brute' expression. (Chap. 65, p. 265)

The allusion to assassination of Julius Ceasar in Shakespeare's play is quite clear and it needs no elaboration.Melville mocks the mental capacity of the epicures, which is so poor that by eating a calf's head, they are able at least to discriminate between calves' heads and their own.

The Biblical teaching 'Judge not that ye be not judged' has a prominent place in Shakespeare's scale of values. To put it in a more mundane language, we are all tarred with the same brush when it comes to human weakness. Shakespeare's rhetoric that presents this view is well known. In *Moby Dick*, Melville exposes the hollowness of the men who condemn the cannibals. This topic is the climax of the chapter "The Whale as a Dish". One thing leads to another and the narrator sails to the topics of calf's brain and finally to cannibals. Throughout, he brings into play his cheeky sense of humour. His rhetoric has a close resemblance to that of Shakespeare's Lear.

> Cannibal? Who is not a cannibal? I tell you it will be more tolerable for the Fejee that salted down a lean missionary in his cellar against a coming famine; it will be more tolerable for that provident Fejee, I say, in the Day of Judgement, than for thee, civilized enlightened gourmand, who nailest geese to the ground and feastest on their bloated livers in thy pate-de-foie-gras. (Chap. 65, p. 266)

Has man any moral right to sit in judgement over a fellow human being including a cannibal? No, says Ishmael, the narrator of the story. First, the question, then exposure of the guilt or weakness of the man who condemns and finally turning the judgement on the judging party itself—these three elements can be distinctly seen in this rhetoric. Now place by its side the tirade of King Lear in Shakespeare's play.

> Thou rascal beadle, hold thy bloody hand
> Why dost thou lash that whore? strip thy own back;
> Thou hotly lusts to use her in that kind
> For which thou whipp'st her. The usurer hangs the cozener.
> None does offend, none, I say none. (IV.vi.159-63)

Humour and tirade go hand in hand in some chapters of this great American masterpiece. One such chapter is called fast-fish and loose-fish in which the author discusses the various laws and regulations governing the ownership of the whales hunted on the high seas. The fast fish, according to him, may cause legal complications if the whale is hunted by one vessel, but taken possession of by another. In contrast, the dispute about the loose fish does not lead to any hair-splitting interpretation of law, because a loose fish is a waif possessed by nobody. Ishmael, the narrator goes on piling one rhetorical question upon another, asking whether this or that is not a loose fish and finally comes to the question:

> What is the great globe itself but a loose fish? (Chap. 89)

In a very uncommon collocation, the author combines the question of loose fish with the phrase the "great globe itself," taken from Prospero's speech in *The Tempest* (IV.i.128) which is suffused with the philosophical concept of reality and unreality.

The intersection of the dream world and the humdrum world is a well known characteristic of Shakespeare's view of life. The linking of the sentimental and the mundane world can be seen in *Moby Dick* also. In a musical the sailors drink, sing and dance. When some sailors sing a song about Spanish ladies and bid farewell to them in the form of their song, another sailor cautions them in prose:

> Oh don't be sentimental; it's bad for digestion. Take a tonic, follow me. (Chap. 40)

This scene in the novel reminds us of the mutual involvement of the world of the Athenian craftsmen and the dream world of the fairies in Shakespeare's *The Midsummer Night's Dream.*

Many a time, Shakespeare employs pun in situations in which verbal ingenuity looks like odd one out. In *Richard II*, when the king visits the ailing Duke of Lancaster who is also known as John of Gaunt, he addresses him with the words "how's it with the aged Gaunt?" The dying duke replies

> Old Gaunt indeed: and gaunt in being old: (II.i.74)

In *Moby Dick*, we have a sailor who cannot and does not want to join the dance of the merry sailors because he is old and says to them rather peevishly:

> Well, well, beelike the whole world's a ball, as you scholars have it: and so it is right to make one ball room of it. Dance on lads, you're young; I was once. (Chap. 40, p. 153)

The word "ball" is used in two different senses.

According to the Bible, all men are likely to err and, therefore, we are all in need of God's mercy. This Christian teaching is echoed in Shakespeare's *The Merchant of Venice*, *Measure for Meas-*

ure and *Titus Andronicus*. The most celebrated and frequently quoted is the plea for mercy in *The Merchant of Venice*.

> Therefore, Jew
> Though justice is thy plea, consider this
> That in the course of justice, none of us
> Should see salvation; we do pray for mercy,
> And that same prayer should teach us all to render
> The deeds of mercy. (IV.i.197-202)

Portia's eloquent and noble exhortation is preceded by her declaration that mercy is a divine quality. In this exhortation to Shylock, she states that all human beings are in need of God's mercy without which we cannot hope for salvation. In *Moby Dick*, a similar view is presented. Ishmael refrains from judging Queequeg's religion, though he and other sailors are Christians, and regard him as a pagan non-Christian.

> Qeequeg thought that he knew what he was about, I suppose; he seemed to be content; and there let him rest. All our arguing with him would not avail; let him be, I say; and heaven have mercy on us all—Presbyterians and pagans alike—for we are all dreadfully cracked about the head, and sadly need mending. (Chap. 17)

Incidentally, this passage is also a plea for religious tolerance and co-existence of religions.

If we take the stand that all are offenders, can a judge who is a judicial authority be an exception? Neither Shakespeare nor Melville would answer this question with a yes.

> The usurer hangs the cozener. . . .
> The strong lance of justice hurtless brakes:
> (*King Lear*, IV.vi.163-66)

Ahab who is on a do-or-die mission becomes meditative in his tryst with destiny. His speech like that of Lear is more a soliloquy than a speech.

> Where do murderers go, man? Who's to doom, when the

judge himself is dragged to the bar? (Chap. 133, p. 476)

The thought is shared by *King Lear* and *Moby Dick*.

Ishmael, the narrator of the story, seeks accommodation in an inn when he is stranded in New Bedford during a stormy night. The snow and the ice of the freezing northern climate rouse his sympathies for the less fortunate people who have to spend even such nights outdoor:

> Poor Lazarus there, chattering his teeth against the curb stone for his pillow, and shaking off his tatters with his shiverings, he might plug up both ears with rags, and put a corn cob into his mouth, and yet that would not keep out the tempestuous Euroclydon. (Chap. 2)

The sympathetic feeling for the destitutes, the image of storm, rags and tatters bear the influence of Lear's exclamation during the storm when he is persuaded to seek shelter in a hovel.

> Poor naked wretches, whereso'er you are,
> That abide the pelting of this pitiless storm,
> How shall your houseless heads and unfed sides,
> Your looped and windowed raggedness, defend you
> From seasons such as this. (III.iv.28-32)

Throughout the history of civilization, man has attached great importance to external forms and equipments. Appearances outside man's private world do count, though their effects are superficial when they are not matched by inner strength. King Lear sees a contrast between the external appearance of a civilized man who is a product of culture and the crude trappings of a primitive man who may be a noble savage, but who is bereft of external shows.

Ishamel seems to believe that external appearance, however paltry by itself, does have practical importance. It invests man with a certain aura of superiority, if not with supremacy. To put it in his own words, "for be a man's intellectual superiority that it will, it can never assume the practical, available supremacy over other men, without the idea of some sort of external art and entrenchments, always in themselves, more or less, paltry and base."

Melville has probably derived this thought from Shakespeare's play, *King Lear* in which the importance of form, usage and trappings is emphasized by Lear more than once. When Regan wants his hundred knights dismissed and tells him that he is not in need of knights at all, since she will take care of him, Lear replies:

> O reason not the need! Our basest beggars
> Are in the poorest things superfluous.
> Allow not nature more than nature needs,
> Man's life is cheap as beast's. Thou art a lady;
> If only to go warm were gorgeous,
> Why nature needs not what thou gorgeous wear'st
> Which scarcely keep thou warm. (II.iv.267-73)

There is an emphasis here as in *Moby Dick* on what civilization is able to add to Nature. Man does not like to give him more than what nature gives him. Without what civilization and progress have contributed, man is no more than a beast or primitive man. Melville goes to the extent of saying that these external trappings can impart potency to imbecility when "political superstitions" invest them. Shakespeare puts it more succinctly when he makes Lear say that 'a dog's obeyed in office.'

Temporal authority may need external paraphernalia but not the real regal authority. This aspect of the situation can be seen in Portia's speech on mercy, when she maintains that the sceptre and the throne are but the trappings of temporal authority. Melville brings in this subject when he describes the formality of behaviour in the hierarchy of sailors in the whale-hunting ship.

The position of Pip in *Moby Dick* is analogous to that of the Fool in *King Lear*, particularly after his recovery from the sea. As Ahab's destiny gradually closes in upon him, he is particular that Pip should continue to live.

> Lad, lad, I tell thee, thou must not follow Ahab now, The hour is coming when Ahab would not scare thee from him, yet would not have thee by him. There is that in thee, poor lad, which I feel too curing to my malady. (Chap. 129)

The chapter is structured like a scene in a drama. It begins with a stage direction which is followed by a dialogue and a soliloquy. This part of the chapter can be compared with Lear's expression of pity for the Fool.

> Poor fool and knave, I have one part in my heart
> That's sorry yet for thee. (III.ii.72-73)

These are the words of the king when he is persuaded to get into a hovel to seek protection from the thunder-storm and rain. Lear, whose authoritarian nature only had been in evidence so far, begins now to show signs of sympathy and pity for the needy, after his traumatic experience in the storm. He asks the Fool to enter the hovel first and is very solicitous about his condition, since the latter is much younger and more delicate. Captain Ahab who is also very authoritarian by nature also exhibits his concern for Pip who is young and weak. Pip is described as a little Negro lad, five feet high, hang-dog look and cowardly (Chap. 29). He bears resemblance to the Fool in *King Lear*. Both the Fool and the negro lad utter soliloquies at the end of the respective scenes and both refer to a certain deplorable state. The Fool satirizes the topsyturvydom of the moral world and Pip, imitating the maritime officers' style, deplores cowardice.

"Sympathy" is one of the most interesting chapters in *Moby Dick* and almost the whole chapter is Ahab's soliloquy which ranges from self-dramatization to speculation about fate. While Ahab is not pessimistic like the Duke of Gloucester in *King Lear*, his view of man and providence reminds us of the philosophy of the prince of Denmark after he returns from the voyage. The captain of the American ship asks Starbuck what it was that was driving him to the sea again and again in search of the white whale, while all the time, in his heart of hearts he was not so inclined. He answers the question himself.

> By heaven, man, we are turned round and round in this world, like yonder windlass, and Fate is the handspike. (Chap. 132, p. 476)

We can place this philosophical view beside Hamlet's remark

> There's a divinity that shapes our ends
> Rough-hew them how we will. (*Hamlet*, V.ii.11-12)

Both Hamlet and Ahab are single-mindedly engaged in the pursuit of revenge. They utter soliloquies frequently and towards the end of their lives develop near-fatalistic view of life.

The captain who has sworn revenge upon the white whale calls upon the other sailors to swear death to Moby Dick, the whale. Here Ahab resembles Hamlet who calls upon the guards and Horatio to swear that they will not breathe a word to anybody about Hamlet's meeting with the ghost. They swear both in *Hamlet* and *Moby Dick* and disperse. In the background of Hamlet's meeting with the ghost, we hear the boisterous carousing by Claudius and his favourite courtiers. In *Moby Dick*, Starbuck who is speaking a monologue covering a whole chapter, hears the noise of the drunken revelry of the harpooners.

> Hark the infernal orgies! that revelry is forward. (Chap. 38, p. 149)

In both Hamlet and Ahab, we see a certain denial of life. This similarity is quite striking. The gay and creative things of life, society and Nature do not interest Hamlet and in this respect, Ahab resembles Hamlet. The magnificent obsessions of Hamlet's mind prevent him from enjoying life and the prince is aware that he is no longer what he was before the unhappy events in the royal life of Denmark came to pass. The bleakness within his character paints the external world in sombre colours. When he is provoked by Rosencrantz and Guildenstern, the prince says:

> I have of late—but wherefore I know not—lost all my mirth, foregone all custom of exercise; and indeed it goes so heavily with my disposition that this goodly frame, the earth seems to me a sterile promontory; this excellent canopy, the air, look you, this brave o'erhanging firmament, this majestical roof fretted with golden fire—why it appeareth no other thing to me than a foul and pestilement congregation of foul vapours. (II.ii.296-304)

Hamlet concedes that the lights, shapes and colours of this universe are splendid, but he has lost interest in them. Place Ahab's soliloquy by the side of this self analysis:

> Dry heat upon my brow? Oh. time was when as sunrise nobly spurred me, so the sunrise soothed. No more. This lovely light, it lights not me; all the loveliness is anguish to me, since I can never enjoy. (Chap. 37, p. 148)

Ahab's sole passion in life is revenge against the white whale which had chewed away his foot, rendering him a one-legged man. In this revenge-oriented life, no other thing interests him unless it helps him avenge the loss of his leg. Nature's colours and shapes do not have any attraction for him.

However, Melville has not made captain Ahab a copy of Hamlet. There is neither irresoluteness nor procrastination in his character and there is no feeling that he is not equal to the task that he has undertaken. The latter feature can be found in the character of Starbuck, one of his shipmates. Just as the prince of Denmark pities the ghost, Starbuck pities the captain. In the chapter called "Dusk," Starbuck broods over his ties with the captain who wants revenge.

> For in his eyes I read some lucid woe would shrivel me up, had I it. (Chap. 38)

Starbuck is enjoined to swear death to Moby Dick and he is sometimes afraid that he is not equal to the task

> Will I, nill I, the ineffable thing has tied me to him; tows me, with a cable I have no knife to cut. (Chap. 38)

We can reasonably compare this exclamation in Starbuck's soliloquy which occupies the entire chapter with Hamlet's exclamation which conveys his sense of failure and helplessness after the mission of revenge is entrusted to him by the ghost.

> The time is out of joint. O cursed spite.
> That ever I was born to set it right. (I.v.188-89)

Ahab is quite conscious of the fact that the others consider him to be mad.

> They think me mad—Starbuck does; but I am demoniac, I

> am madness maddened! That wild madness that's only calm to comprehend itself. (Chap. 37)

Shakespeare's influence can be seen in the philosophical utterances and transcendental dimensions of the novel. Both Ishmael, the narrator of the story, and Hamlet, the prince of Denmark, indulge in romantic idealization of man, knowing fully well the other side of man. Ishmael is aware of the fact that though Starbuck, next in command to captain Ahab, is brave, he does modify bravery with discretion. Nevertheless, he speaks of man in glowing terms.

> man may have mean and meagre faces; but man, in the ideal, is so noble and so sparkling, such a grand and glowing creature, that over any ignominious blemish in him all his fellows should run to throw their costliest robes. That immaculate manliness we feel within ourselves, so far within us, that it remains intact though all the outer character seems gone. (Chap. 26, p. 102)

Place Hamlet's description of man beside this glowing idealization.

> What a piece of work is man! How noble in reason! how infinite in faculties! in form and moving, how express and admirable! in action how like an angel! in apprehension how like a god! (II.ii.304-8)

Ishmael goes on like Hamlet to compare the august dignity of man with that of God himself. Ishmael knows Starbuck's limitations and his assessment of man has some political overtones; it begins with Ishmael's attack on joint stock companies and ends with his discovery of the dignity of manual labour which he calls democratic dignity, reminding us of John Ruskin's writings.

There is something common in the intense hostility which underlines Ahab's and Hamlet's attitudes towards the objects of their revenge. The targets of their revenge represent undiluted evil. The whole beings of Ahab and Hamlet revolt against Moby Dick and Claudius respectively. Ishmael says:

> Small reason was there to doubt, then, that ever since that almost fatal encounter, Ahab had cherished a wild vindictive-

> ness against the whale, all the more fell for that in his frantic morbidness he at last came to identify with him, not only all his bodily woes, but all his intellectual and spiritual exasperations. (Chap. 41, p. 160)

Hamlet cherishes the same uncompromising vindictiveness against Claudius whom he identifies with all that is evil. One can see the intense morbidity of Hamlet's hatred when he abuses Claudius in the presence of his mother:

> A murderer and a villain
> A slave that is not twentieth part the tithe
> Of your precedent lord; a vice of kings;
> A cutpurse of the empire and the rule,
> That from a shelf the precious diadem stole
> And put it in his pocket. (III.iv.97-102)

Hamlet's intellectual and spiritual consciousness is obsessed with what he regards as the evil nature of Claudius, though after gaining the throne, Claudius has done no harm to anybody including Hamlet and conducts himself with dignity while handling domestic and foreign affairs. Hamlet employs the strongest possible invectives to attack Claudius. He calls Claudius an "incestuous, murder'ous, damned Dane" at the time of stabbing him to death. Nobody in the play except Hamlet regards the relation of Claudius with Gertrude as adulterous or incestuous. Marriage with a brother's wife was not regarded incestuous during the time of Hamlet or else the church would not have been a party to that marriage. All this shows that Hamlet is intellectually and morally exasperated by Claudius. Like Hamlet, Ahab identifies the target of his emotion with evil itself.

The transcendental character of the novel unfolds itself in some unexpected regions. Melville describes the career of the ship's blacksmith who has ruined himself and his family by opening the mouth of the bottle in his old age. One after another, his wife and children are snatched away by death and the author regards the craftsman's own death as a possible relief to him.

> Death seems the only desirable sequel for a career like this: but death is only a launching into the region of the strange

> untried; it is but the first salutation to the possibilities of the immense remote, the wild, the watery, the unshored; therefore, to the death-longing eyes of such a man, who still have left in them some interior compunctions against suicide. (Chap. 112, p. 428)

The prince of Denmark yearns for death, if necessary, through suicide, but is not sure what lies beyond the boundary of life. The longing for death and the internal compunction against suicide in the chapter "The Blacksmith" are reminiscent of the sentiments and doubts in the very first soliloquy of Hamlet:

> O, that this too too solid flesh would melt
> Thaw and resolve itself into a dew
> Or the Everlasting had not fix'd
> His canon 'gainst self-slaughter! (I.i.129-32)

Hamlet's weary longing to get rid of his body and the wish that God had not forbidden suicide have clearly made their way into Melville's *Moby Dick*. Hamlet's description of life beyond death is also reflected in the passage of *Moby-Dick* quoted above.

> But that dread of something after death—
> The undiscover'd country, from whose bourn
> No traveller returns—puzzles the will (III.i.78-80)

Hamlet's wish that the gross and solid flesh would melt like an icicle can be compared with the longing of the captain of *Pequod,* a man of indomitable spirit and tenacity. His leg had been chewed off by Moby Dick and he had a replacement in the form of an artificial leg made of a whale bone. There comes a time when this leg also has to be replaced and he depends upon a carpenter for this. We can appreciate the captain's impatience during his final voyage in which he looks more like a spirit than like a body.

> and yet I owe for the flesh in the tongue I brag with. By the heavens I'll get a crucible, and into it, and dissolve myself to one small, compendious vertebra, so. (Chap. 108, p. 416)

Both Hamlet and Ahab are impatient with flesh. In the chapter,

"Sphynx," the pursuer of revenge takes a deep look at the head of a whale which had been captured and decapitated. Death is a mystery to Ahab and he wonders what has happened to what the dead had known.

> "Speak, thou vast and memorable head" muttered Ahab, which though ungarnished with a beard, yet here and there lookest hoary with mosses; "speak mighty head and tell us the secure thing that is in thee." (Chap. 70, p. 274)

Ahab speaks of the home of the whales, the bottom of the sea which is the graveyard of the ships, lovers who had committed suicide and the shipmates who had been murdered. He speaks of the floor of the sea as a place littered with the bones of those killed in the sea. But the mystery that pervades the mind of the beholder when he sees the remains of the dead is evidently derived from the musings of Hamlet in Elsinore's graveyard:

> Where be your jibes now, your gambols, your songs, your flashes of merriment that were wont to set the table on a roar? (V.i.182-84)

In a digression covering a whole chapter, the author presents the beauty and horror of white hue. If the absence of colour results in whiteness, colour can be denigrated as much as whiteness in the writings of natural philosophers.

> Nature absolutely paints like harlots whose allurements cover nothing but the charnel house within. (Chap. 42, p. 171)

The above comment can be compared with Hamlet's remarks in Elsinore's graveyard:

> Now get you to my lady's chamber and tell her let her paint an inch thick, to this favour she must come; (V.i.185-87)

Like Hamlet, Ishmael also speaks of fine ladies making themselves up and both speak of the reality beneath that make-up, that is, the skull. Charnel house is the place where the bones of the dead are preserved. Both distance themselves from worldliness and talk philosophically at the sight of the cosmetic make-up.

Like the ghost in *Hamlet*, the whale in *Moby Dick* appears only at night and inspires superstitious dread.

> For a time, there reigned too, a sense of peculiar dread at the flitting apparition, as if it were treacherously beckoning us on and on, in order that the monster might turn round upon us, and rend us at last in the remotest and savage seas. (Chap. 50, p. 205)

The key words here are "peculiar dread," "beckon," "apparition" and "monster." The seamen look upon the whale as a supernatural being, and they fear that beckoning them, it may take them to remote seas and destroy them. The man at the topmost mast-head raises the alarm and captain Ahab, the avenger, is called.

In *Hamlet* also, the ghost is described as an apparition; it appears and disappears in the view of the night guards and Horatio. In a subsequent scene, the ghost beckons Hamlet to go with it. Horatio expresses the superstitious dread that the ghost might draw Hamlet to a remote place, flood or a dreadful summit in order to do him harm and he does his best to prevent Hamlet from going with the ghost. The message is conveyed to Hamlet who is the avenger in the play. The night guards are distilled

> Almost to jelly with the act of fear. (I.ii.204-5)

T.S. Eliot says that Shakespeare's tragic heroes have a weakness for self-dramatization and self-pity. This trait of a tragic hero is traced by Eliot to classical and pre-Christian tragedians like Seneca. The prince of Denmark, while drawing his last breath, speaks of his 'wounded name' and exhorts Horatio to absent himself from felicity awhile to tell the world Hamlet's story.

> O God! Horatio, what a wounded name,
> Things standing thus unknown, shall live behind me.
> If thou didst hold me in thy heart,
> Absent thee from felicity awhile,
> And in this harsh world draw thy breath in pain
> To tell my story. (V.ii.336-41)

What we notice here is a kind of self-consciousness. Hamlet, like any other tragic hero of Shakespeare's plays, has suffered, but has also caused suffering to others. This is what a tragic hero does in spite of his being great in other respects. Hamlet is responsible for the suffering of Ophelia, and he has needlessly caused the death of Polonius after insulting him several times, but he pities himself for leaving behind what he regards as his wounded name, without thinking of Ophelia or Polonius at all.

Even King Lear who says that he asks for Cordelia's forgiveness refers repeatedly to his old age and sorrows at the end of his tragic career. He emphasizes his own suffering even while saying that Cordelia is a soul in bliss:

> Thou art a soul in bliss; but I am bound
> Upon a wheel of fire, that my own tears
> Do scald me like molten lead. (IV.vii.46-48)

The stress is less on the sufferings Lear has caused to others and more on his own sorrows and sufferings, his physical frailty and old age.

The character of Othello is not free from this trait. The moor is aware that his crime is unforgivable and that on the Day of Judgement, Desdemona's look will hurl him down from heaven.

> When we shall meet at compt
> This look of thine will hurl my soul from heaven,
> And fiends will snatch at it. (V.ii.272-74)

But Othello's self-dramatization is even more obtrusive than that of Hamlet or Lear. When he has reached his journey's end, he is very particular about how his survivors should speak of him!

> Then must you speak
> Of one that loved not wisely but too well;
> Of one not easily jealous, but being wrought
> Perplexed in the extreme; of one whose subdued eyes
> Albeit unused to the melting mood,
> Drop tears as fast as the Arabian trees
> Their medicinal gum. Set you down this;
> And say besides, that in Aleppo once,

> Where a malignant and turbuned Turk
> Beat a Venetian and traduc'd his state,
> I took by the throat the circumcised dog,
> And smote him thus. (V.ii.342-53)

Othello's speech emphasizes his repentance and achievement, but throughout he is the hero of his own speech. In fact his own suffering and patriotism—he could not bear any insult to Venice by a foreigner—are dramatized here. Othello is keen on setting his record straight and on the image he is leaving behind.

In *The Merchant of Venice,* Antonio speaks of his own suffering and never for a moment speaks of the insults he had heaped on Shylock and of the bond he had signed according to which he is liable to give him a pound of his flesh.

> I do oppose
> My patience to his fury, and am armed
> To suffer with a quickness of spirit
> The very tyranny and rage of his. (IV.i.10-13)

The Christian merchant's speech does not speak of the tyranny of persecution of the Jews, but of the tyranny and rage of the Jew to whom he went for a loan and signed the agreement voluntarily. On the contrary, he speaks of suffering to which he would be subjected and the quietness of spirit with which he is going to face it. Self-dramatization and self-pity are two prominent features of the self-consciousness of the Shakespearean heroes when they speak about themselves at the tragic end of their lives. What they lack is humility.

Now let us place beside these examples the speech of the hero of *Moby Dick*. Nearly half the chapter called "Symphony" comprises Ahab's speech which is more like a soliloquy than like a part of the dialogue with Starbuck, his shipmate. The pensive air, the gentle sea and clear blue firmament induce in the strong-willed captain a gentle and pensive mood in which he starts reminiscing:

> Forty—forty—forty years ago! Forty years of continual whaling! Forty years of privation, and peril and storm-time! forty years of pitiless sea! for forty years has Ahab forgotten the peaceful land, for forty years to make war on the horrors of

> the deep! Aye and yes, Starbuck, out of those forty years I have not spent three ashore. When I think of this life I have led; the desolation of solitude it has been. . . . Oh, weariness! heaviness! . . . When the poorest landsman has had fresh fruit to his daily hand, and broken the world's fresh bread to my mouldy crusts—away, whole oceans away, from the young girl—wife I wedded past fifty, and sailed for Cape Horn the next day, leaving but one dent in my marriage pillow . . . and then, the madness, the frenzy, the boiling blood and the smoking brow with which for a thousand lowerings old Ahab has furiously, foamingly chased his prey—more a demon than a man. (Chap. 132, pp. 474-75)

The captain has been sailing and fighting the whales for forty years and this has resulted in his separation from his family. He has been a stranger to the gentle sentiments of family life, though married. His professional life was hard and dangerous. But the captain does not think of the shipmates whose life and limbs he is risking for the sake of his personal revenge on Moby Dick. In fact, when the white whale is finally attacked, all the sailors except Ishmael lose their lives. Ishmael alone survives to tell the story.

Moby Dick is written in a variety of styles. It is an all male novel and there is no room in it for love, passion or adultery. The conflict in the novel is the opposition between the thinking man and the unthinking Nature. Here man's tragedy is also man's triumph. Both *Hamlet* and *Moby Dick* are stories of revenge. But Ahab is no Hamlet. The captain of *Pequod* chases the white whale with a single-minded determination and pays the supreme price.

We may conclude by saying that Melville is indebted to Shakespeare in his use of language, rhetoric and figures of speech in his masterpiece *Moby Dick*.

Shakespeare's *Hamlet* and Osborne's *Look Back in Anger*: A Comparative Study

I am not suggesting in this essay that the themes of *Hamlet* authored by Shakespeare and *Look Back in Anger* authored by Osborne are exactly the same. Jimmy Porter, the protagonist in *Look Back in Anger* is angry with the older generation and the upper classes. There is a leftist streak in his character, typical of the post-war generation and the phase of cold war. Jimmy is angry because the upper class is complacent and the church is indifferent, according to him. The very sight of his young wife ironing his and her clothes day after day annoys him because she comes from a class which is smug and complacent. He is finally reconciled to her because she experiences suffering when her child is born dead.

The theme of *Hamlet* is different. It is not political: it is transcendental. There is no class conflict, no lost cause and no helplessness of the working class. The theme is the tragedy of a young man who is angry because his mother behaves like a whore, and his uncle-king is a murderer. Hamlet is angry with himself also, because he does not act except when he is provoked and is governed by emotion. As a result, he is a lonely man and even the mission entrusted to him by his father's ghost does not turn him into a man of action. The world is out of joint and he regrets that he has been charged with the mission of setting it right. He is an introspective type and acts rashly, one should say, only when he is subjected to ungovernable emotion and when he encounters the object of that emotion.

So far, we have seen a contrast in themes, but we can also discern a significant resemblance between the two plays, though there is no one-to-one correspondence. Jimmy Porter has zeal and curiosity: he loves to fight for a cause. His frequent tirades are comparable to Hamlet's frequent soliloquies. That Shakespeare was very much in John Osborne's mind is clear from the text of the play, *Look Back in Anger*. Most of the speeches of Jimmy Porter are, no doubt, fulminations and tirades directed against an individual or the class represented by him or her. The news that Helena Charles is coming to stay with Jimmy Porter and his wife sets off a tirade, after he calls her a bitch. He wonders what the motive of her coming is and goes on to add: "Few minutes ago things didn't seem so bad either, I've just about had enough of this 'expense of spirit' lark, as far as women are concerned." (Act I, p. 35) This is an obvious reference to William Shakespeare's sonnet, one hundred and twenty nine, addressed to his dark mistress, in which he defines "lust in action." This, of course, is a literary allusion. But there is a direct reference to Shakespeare himself in which Jimmy Porter lampoons the American professors who do research on Shakespeare and draw fanciful conclusions about him.

Jimmy Porter is iconoclastic, rebellious and high-strung. He is angry at the upper class and equally angry at the previous generation. When he finds nothing to be angry about, he turns his anger against Sunday newspapers which he and Cliff are reading. He is bored and, therefore, angry. "Why do I do this every Sunday? Even the book reviews seem to be the same as last week's. Different books, same reviews." (Act I, p. 10) Everything appears to be futile and unprofitable. This is what we see or read as the play opens. This can be compared to what Hamlet feels as the play of Shakespeare opens:

> How weary, stale, flat and unprofitable
> Seem to me all the uses of this world! (I.ii.133-34)

The young prince finds all the customs and practices of this world stale, flat and unprofitable. There were no newspapers in the age of Hamlet, and if there were, the readers can be certain that they too would have come under the category of the 'uses of this world.' Hamlet is angry at so many objects including the new king and his own twice-married mother, but till he is able to act, he turns his emotions against the ways and customs of this world in very much the same way as Jimmy Porter who turns his discontent against the Sunday newspapers.

Unlike Hamlet, Jimmy is a married man, though young. The very concentration with which Alison presses the clothes like a typical housewife is enough to provoke him to anger. The immediate provocation can rarely conceal the incompatibility of their marriage. Alison's indifference to Jimmy Porter's periodic outbursts of anger makes him even more angry. He starts insulting her in a rude language. Like Jimmy, Hamlet heaps insults upon Ophelia. Like Jimmy and Alison, Hamlet and Ophelia would have been an incompatible pair, though for a different reason, if they had married. Hamlet is emotional, sensitive and excitable. He is certainly heartless like Jimmy in treating his girl, and like him, he nags her persistently.

> Hamlet: Oh, oh. Are you honest?
> Ophelia: My lord?
> Hamlet: Are you fair? (III.i.103-5)

It is easy to see how insulting these remarks are; strictly speaking, they are questions for badgering Ophelia. She is an irritable object for him. She is a protected girl like Alison and she is unable to enter into sympathy with Hamlet even when he is in great distress, following the death of his father and the hasty second marriage of his mother. Ophelia is not able to rise to the occasion, though it must be conceded that Hamlet is a difficult man.

The excitable nature of Hamlet can explode into an ungovernable temper, if he is crossed. When Horatio and Marcellus try to prevent Hamlet all but physically from going with the ghost on the fort. Hamlet is infuriated, though Horatio, and Marcellus did so only with good intentions. Hamlet reacts with a fury which is astonishing.

> Still I am called. Unhand me, gentlemen,
> By heaven, I'll make a ghost of him that lets me.
> I say, away; Go on; I'll follow thee. (I.iv.84-86)

Compare this with Jimmy Porter's temper. His perpetual restlessness and anger can turn into fury if he is crossed. The role of Cliff corresponds to that of Horatio in *Hamlet*. He is Jimmy's well-wisher and friend; like Horatio, he is more a disinterested observer than a participant in the play. He intercedes on behalf of Alison and asks Jimmy to leave her alone. When Jimmy doesn't, he places his leg on him from behind the newspaper he is reading. At this

Jimmy becomes incredibly furious and yells at Cliff: "Do that again, you ruffian, and I'll pull your ears off." (Act I, p. 11) It must be conceded, however, that Cliff does intervene a little more than Horatio in Shakespeare's play. Times and attitudes are different and much water had flown down the Thames since *Hamlet* was written.

The young Hamlet's antipathy to Polonius, Ophelia's father, is well known. When in answer to his question where her father is, she says that he is at home—a lie, of course—Hamlet hits back: "Let the doors be shut upon him, that he may play the fool nowhere but in's own house." (III.i.132-33)

This is not the only occasion when Hamlet makes insulting remarks about the old man. In Hamlet's view, Polonius is a tedious, meddlesome, old fool. He is scornful towards the old man, and on one occasion, after Polonius leaves—he had come to test Hamlet's sanity of mind—the prince exclaims, "These tedious old fools!" (II.ii.219) In fact, this exclamation comes close on the heels of Hamlet's imaginary description of old men and the description itself is contemptuous. When Polonius asks Hamlet what he is reading, the prince replies: "Slanders, Sir; for the satirical rogue here says that old men have grey beards; that their faces are wrinkled . . . and that they have plentiful lack of wit, together with weak hams. . . ." (II.ii.196-200)

Why does Hamlet develop this hostility towards old people? It is obvious that he sees his confrontation with Polonius as a confrontation between himself and the older generation. Two others to whom he has a pet aversion, namely, Claudius and Gertrude are not young either. When Hamlet kills Polonius by mistake, even his old age does not deter him from exclaiming: "Thou wretched, rash, intruding fool, farewell!" (III.iv.74)

Hamlet's counterpart in *Look Back in Anger* exhibits a resentful attitude towards Alison's father. Much time is spent in the opening scene on reading newspapers and he reads aloud a certain statement by the Bishop of Bromley who says he is accused by someone of supporting the rich against the poor. Denying this accusation, the Bishop says as quoted by Jimmy: "This idea has been persistently and wickedly fostered by the working class!" (Act I, pp. 13-14) Quoting this, Jimmy Porter turns to Alison and asks her whether her father could have written it and remarks "Sounds rather like Daddy, don't you think?" When she doubts it, he asks "Is the Bishop of Bromley his nom de plume, do you think?"

Jimmy Porter's aversion to Alison's father who had opposed their marriage like Hamlet's aversion to Polonius surfaces again and again in the play. Perhaps, the remote origin of this resentment lies in the conflict of class interests. Daddy, as he calls his father-in-law, belongs to the upper class and Jimmy to the working class.

A curious point of resemblance between the Shakespearean play and this modern play is the use of the word, *bend* in its noun form by both Hamlet and Jimmy Porter, when they express their anger and impatience. Hamlet is aware that Polonius, Rosencrantz and Guildenstern are curious about his state of mind and are prying into it. He is under a self-imposed compulsion to outdo them in the game of pretending to behave and talk like a fool. After teasing Polonius in this game, Hamlet exclaims in an aside, "They fool me to the top of my bend." (III.ii.375) Evidently, Hamlet feels that his nerves are giving out. Compare this with Jimmy Porter's exclamation when he becomes impatient with what he regards as the listlessness and lack of enthusiasm on the part of even his wife and friend: "You two will drive me round the bend soon—I know it as sure as I am sitting here." (Act I, p. 15) We can see how both Hamlet and Jimmy reach the limit of endurance and how they feel that their nerves are giving out. They both use the noun form of the word *bend* in similar states of mind. This cannot be a sheer coincidence.

Part of the trouble of Hamlet is that he experiences a sense of isolation. The people who have anything to do with him fail to enter into sympathy with him. Their concerns are not his, and his concerns are not theirs. In *Look Back in Anger* also, we cannot fail to notice that the central character nurses a sense of isolation and that nobody is able to enter his world to sympathise with him. Cliff, like Horatio, is, no doubt, a balanced man, but neutral for all intents and purposes like Horatio.

Shakespeare's antipathy to sycophancy is well known and he gives expression to it through the characters created by him in more than one play. No wonder, a play of great psychological interest like *Hamlet* is also used by him to communicate his sympathies and antipathies. The prince of Denmark does not overtly charge Rosencrantz, Guildenstern and Polonius with sycophancy, but he knows that they are not free from it. His own praise of Horatio is no flattery.

Why should the poor be flatter'd?
No, let the candied tongue lick absurd pomp,
And crook the pregnant hinges of the knee
Where thrift may follow fawning. (III.ii.59-62)

There is no need to comment on the vivid images of flattery here, because our present concern is to note the attitude towards sycophancy shared by Hamlet and Jimmy. Like Ophelia, Hamlet's love, Alison, the young wife of Jimmy Porter, has a brother whom Jimmy dislikes, though not for personal reasons. It is the class and attitudes of Nigel that invite Jimmy's antipathy. Clubbing Alison and her mother with him, Jimmy makes them the target of his tirade: "Nigel and Alison. They're what they sound like: sycophantic, phlegmatic and pusillanimous." (Act I, p. 21) It must be remembered, of course, that sycophancy in the royal court is not exactly the same as the sycophancy in a democratic society. But this society is not classless and sycophancy is still useful. What is relevant is that Hamlet and Jimmy share the same set of values, while their situations are not identical.

Hamlet's cynicism towards women in general and Ophelia and Gertrude in particular is well known. Ophelia's move to return his gifts to him is enough to send him into a rage of cynicism.

Hamlet: Oh! Oh! Are you honest?
Ophelia: My lord?
Hamlet: Are you fair?
Ophelia: What means your lordship?
Hamlet: That if you be honest and fair, honesty should admit no discourse to your beauty.
Ophelia: Could beauty, my lord, have better commerce than with honesty?
Hamlet: Ay, truly; for the power of beauty will sooner transform honesty from what it is to a bawd than the force of honesty can translate beauty into his likeness. (III.i.103-12)

Hamlet who is in an angry mood is associating his love, Ophelia with dishonesty, and, what is interesting, he says so directly, knowing fully well that it would hurt her. He persists in doing so, as if he enjoyed it. In *Look Back in Anger*, Hamlet's counterpart is in a similar angry mood and attacks Alison, his love and wife persistently, not talking to her directly as Hamlet does, but in her immediate presence, with as much cynicism as Hamlet. Alison lacks firmness of mind according to Jimmy—in this respect Ophelia is not different—who takes up a dictionary, looks up for the word pusillanimous and begins his fulmination: "Here it is, I quote: Pusillanimous. Adjective. Wanting of firmness, of small courage, having a little mind, mean spirited, cowardly, timid of mind. From the Latin Pusillus, very little, and animus, the mind. That's my wife. That's her. Isn't it?" (Act I, p. 22)

What Jimmy identifies Alison with is not exactly the same as what is attributed to Ophelia by Hamlet. But there is no doubt that the daughter of Polonius is timid of mind and that another phrase seen above, *wanting of firmness* can also be attributed to her without being unfair to her. What is very significant is that both Hamlet and Jimmy Porter are hurting their girls with a vengeance and that both are rude and cynical.

Hamlet's attack on Ophelia is supplemented by his tirade against women in general. He has, it must be admitted, a penchant for generalization. What is important in this context is Hamlet's fulmination against fair sex itself. In the famous 'nunnery scene' the prince of Denmark turns his wrath against women in general: "I have heard of your paintings too, well enough; God hath given you one face, and you make yourselves another. You jig and amble, and you lisp, and nickname God's creatures, and make your wantonness your ignorance. Go to, I'll no more o't: it hath made me mad." (III.i.143-48)

The hero of *Look Back in Anger* too turns his attack on Alison, his wife, into an attack on women in general. Alison's routine work of ironing the clothes including those of Jimmy himself annoys him and brings out his anger. He finds in Cliff an audience for his tirade against women: "I watch for her to do the same thing every night. The way she jumps on the bed, as if she were stamping on someone's face, and draws the curtain back with a great clatter, in that destructive way of hers. It's like someone launching a battleship. Have you ever noticed how noisy women are? Have you? The way they kick the floor about, simply walking over it? Or have you watched them sitting at their dressing tables, dropping their weapons and banging down their bits of boxes and brushes and lipsticks?" (Act I, p. 24)

The sight of Laertes leaping into the grave of Ophelia and his histrionic demonstration of grief infuriates Hamlet and he emerges into the scene of the funeral, only to leap into the same grave to challenge Laertes's claim that he loved Ophelia most and, therefore, he was the most grief-stricken of all the survivors. Both are in an emotional state and the result of their close encounter can easily be guessed. Laertes grips Hamlet in his arm aggressively and the latter attempts to free himself, threatening Laertes with grave consequences.

> I prithee take thy fingers from my throat;
> For, though I am not splenitive and rash,
> Yet have I in me something dangerous,
> Which let thy wiseness fear. Hold off thy hand.
>
> (V.i.252-55)

Let us compare this confrontation and threat with what happens in *Look Back in Anger*. Jimmy Porter, the central character, persists in insulting Alison in particular and women in general. His friend, Cliff who is young like Laertes, but more like Horatio in character, cannot bear it and he pushes Jimmy round the floor and grips him like a vice. Jimmy makes a determined bid to free himself and warns Cliff: "Your teeth will be out in a minute, if you don't let me go!" (Act I, p. 26)

We can see how the details of the two scenes in *Hamlet* and *Look Back in Anger* correspond to each other. The dispute is about the suffering caused to a young woman by the hero. It is a young man who grapples with the hero and holds him in his grip. Thirdly, the hero who tries to free himself warns him of dire consequences. Hamlet's response is, no doubt, a little more complex in that he speaks of a dangerous trait in his own character, while Jimmy does not. But it looks as if Horatio had acted like Laertes in *Look Back in Anger*.

Hamlet is sarcastic about Ophelia's virginity which she has assiduously preserved at the advice of her father who thought that Hamlet might desert her. This is one of the things that make the prince angry and Ophelia who is a ploy used by her father becomes unwittingly the victim of Hamlet's anger. Hamlet advises her to go to a nunnery and become a nun instead of marrying a sinner like him: "Get thee to a nunnery. Why should thou be a breeder of sinners? I am myself indifferent honest, but yet I could accuse me of such things that it were better my mother had not borne me." (III.i.121-24)

This can be compared to what Jimmy Porter says to Alison in *Look Back in Anger*. We do not have his direct speech here, but we have it as reported by Alison, his girl when she is talking to Cliff, the Horatio of this modern play who for once had acted like Laertes: "We knew each other such a short time, everything moved at such a pace, we didn't have much opportunity. And, afterwards, he actually taunted me with my virginity. He was quite angry about it, as if I had deceived him in some strange way." (Act I, p. 30)

It is true that there is no one-to-one correspondence between the two plays. The modern play has a modern sensibility in the sense that the question of class morality—the loose morality of the working class and the strict morality of the upper class—comes into the view here. But the association of anger, virginity, taunting of the girls and even the thought of deception with the hero's relation with the girl are quite significant. In the heart of comparison we find the girl's adherence to virginity and the innuendo of the girl's parents about the morality of the young men in love with them. What we find in *Look Back in Anger* and not in *Hamlet* is the modern concept of class morality and the attitudes of the classes.

Hamlet is not married and he would have married Ophelia—his mother would have liked to see her as her son's wife—if certain things including the suspicion of Ophelia's father had not come in the way. Polonius had feared that Hamlet might desert Ophelia after she had lost her virginity and that he could afford to do so, because he belonged to the royal family, while she did not. In *Look Back in Anger*, the young man faces the hostility of Alison's parents to his proposal to marry Alison. Jimmy resents their attitude: "Mummy and Daddy turn pale, and face east everytime they remember she's married me." (Act I, p. 31) We can see the undercurrent of Jimmy Porter's anger and sarcasm. Alison's parents including her father are suspicious towards Jimmy Porter whose character, they thought, was loose because he belonged to the working class. As I said earlier, there is no sign of class conflict and no sign of any aspersion cast on the fidelity of a working class man in *Hamlet*. But what the two plays share is a set of attitudes which include the older generation's opposition: the doubt they express about the young man's fidelity and the young man's sarcasm.

The readers of Shakespeare's play are likely to ask the question whether Hamlet is not, when all is said, a puritan at heart. Why, otherwise, should Hamlet repeatedly censure his mother's sexual life, when all her offence was remarriage after the death of her husband? He denounces it to the face of his mother herself:

> Rebellious hell,
> If thou canst mutiny in a matron's bones,
> To flaming youth, let virtue be as wax
> and melt in her own fire; (III.iv.83-86)

Why should Hamlet object to the enjoyment of sex by the middle-aged people and regard it as wicked? He even goes to the extent of saying that in such people, reason itself is playing pander to their desire. In the graveyard scene, he addresses the skull thrown up by the Sexton and asks it to go to a lady's chamber and tell her that to this state she will come ultimately, however thickly she might paint her face. In the closet scene, Hamlet tells his own mother how her husband might caress her body by pinching her cheek, patting her neck and kissing her sexily, as if they are dirty things.

Jimmy Porter notices the gestures of love in which his own wife and his friend Cliff indulge, but instead of becoming jealous, he only condemns their indulgence in sex! He tells them that they look silly "slobbering over each other" and goes on to say to Cliff: "You are just a sexy little Welshman, and you know it!" To this objection, Cliff's calm answer is that Jimmy is "just a puritan at heart." (Act I, p. 31)

It is curious that Jimmy Porter is not jealous and angry, though he is angry most of the time over more basic issues, but only expresses his disgust, since he cannot bear the sight of caressing! The reader can be pardoned if he concludes that both Hamlet and Jimmy, though young, are puritans at heart.

Hamlet knows his own character as much as his critics do and like a true gentleman begs Laertes's pardon for having wronged him, a little while before the fencing match begins:

> Give me your pardon, Sir, I have done you wrong:
> But pardon't, as you are a gentleman.

This presence knows,
And you must needs have heard how I am punish'd
with a sore distraction. (V.ii.217-21)

Hamlet finds himself in the grip of emotion whenever he is provoked and he is painfully aware of this weakness which he regards as a violent perturbation of mind. Compare this with what Jimmy Porter says to Alison after he has hurt her. The angry young man feels sorry and says so to Alison, and, what is incredible, admits he did so on purpose: "I've got to hit out somehow. Nearly four years of being in the same room with you, night and day, and I still can't stop my sweat breaking out when I see you doing something as ordinary as leaning over an iron board." (Act I, p. 33) What is pertinent here is not the reason given by Jimmy Porter, but his frank admission that he is in the grip of the emotion of anger. Jimmy's apology to Alison and his admission that he cannot help getting angry remind one of a similar situation, apology and admission of this trait by Hamlet. Neither Hamlet nor Jimmy Porter states the reason for his emotion. Jimmy Porter tries to find a reason for his angry outbursts: for example, he says rather haltingly that he has a lot of old stock presumably in his shop of sweets—and that nobody wants it. We may note incidentally, that Hamlet also speaks of *old stock* in his outburst against Ophelia, but this phrase has a different meaning in his speech.

Both Hamlet and Jimmy Porter experience a sense of isolation and suspect the activities of the people who belong to a world to which they do not belong. When we do not have rapport with some people and still they seem to be sympathetic towards us, though we are alone, it is natural that we suspect them. No wonder, Hamlet is suspicious of the communication that is being sent to the king of England with Rosencrantz and Guildenstern who are accompanying him. What are the contents of this communication? Is Hamlet going to be betrayed? Is he going to be the victim of perfidy? Hamlet does not mind purloining the letters when Rosencrantz and Guildenstern are not in their cabin one night. He searches their baggage and takes out the letters. Unethical? Yes. But Hamlet is not very much bothered and thinks that the end justifies the means:

Up from my cabin,
My sea-gown scarf'd about me, in the dark

Grop'd I to find them; had my desire;
Finger'd their packet and in fine withdrew
To my own cabin, making me so bold,
My fears forgetting manners, to unseal
Their grand commission. (V.ii.13-18)

Let us place this speech side by side with the speech of Jimmy Porter who like Hamlet justifies his looking into the handbags, cases and even trunks of Alison to find out whether there is any letter containing references to him. Cliff is Horatio's counterpart in *Look Back in Anger* and the modern Hamlet feels it necessary to defend his action when Cliff demurs:

> You're quite right. But do you know something? Living night and day with another human being has made me predatory and suspicious. I know that the only way of finding out exactly what's going on is to catch them when they don't know you're looking. When she goes out, I go through everything—trunks, cases, drawers, bookcase, everything. Why? To see if there is something of me somewhere, a reference to me. I want to know, if I am being betrayed. (Act I, p. 36)

All the details in this comparison do not correspond to one another; but basically, the attitudes and the actions are the same. Hamlet and Jimmy are suspicious. They have to defend their actions in their talks with their confidants—Horatio and Cliff—and they fear that they may be betrayed by those who are hostile to them. Searching other people's belongings does not bother their scruples. As a reader I feel that if Ophelia had married Hamlet against the will of her father, Hamlet would have done what Jimmy Porter does in *Look Back*. Correspondingly, Jimmy Porter would have done what Hamlet did if he were in Hamlet's situation. As it happens, their actions and basic attitudes are the same.

We are all prone to use the words, *mad, madness* and *psychology* in a loose sense which is rather metaphorical and not professional. Hamlet's mother who knows her son's character quite well exclaims "This is mere madness!" (V.i.278) when Hamlet leaps recklessly into the grave of Ophelia and challenges the love of Laertes who had earlier leaped into the same grave. A little while earlier, Claudius himself had reacted saying, "O, he is mad,

Laertes!" (V.i.266) The references are obviously to Hamlet's emotional and rash actions when he is provoked. Both Gertrude and Claudius know that Hamlet is no lunatic. *In Look Back in Anger*, Helena whose initial reaction to Jimmy's frequent angry outbursts is scornful, exhorts Alison to leave Jimmy. She tells her friend that either Jimmy should learn to behave like anyone else and look after her or "You must get out of this madhouse." (Act I, p. 47) It is evident that Helena has in mind only Jimmy's frequent tirades and insults.

When the play opens, Hamlet has already lost his father. In a curious way, Jimmy too has lost his father, and his mother has survived him. In both the plays, the deceased fathers are heroes to their sons.

Hamlet is angry with Polonius, his bete noire because he is opposed to his love for Ophelia though his opposition is based on a worldly man's suspicion and not on class interests. Taking advantage of his disguise as a madman, he starts insulting the old courtier. He lampoons Polonius to his face when the latter asks him what he is reading. Hamlet's reply is

> Slanders, Sir; for the satirical rogue says here that old men have grey beards; that their faces are wrinkled; their eyes purging thick amber and plum-tree gum; and that they have plentiful lack of wit, together with most weak hams—all which, Sir, though I am most powerfully and potently believe, yet I hold it not honesty to have it thus set down; for yourself, sir, shall grow old as I am, if like a crab, you could go backward. (II.ii.196-204)

Hamlet's attack on the old man is outrageous because it is marked by disgusting images.

Jimmy Porter's attack on Alison's mother is equally outrageous and disgusting. What is significant here is the young man's anger and the disgusting images he uses to vent his anger. Jimmy does not confront Alison's mother and in this respect, Hamlet's situation is different. But there is a proxy, as it were, because her daughter is present and Jimmy describes her in a very insulting language:

> Mummy and I took one quick look at each other, and from then on, the age of chivalry was dead. I knew that, to protect

> her innocent young, she wouldn't hesitate to cheat, lie, bully and blackmail. Threatened with me, a young man, without money, background or even looks, she'd bellow like a rhinoceros in labour—enough to make every male rhino for miles turn white, and pledge himself to celibacy.
>
> (Act II, p. 52)

The new contemporary sensibility, no doubt, involves here the hostility between the working class and the middle class with its smug security and complacency. But what is important is that the young man, like Hamlet, is hostile to the elder generation and uses disgusting images to express his hostility. Jimmy may not be satirical, but he is certainly blunt and more contemptuous.

Comparisons and contrasts cannot be separated into air-tight compartments in all cases. Sometimes, there is contrast within comparison, just as there is comparison within contrast. In Shakespeare's play, it is Polonius who probes into Hamlet's affairs like a private detective and it is Claudius who engages the services of Rosencrantz and Guildenstern, just as one would engage the services of private detectives these days. Their job is to probe Hamlet's affairs and discover the reasons for his strange behaviour. What is equally important, it is the father of Ophelia, Hamlet's flame, who zealously offers his services to the king of making a secret investigation of Hamlet's transformation.

> Take this from this, if this be otherwise.
> If circumstances lead me, I will find
> Where the truth is hid, though it were hid indeed
> Within the centre. (II.ii.156-59)

Polonius, the overzealous courtier, goes to work like a professional detective by 'loosing' his daughter to Hamlet, when Hamlet walks in the lobby and watches Hamlet's responses with the king by his side.

In *Look Back in Anger*, it is not Alison's father, but her mother who arranges surveillance on Jimmy Porter's movements. In one of his tirades provoked by the presence of Helena, Jimmy recalls what Alison's mother did, when she could not appreciate his long hair: "So she hires detectives to watch me, to see if she can't somehow get me into the *News of the World*." (Act II, p. 52) In both the plays, it is a parent who is opposed to his daughter's love and it is this parent that keeps a watch on the young man's behaviour and movements. What is also basic in this comparison is that the young man kept under surveillance knows it and this surveillance fuels the fire of the young man's hostility towards the older generation.

As far as characters are concerned, the resemblance is a major factor. This is of basic importance, because it explains why Hamlet and Jimmy are both angry young men. Both the young men have high regard for their fathers and scant regard for their mothers. Hamlet idealises his father and regards his mother's love for her second husband as a bestial passion. Both Hamlet and Jimmy denigrate their mothers whose characters are superficial. They believe that these ladies did not love their husbands truly, because they had other interests. Jimmy Porter's father has come back from the Spanish civil war of which he is an unknown hero. In any case, he is a hero to his son. He recalls in his talk with Helena who has turned into a sympathetic listener, though she was critical in the beginning:

> For twelve months, I watched my father dying—when I was ten years old. He'd come back from the war in Spain, you see. And some god-fearing gentlemen had made such a mess of him he didn't have long left to live. Everyone knew it—even I knew it. But you see I was the only one who cared. His family was embarrassed by the whole business. Embarrassed and irritated. As for my mother, all she could think about was the fact that she had allied herself to a man who seemed to be on the wrong side in all things. My mother was all for being associated with minorities, provided they were smart, fashionable ones. (Act II, p. 57)

We must note that like Jimmy Porter, Hamlet is the only man in the family who cared for his father. There is hardly any reference to him in the speeches of Claudius, Gertrude and Polonius, though he was the hero of the war with Norway. In either play, there is hardly any love lost between the husband and wife. The only man who has any sense of values is their son.

The resemblance between the two plays extends to the parental objection to the marriage of the girl with the young man with whom she is in love. Polonius disapproves of Ophelia's romance with

Hamlet who belongs to a class different from hers. In fact, he belongs to royalty. Polonius tries to dissuade his daughter from accepting Hamlet's love.

> For Lord Hamlet,
> Believe so much in him, that he is young,
> And with a larger tether may he walk
> Than may be given to you. In few, Ophelia,
> Do not believe in his vows; for they are brokers,
> Not of that dye which their investments show,
> But mere implorators of unholy suits. . . . (I.iii.123-29)

The readers can easily discern the worldly wisdom and cynicism underlining these words of advice. Hamlet is young and, therefore, his love is like a flame that gives more heat than light. Secondly, Hamlet is a prince and can afford to trifle with a mere chamberlain's daughter and let her down, after seducing her.

In *Look Back in Anger*, the father of the girl is opposed to her marriage with the young man whom she has decided to marry. Unlike Ophelia, Alison's mother is alive and she is much more determined in her opposition to her daughter's marriage with Jimmy Porter. Col. Redfern, Alison's father wonders whether he and his wife went too far in their opposition: "I didn't approve of Jimmy at all, and I don't suppose I ever would, but looking back upon it, I think it would have been better, for all concerned, if we had never attempted to interfere. At least, it would have been a little more dignified." (Act II, p. 65)

Col. Redfern, like Polonius, attempts to stop the marriage. Their characters are, however, poles apart. Alison's father is not cynical or worldly. He is more balanced and sensible. Their reasons are different. In *Look Back in Anger*, the marriage does take place, unlike what happens in *Hamlet*, not only because the times are different, but also because Alison is much more determined than Ophelia, Again, the question of class is placed upside down here. Jimmy, unlike Hamlet, comes from a lower class, from the working class to be precise. The parental opposition smacks of the upper class attitude, but the basic similarity lies in the elders' opposition which results in the young man's hostility to the older generation. Even the motives of the young man are questioned, but in the modern play, it is not the father but the mother who questions the motives of the young suitor.

In *Hamlet*, Horatio's character is unique in the true and literal sense, because there is none like him in that play and we must turn to *Look Back in Anger* to find someone like him. He is non-aligned, disinterested and dispassionate, though his sympathies are with Hamlet. No wonder, Hamlet who is a slave of emotion finds him an admirable character. He says so to Horatio himself:

> for thou hast been
> As one, in suff'ring all, that suffers nothing;
> A man that fortune's buffets and rewards
> Hast ta'en with equal thanks (III.ii.66-69)

In *Look Back in Anger*, Jimmy Porter too has a friend and confidant in Cliff who is a detached and impartial observer like Horatio and like the latter, has the poise and equanimity which Hamlet sees in Horatio. Helena, the passionate champion of Alison, blames him for his detachment.

To use an image from *Bhagavadgita*, both Cliff and Horatio are like a drop of water on a lotus leaf. They are in the midst of action, but they maintain a certain degree of objectivity and poise. Cliff does not always share Jimmy's ideas or support Jimmy's actions, but his sympathies are always with Jimmy. As for Alison, he loves her and his love is not purely Platonic, but at the same time, he is a sort of what he calls a no man's land between Alison and her husband. Horatio in the play of Shakespeare does not practise negative neutrality, either. He does co-operate with Hamlet, because his sympathies are with him. We must concede that he does take the initiative of taking Hamlet to the ghost of his father and at Hamlet's request, he watches Claudius's response during the play arranged by Hamlet. At the same time, he does intervene to separate Hamlet and Laertes when they confront each other in the grave of Ophelia. He does not automatically or blindly take the side of Hamlet in this unseemly confrontation. Hamlet's action of sending Rosencrantz and Guildenstern to the executioner's axe does not meet with his approval, though this disapproval is hinted only in a brief and cryptic remark. When Hamlet has a premonition of the coming event and says so, Horatio tries to persuade Hamlet to get the encounter with Laertes put off.

As Cliff likes Jimmy and is on his side, Horatio likes Hamlet and is on his side. When Hamlet is dying at the end of his match with Laertes, Horatio tries to take his own life after a very touching prayer for the peace of Hamlet's soul. When the news is brought that the instructions of Claudius had been carried out in England and that Rosencrantz and Guildenstern were dead, Horatio remarks even in the midst of those tragic and solemn moments that no such instructions had been given by the king. Truly, Horatio and Cliff have a lot of things in common.

While elaborating the comparisons, I have dwelt upon the contrasts also. Jimmy Porter is married, while Hamlet is not. Jimmy marries Alison regardless of the opposition by her parents, but Hamlet does not persuade Ophelia to accept him, because something else also claims his attention. Hamlet dies, but Jimmy does not; only his child dies. Jimmy comes from the working class, and his fulminations are directed against both the upper class and the elder generation. In *Hamlet*, there is no room for conflict of class interests.

Jimmy directs his anger not only against the upper class, but also against the church and the religion which are in his view collocated with rightists and upper class. Hamlet is not against them and he does not share Jimmy's irreverent attitude towards the supernatural. Far from it, Hamlet tells Horatio that there are more things in heaven and earth than in his philosophy. The prince of Denmark does not entertain any anti-clerical attitude and starts believing that there is a divinity that shapes our ends rough-hew them how we will and that there is special providence in the fall of a sparrow. Jimmy Porter is at times, sentimental, if not maudlin, but Hamlet is not.

There is no denying that John Osborne is not a plagiarist. In fact, the themes of the two plays are different. for each play is known for its own sensibility. When all is said, the reader must note the employment of a Shakespearean technique in the play, *Look Back in Anger*. Helena, a friend of Alison, is the first character in the play to question Jimmy's right to say the things which he is saying and to defend those whom he attacks without justification. One such outburst had started with Alison's agreeing to accompany Helena to the Church. Helena asks Jimmy how such an innocuous and common thing could call for an angry tirade by him. Jimmy Porter does not calm down and persists in his insults. Helena does not give in meekly and asks him: "You think the world's treated you pretty badly, don't you?" At this, Alison intervenes to make a humorous, sarcastic and tongue-in-the-cheek comment: "Oh, don't try and take his suffering away from him—he would be lost without it." (Act II, Scene I, p. 54) Such a counterpoint is not much in evidence in Hamlet, though Shakespeare is well known for counterpoint or dual vision in his plays. Hamlet's soliloquies dominate the play and there is no one to express the opposite point of view either seriously or humorously. This may be due to the fact that all are puzzled by Hamlet's 'antic disposition' which he has cleverly put on. His emotional excesses seen in the form of rash and reckless actions are at best explained by his mother to save her son. Here is the only comment on Hamlet's psychology:

> This is mere madness;
> And thus awhile the fit will work on him;
> Anon, as patient as the female dove
> When that her golden couplets are disclos'd,
> His silence will sit brooding. (V.i.278-82)

Gertrude is partly right, but this is no ironic or direct questioning of the justification for Hamlet's tirades and rash actions. This is no counterpoint to a point. However, even after studying all the differences between the two plays, the reader cannot resist the conclusion that one can see the impress of *Hamlet* on *Look Back in Anger*.

Both Hamlet and Jimmy Porter are slaves of passion, if by passion we mean ungovernable emotion of anger. They are both sadistic and emotional. They indulge even in sentimental self-pity. But John Osborne's play is no carbon copy of *Hamlet*. I am aware that Jimmy Porter is a leftist and certainly an iconoclastic rebel unlike Hamlet. However, Shakespeare's *Hamlet* has such powerful magnetism that John Osborne saw in its hero the archetype for the character of the angry young man who rebels against the older generation and who is puzzled by his own emotion of anger which seems to govern him sometimes. I have no doubt in my mind that the twentieth century play is indebted to *Hamlet* without being a copy of the latter. If Hamlet were in the position of Jimmy Porter, he would have acted very much like the latter. The converse is equally true, I believe. The resemblances which I have studied above cannot be dismissed as purely accidental.

His (Shakespeare's) Grammar and Our Grammar

The phrase "his grammar" means in this essay a set of grammatical features in the plays of Shakespeare, which are at variance with the rules of modern English grammar. The phrase "our grammar" means in this essay the corresponding grammatical features and the rules of grammar which we in India have derived from well-known text books of grammar and models of English prose, written and published in the twentieth century. The body of this essay consists of the differences between Shakespeare's grammar and our grammar. The differences are illustrated by quoting the concerned sentences from Shakespeare's plays and by noting the way in which we in modern times are expected by our grammarians to rewrite them.

A careful study of the plays of Shakespeare with our focus on what is grammatically acceptable will bring to light nearly a hundred types of what today looks either as odd or unacceptable from the point of view of modern grammar. It is necessary to say one more thing in this context on the scope of this essay. Vocabulary and orthography are outside its scope; and the focus of the essay is only what is grammatically unacceptable today. The reasons for saying so are also explained in each case. No aesthetic judgement is made.

Roughly speaking, the year 1500 marks the beginning of modern English and the end of medieval English. The sentence modifier, "roughly speaking," sounds a note of caution and this participial phrase is necessary to anticipate the statement that Middle English and Renaissance English cannot be separated into watertight compartments. Vestiges of Middle English continued beyond the year 1500 for a little more time, but to all intents and purposes, the Renaissance English can be clearly marked off from the former.

William Caxton and William, the Conqueror, have more than

their first name in common. Both of them in their respective periods were directly or indirectly responsible for the growth of English language. In 1476, William Caxton who set up the first printing press in England might not have known that the process of printing from movable types would affect the course of the development of English language, for, after all, he was a technical man and not a writer. But that was precisely the influence of his printing press on English language, though to bracket him with William the Conqueror (1027-1087) in all respects would be an irrelevant comparison.

A fall-out of the introduction of the printing press was the rapid dissemination of knowledge through books which swiftly replaced the laboriously copied manuscripts. By 1640, twenty thousand titles had appeared and what was till then the luxury of a few people was now within the reach of all and sundry. It is difficult to exaggerate the influence of the printing process on language, particularly in the decade following its invention and general use. No other development can equal it in the matter of promoting a standard and uniform language.

The Renaissance or the Revival of Art and Learning could not but involve the commoners and it is not surprising that more and more people acquired literacy. This movement of literacy was given a forceful fillip by the printing press of movable types which could turn out thousands of copies which were exactly similar. Ability to read and write was much more easy to acquire now than ever before. The neo-literates moved up the social ladder and it was natural that they should imitate the language and culture of the upper classes. This social dynamics was triggered by the printing press through the spread of literacy. William Shakespeare was born against this background.

The neo-classical language in England was, of course, English and it was not without struggle that English won recognition as a medium of serious thought. Greek and Latin, the two ancient classical languages of Europe, particularly Latin, had till the sixteenth century occupied the centrestage and English was relegated to the side wing. In the Middle Ages, French, a Latin-based language, was the official language of England and hence English was the linguistic Cinderalla. But struggle for recognition of English as a medium of various subjects had been carried on more or less successfully by the English enthusiasts before Shakespeare arrived on the scene to set the Thames on fire, though a knowledge of Latin and Greek was still considered to be a cultural and linguistic asset. Remember Ben Jonson's "thou had small Latine, and less Greeke."

The scholars of the previous generation did entertain the notion that English language was not suitable or rich enough to be the medium of science and humanities, whereas the classical languages, according to them, had nearly reached the acme of perfection. Therefore, a writer of this pre-Shakespearean generation took up the gauntlet on behalf of his native English. Sir Thomas Elyot (1490-1546), a writer of books on education and political science, was himself a bit apologetic when he wrote an English translation of a Greek work, but a year later, in 1534, when he wrote the book, *Castle of Health*, he was forthright in his defence of writing in English: "If physicians be angry, that I have written physicke in English, let them remember that the Greeks wrote in Greke, the Romans in Latine, Avicenna, and others in Arabike, which were their own proper and material tongues. And if thei had bene as much attached with envie and covetise, as some now seems to be thei wolde have devised some particular language, with a strange cipher or form of letters, wherein thei would have written their scyence, which language or letters no man should have knowen that had not professed or practised physicke." Note the quaint punctuation and spelling. Elyot's logic was very convincing. The champions of English in England had done their work by the time Shakespeare started writing the plays for which he is known all the world over. English language was ready for him.

Let me once again state that this essay does not dwell on vocabulary, orthography or the phonological aspects of Shakespeare's English. Its scope is limited to those features of Shakespeare's English which have a bearing on grammar. By his time, inflections which prominently characterize Middle English and Old English had been reduced to almost modern proportions. The survival of "eyen" for the plural noun, "eyes," is only one of the few exceptions like "shoon" for "shoes." Their appearance even in his plays is not frequent: it is only occasional. In any case, the study of the disappearance of inflections in Elizabethan English is not within the scope of this essay which discusses only those features of Shakespeare's English that are not permitted today by the rules of modern English grammar as learnt in India. These features are, let me say at the outset, arranged in the alphabetical order and each example is followed by an explanation for the sake of clarity.

The classification I have made cannot prevent overlapping, since some items can be placed under more than one head. For example, the very first item here, namely, "Adverbial Clause," can be included with equal justification in two different groups, tense and subjunctive mood. It all depends upon the angle from which we look at the various grammatical features here.

Adverbial Clause: Tense

Brabantio: If she confess that she was half the wooed
Destruction on my head, if my bad blame
Light on the man! (*Othello*, I.iii.117-19)

The plural verb "confess" attracts our attention here. It is the verb in the first adverbial clause. Its NP/Subject is "she" which is singular in number, but its verb "confess" is plural or to put it in a different manner, the verb is in its base form. This particular example is taken from the speech of Brabantio who is bitterly complaining to the duke that the black moor had enticed his daughter into marriage with him. The absence of tense and number in the verb "confess" which is used as a non-finite verb should be noted in this adverbial clause of condition. We can see a similar example in *Henry V* (II.ii.19), *As You Like It* (I.i.118-19), *Much Ado About Nothing* (I.i.59-63) and in quite a few other plays. What is interesting in the example taken from *Much Ado About Nothing* is that even the verb "have" (not the auxiliary "have") is without tense and number. These are all examples of adverbial clause of condition. Today, however, according to the rules of modern English grammar, we must rewrite the example by replacing "confess" with "confesses," its singular form. Let us now take a look at a few other types of adverbial clause.

Countess: (reading a letter from her son, Bertram): You shall hear
I am run away; know it before the report come.
(*All's Well That Ends Well*, III.ii.2)

Here the sentence ends with the adverbial clause of time. In this clause too, its verb "come" is conspicuous because it has no tense and number. Today, as in the first example, we are required to add the singular morpheme to the verb and make it singular, as its Noun Phrase/Subject "the report" is singular. But Shakespeare's English has no such rule of grammar, whether the adverbial clause is related to condition as in the first example or time as in this example. Shakespeare uses the basic form of the verb.

Beatrice: Yes, faith; it is my cousin's duty to make curtsy, and say, 'Father, as it please you';
(*Much Ado About Nothing*, II.i.47)

This example is taken from a speech of Beatrice in an exchange of pleasantries with Leonato, Hero and others. She makes this observation about her cousin, Hero who, according to her, should take the advice of her father. Notice the absence of tense in the clause "as it please you." This is an Adverbial clause of manner and what we have said about the other two types of adverbial clause is equally applicable here. While "it" is the NP/Subject, its verb "please" does not have the singular morpheme "s." The verb, evidently, is in its base form. The verb is non-finite in form. Today, we are required to add the morpheme "s" and make the verb singular. Is there any other class of adverbial clause which is an equally good example of the verb of this kind?

Iago: Now, whether he kill Cassio
Or Cassio him, or each do kill the other,
Every way makes my gain: (*Othello*, V.i.12-14)

In the passage quoted above, we notice an adverbial clause of concession, but here also we find the singular morpheme "s" absent in the verb "kill," though its Noun Phrase/subject is singular number. This is the fourth type of adverbial clause in which Shakespeare uses the verb in its base form. A twentieth century English professor will write or say "kills" and not "kill." Regarding the classification of the adverbial clause, some may argue that this clause "whether he kill" is not one of concession, but of condition. Others may take the middle position and maintain that it is a clause of conceded condition. Therefore, let us consider now a regular adverbial clause of concession and supposition.

3rd Gentleman: But this same Cassio, though he speak of comfort
Touching the Turkish loss, he looks sadly
And prays the moor be safe. (*Othello*, II.i.31-33)

The absence of singular morpheme "s" is quite evident in the verb "speak" in the adverbial clause of concession, "though he speak" although the NP/subject "he" is singular number. We have thus seen five different types of the adverbial clause in each one of which the playwright has used a non-finite verb, that is, the verb in its base form. These examples are taken from different plays. In modern English, every one of these verbs must include the number morpheme—ordinarily, it is "s"—to make the verb singular. That is the rule.

Adverbial Clause: Modal Auxiliary

King Richard: This earth shall have a feeling and these stones
Prove armed soldiers, ere her native king
Shall falter under foul rebellion's arms.
(*Richard II*, III.ii.24-26)

Evidently, the clause "ere her native king shall falter" is an adverbial clause of time. Today, the inclusion of the modal auxiliary "shall" or "will" in such a clause is not permitted. W. Stannard Allen says in his book *Living English Structure* (Longmans, 137): "No future after temporal conjunctions. Although, the main clause is future, the presence of 'when,' 'until,' 'as soon as,' 'before,' 'after,' etc. is sufficient to indicate futurity, and such clauses remain in the present tense."

Friar: So will it fare with Claudio:
When he shall hear she died upon his words,
The idea of her life shall directly creep
Into the study of his imagination.
(*Much Ado About Nothing*, IV.i.222-25)

The adverbial clause of time in the second line includes the modal auxiliary "shall." This is not permissible, according to modern English grammar. The conjunction "when" itself indicates futurity and, therefore, the presence of "shall" or "will" for that matter will make the sentence ungrammatical. W. Stannard Allen (*Living English Structure*, p. 152) says that "like the clauses beginning with 'when,' 'as soon as' etc. 'if' clauses also have no 'shall,' 'will,' 'should,' 'would,' in them." It is evident that the grammar of Renaissance English is different in this respect also. Similar examples can be found in the same play, V.i.29-31 and in *King Lear*, V.i.46-48. Now let us turn to the "if" clause.

Jeweller: If he will touch the estimate. But for that.
(*Timon of Athens*, I.i.15)

Modern English grammar does not permit the inclusion of the Modal Auxiliary "shall," "will," "should" or "would" in the Adverbial Clause of condition, beginning with "if." Similar examples can be found in *Antony and Cleopatra*, II.ii.52-54, *Much Ado About Nothing*, II.i.335-37 and *Macbeth*, II.i.67-70.

Distinction between "Shall" and "Will"

Philo: Look where they come;
Take good note, and you shall see in him
The triple pillar of the world transformed
Into a strumpet's fool. (*Antony and Cleopatra*, I.i.10-12)

It is evident from the above example that Shakespeare does not see any distinction between the modal auxiliaries, "shall" and "will." He uses "shall" in the sentence in which the subject is the second person. In modern English, the use of the auxiliary "shall" in such a sentence makes the action imperative. It is only in the first person that the word "shall" means just a proposed action. It is a somewhat colourless word in the first person, but in the second and the third person it conveys a sense of command. It is clear from the play that Philo is not ordering Demetrius to take a look at Antony when he arrives with Cleopatra. The writers during the time of Shakespeare did not observe any distinction between "shall" and "will." Similar examples can be found in *All's Well That Ends Well*, III.v.129 and *Othello*, II.iii.296-97.

Modern English grammar makes a careful distinction between "shall" and "will." It is interesting to note that it all began in

1653 itself, when a grammarian, John Allis, proposed a clear-cut distinction between the two auxiliaries. Evidently it took quite some time for it to become a rule and the case underlines the fact that it is easier to make changes in vocabulary than in grammar.

Another Auxiliary: "Can"

Lepidus: Tomorrow Caesar,
I shall be furnished to inform you rightly
Both by what sea or land I can be able
To front this present time.
(*Antony and Cleopatra*, I.iv.77-78)

The oddity that we notice here is the association of the auxiliary "can" with the adjective "able." The meaning of the word "can" when used as an auxiliary is "to be able" or "to have the capacity," according to the Oxford English Dictionary. We do not add this auxiliary to the adjective "able." Such a thing is regarded as ungrammatical.

Articles

Bolingbroke: That Mowbray hath received eight thousand nobles
In name of lendings for your highness' soldiers
The which he hath detained for lewd employments
(*Richard II,* I.i.88-90)

The Definite Article "the" at the beginning of the last line looks an odd one out. We do not use the article for modifying the Relative Pronoun which starts the Relative Clause. Shakespeare's use of the Definite Article is the relic of the Middle Ages which did not have the Relative Pronoun Proper, but made use of the Definite Article. In the Renaissance English, Relative Pronouns made their appearance, but when the Relative Pronoun was "which," the use of the Definite Article was continued. This peculiarity was the hang-over of the medieval English. The modern grammar does not permit such a combination. For other examples of this kind, we can turn to *Antony and Cleopatra*, III.i.27-29 and *As You Like It*, II.vii.38-42, among others. There are many examples and in all these cases, the Relative Pronoun is "which." Incidentally, we may also notice the conspicuous absence of the article, "the," before the noun, "name," at the beginning of the second line. The noun specifies something here and, therefore, the Definite Article is necessary.

Helena: 'Tis pity. (*All's Well That Ends Well,* I.i.175)

The author drops the Indefinite Article, though it is necessary to place it before the word "pity." Another example of the absence of a necessary article can be found in *As You Like It*, I.4-6. The system of articles had not been perfected by the time of Shakespeare.

Gonzalo: O, look, Sir; Here is more of us:
I prophesied, if a gallows were on land
This fellow could not drown.
(*The Tempest*, V.i.217-19)

The presence of the Indefinite Article in the second line looks ungrammatical today. The word "gallows" was treated as both singular and plural in Shakespeare's age. Today it is plural only and the article which suits only singular nouns should not be used.

Biron: Never durst poet touch a pen to write
Until his ink were temper'd with love's signs.
(*Love's Labour's Lost*, IV.iii.343-44)

It looks as though Shakespeare uses an article where it is not to be used and does not use an article where it is necessary! What we notice here is the absence of the Indefinite Article "a" between the second and the third word in the first line. It is considered so essential today that an English teacher penalizes his pupil if he drops it. An article is such an important part of English language that nowadays, grammarians prefer Noun Phrase to Noun as if a Noun consists in most cases of at least two words, one of them being an article. For another example of this kind, we can turn to *As You Like It*, V.iii.120. I am aware that there are no hard and fast rules guiding the use of articles. But there are clear instances in which one can easily say that they are ungrammatical in the absence of articles.

Antony: I have heard it, Pompey
And I am well studied for a liberal thanks
Which I do owe you.

(*Antony and Cleopatra*, II.vi.47-48)

Again, it is an interesting example of the use of the Indefinite Article which cannot be, strictly speaking, justified. "Liberal thanks" in the second line is a plural noun phrase and the article used is singular. Shakespeare wrote plays which were not meant for printing and publication. How else can we account for the fact that his plays were not printed and published during his life time and that only some pirated editions came out? They were intended for rendering orally on the stage. The meaning of the phrase "liberal thanks" might have appeared singular while the phrase appeared plural in form. But today we do not say a liberal thanks. In fact, the phrase does not need an article at all.

Auxiliaries Again: "is" in the place of "has"

Albany: Sir, this I hear: the king is come to his daughter.

(*King Lear*, V.i.21)

The word order in the sentence above is impossible in modern English. When "is" functions as an auxiliary, it can be followed only by the progressive form of the verb, that is, the "ing" form, if the sentence is not in passive voice. Therefore, today we are required to say "The King has come" if what we say is a basic or kernel sentence like the one spoken by Albany. "Has" should replace "is." Another example is the following exclamation in *Othello*.

Cassio: O, behold,
The riches of the ship is come on shore! (II.i.83-84)

Today we had better say "has come." Here again the verbal is "come," but the observation we have made covers some other verbs also, as when we study examples of active and passive voice in Shakespeare's plays.

Auxiliary Dropped

Cordelia: But yet, alas, stood I within his grace,
I would prefer him to a better place.
So farewell to you both. (*King Lear*, I.i.271-73)

The subordinate clause in the first line is, no doubt, a case of subjunctive mood. Even granting this, the clause should be "had I stood within his grace." The key word here is "had." Shakespeare drops this auxiliary and then inverts the order of the next two words! This is an example of elliptical style.

Modal Auxiliary without the Verb

King Richard: We will ourself in person to this war.
(*Richard II*, I.iv.42)

The absence of the verb or what is called the main verb in the well known traditional grammar can be noticed in the speech quoted above. We have only the Modal Auxiliary "will." This utterance is the king's response to Green's reminder that the Irish nationalists were rebelling against the English rule. Shakespeare has dropped the verb, but has retained only the auxiliary "will." In modern English this deletion of the verb is not possible and a suitable verb like "go" or "proceed" is essential to make the sentence grammatical. A similar grammatical aspect can be found in the following speech of Claudius in *Hamlet*.

Claudius: He shall with speed to England
For the demand of our neglected tribute. (III.i.171-72)

Claudius is refering to his instruction that Hamlet should proceed to England ostensibly to demand the tribute which had not yet been paid. Other similar examples are *Hentry V*, III.i.94, *The Tempest*, III.i.96-98 and *Romeo and Juliet*, III.i.39-41. In all these cases, Shakespeare drops the verbs even out of context. Some scholars point out that what is missing in all such cases is the verb of motion. This view is not correct. It is not the verb of motion that is missing in William's assertion "I will none of your money" in the play *Henry V*, IV.v.57.

"Be" in the place of "is" and its other forms

Hamlet: Where be his quiddities now, his quillets, his cases, his tenures, and his tricks? (*Hamlet*, V.i.95-96)

Today we do not use "be" in the place in which Hamlet in the well-known graveyard scene uses it. We prefer "are," one of the forms of "be." We can give another example.

Benedick: If signior Leonato be her father, she would not have his head on her shoulder for all Messina, as like him as she is. (*Much Ado About Nothing*, I.i.102-4)

Here the basic verb "be" is used in the place of "is." In modern times, the use of "be" is to all intents and purposes confined to the sentences which convey a wish or command concerning someone.

Conjunctions

a) Co-ordinating unlike structures

Marshal: The Duke of Norfolk, sprightfully and bold
Stays but the summons of the appellate trumpet.
(*Richard II*, I.i.3-4)

These lines from the scene of challenge and counter challenge of the nobles of King Richard II is a good example of a conjunction co-ordinating unlike structures. "Sprightfully" is an adverb and "bold" is an adjective. According to the rules of modern English grammar, they cannot be co-ordinated by the conjunction "and" which can only co-ordinate like structures. Perhaps, the hurry and pressure of spoken English on the stage permitted this usage. It can also be treated as a figure of speech. We can cite a few other examples: *Macbeth*, V.iv.141-42, *King Lear*, V.iii.141-45 and *Timon of Athens*, I.i.132.

b) Omission of a part of compound conjunction

Lear: We have this hour a constant will to publish.

Our daughters' several dowers, that future strife
May be prevented now. (*King Lear*, I.i.42-44)

We have here an adverbial clause of purpose and the linker that is used in modern English is the compound conjunction "so that." But we notice the absence of the first word "so" in the above example. We have only "that." Some other examples are *Much Ado About Nothing*, II.i.347, 340, *All's Well That Ends Well*, I.iii.26-27, 34-35 and *Timon of Athens*, IV.iii.381-82.

c) Two conjunctions used together

Iago: Though that his joy be joy
Yet throw such changes of vexation on't
As it may lose some colour. (*Othello*, I.i.72-74)

The oddity lies in the first two words. Both are subordinating conjunctions, but they are strung together. Of these words, "though that," the second is unnecessary; its presence makes the sentence ungrammatical. It passed muster in Shakespeare's time and there are quite a few examples of this kind in his plays: *Othello*, I.i.288. *All's Well That Ends Well*, V.iii.165-66, *King Lear*, II.i.46-49, *Much Ado About Nothing*, V.iv.67-71 and many others scattered all over the plays.

d) Subordinating Conjunction

Iago: But we have reason to cool our raging motions, our carnal stings, our unbitted lusts; whereof, I take this, that you call love, to be a sect or scion.
(*Othello*, I.iii.329-32)

Mark the word "that" in the sentence above. According to the rules of modern English grammar, what we need here is the Relative Pronoun "what." The other word "that" cannot be a Relative Pronoun without its antecedent, that is, the noun which it replaces in the clause. "What" does not require an antecedent in such a grammatical situation. In modern English, we'd better say "I take it that what you call love is a sect or scion." In this sentence, "that" is retained but as a subordinating conjunction.

Helena: O then, give pity
To her whose state is such that cannot choose
But lend and give where she is sure to lose;
That seeks not to find that her search implies,
But riddle-like lives sweetly where it dies!
(*All's Well That Ends Well*, I.iii.208-9)

This example is less complicated, but in this speech also, the subordinating conjunction "that" in the second part of the fourth line must be replaced by the Relative Pronoun "what." The other word cannot be treated as a Relative Pronoun, because we do not find any noun or noun phrase which is its antecedent.

Claudius: For all our thanks,
Now follows that you know: (*Hamlet*, I.ii.16-17)

This is the simplest of the examples of this group. Claudius is telling his councillors that they already know what he is about to tell them. The word "that" is not used in the sentence as a subordinating conjunction, but as a Relative Pronoun. In modern English, we must replace it with "what," because "that" does not have an antecedent in the sentence above.

King: O Gertrude, come away!
The sun no sooner shall the mountain touch
But we shall ship him hence; (*Hamlet*, IV.i.28-30)

In modern English we are all familiar with what is called correlative conjunction. "No sooner than" is one such frequently cited example. The comparative degree in the word "sooner" demands the conjunction "than" and not "but." Similar examples from Shakespeare's plays include *As You Like It*, III.ii.22, *All's Well That Ends Well* I.iii.160-61, *Othello*, I.i.122-27, and *Macbeth*, V.iv.8-11.

Helena: First give me trust the count is my husband,
(*All's Well That Ends Well*, III.vii)

Here we have an instance of a different kind. The conjunction "that" is not found in the sentence. It is necessary to subordinate the second clause to the first. Without the linker "that," the two clauses will be independent of each other. The second is a clause that functions like a noun phrase: it is a clause in apposition to the noun "trust." Please note that the sentence does not belong to the category in which the use of the conjunction is optional. An example of the second kind is the sentence "I know that you are coming" in which the linker "that" can be deleted. Another example of the first kind is Benedick's speech in *Much Ado About Nothing*, V.iv.28-30.

Dauphin: Shall we go send them dinners, and fresh fruits,
And give their fasting horses provender,
And after fight with them? (*Henry V*, IV.ii.59-61)

Today, we find it necessary to place the co-ordinating conjunction "and" between the two finite verbs "go" and "send" in the first line above. Both are similar structures and the conjunction is needed to co-ordinate them. Remember Donne's famous line "go and catch a falling star." Some other examples are *Much Ado About Nothing*, II.iii.192-93, and *Othello*, III.iv.142.

Biron: O, these are barren tasks, too hard to keep,
Not to see ladies, study, fast, not sleep.
(*Love's Labour's Lost*, I.i.47-48)

In the last line, we have a series, some positive and some negative. That is why the adversative conjunction "but" is needed. The first unit in the series is a negative structure and it is followed by two positive structures. For this reason it is necessary to place the conjunction "but" after the noun phrase, "ladies." The last line is also negative again, following two positive units. Therefore, it is necessary to place the conjunction "and" before it.

Double Possessive

Iago: For I mine own gained knowledge should profane
If I would time expend with such a shape
But for my sport and profit. (*Othello*, I.iv.382-84)

This is the speech of Iago who remarks that it would be an insult to his intellect if he spends time on Roderigo, unless Iago has something to gain by it. Granting this assertion on his part, can modern grammer permit the use of the double possessive "mine"? It is only when a noun or noun phrase does not follow the possessive, but understood in the context, that the double possessive is permitted. In fact, it is a compensation for deleting the noun or noun phrase after the possessive. When I ask, "Is this your book?" you can respond by saying "Yes, this is mine." You do not have to say, "Yes, this is my book," The noun, "book" can be deleted and the possessive pronoun "my" is changed into "mine" simultaneously. The double possessive and the noun possessed by another noun or pronoun cannot exist together. They are mutually exclusive. Some other examples are: *All's Well That Ends Well*, III.vi.7-9, *Macbeth*, I.iv.68 and *Pericles*, II.v.50-53.

Double Comparative

Duke: To vouch this, is no proof,
Without more wider and more overt test
Than these thin habits and poor likelihoods
Of modern seeming do prefer against him.
(*Othello*, I.iii.106-9)

The duke has patiently heard the bitter complaint of Brabantio and asks for more solid proof than mere assertion. In this hearing, he wants more wider and more overt test. In the first qualifier, he uses both the comparative morphemes, "more" and "er." The general rule is that we add only one of these morphemes. Another rule says that the bound morpheme "er" only should be added if the word is monosyllabic. The free morpheme "more" can be added to only multi-syllabic words. The playwrights of the Elizabethan age did not follow this rule strictly. Some other examples are *King Lear*, I.i.269-72, *As You Like It*, III.ii.57-58 and *Hamlet*, II.i.9-12. We find the word "worser" in *Romeo and Juliet*.

Double Superlative

Hamlet: I have not art to reckon my groans, but that I love thee
best, O most best, believe it. (*Hamlet*, II.ii.120-22)

The adjective "good" is inflected, of course, in its superlative form, but we can see here not only the bound morpheme "est" added, but also the free morpheme "most." See also *Julius Caesar*, III.ii.183. What Shakespeare has written can also be regarded as a stylistic device.

Double Negative

Pericles: By the gods, I have not;
Never did thought of mine levy offence;
Nor never did my actions yet commence
A deed might gain her love or your displeasure.
(*Pericles*, II.v.50-53)

Here is an example of the well known correlative conjunction. We find Shakespeare using the double negative invariably in the second clause. The first clause does not begin with the conventional "neither," but with "never." In the second clause, the playwright employs two negatives in a row; namely "nor" and "never." According to the rules of grammar today, the first negative conjunction "nor" only is needed. The other, "never," is needlessly added to it. Pericles has not revealed that he is the king of Tyre and is protesting to Simonides that he has done nothing to encourage his daughter's love for him. The statement is emphatic and it is possible that the playwright places two negatives in the second clause for the sake of emphasis. All told, there are three negatives in the sentence. This is not a solitary example. See also *Othello*, IV.ii.5-6, *King Lear*, III.ii.87-88, *Hamlet*, I.ii.118 and *Richard II*, II.ii.310-12. Examples are galore.

Demonstrative Adjective

Lear: But where's my fool? I have not seen him this two days.
(*King Lear*, I.iv.72-73)

The Demonstrative "this" is singular but the noun phrase "two days" is plural. This chain relation is not permitted by modern English grammar. We need here the plural demonstrative "these." There should be concord between the demonstrative adjective and the noun phrase which is modified by it. Another example is *Romeo and Juliet*, V.ii.23-24 where we have the phrase "this three hours." It is interesting to note that the Collins edition, *Shakespeare Tragedies* has printed the phrase as "this three hours," whereas the Oxford University Press has in its *The Complete Works of Shakespeare* printed the same phrase as "these three hours."

Imperative Sentence (See also Transformation)

Timon: Go not you home
Till I have thanked you. (*Timon of Athens*, I.i.245-46)

In contemporary English, the second person "you" is deleted unless it is necessary to include it for a specific reason. In the above example, students of modern English grammar find its inclusion unnecessary. An imperative sentence is a transformation effected by the deletion of the second person pronoun. Some other examples are *Much Ado About Nothing*, I.ii.21, *Pericles*, IV.i.91-92, *King Lear*, III.v.33 and *Othello*, II.iii.1. I must underline the point that the second person pronoun can be included only when it is stressed.

Countess: (Reading a letter) You shall hear that I am run away; know it before the report come.
(*All's Well That Ends Well*, III.ii.21-22)

The countess is reading a letter written by Bertrand who asks her to know something before she hears the report. Nowadays we do not begin an imperative sentence with the verb "know." The most common way of saying the same thing is to mention the second person "you" first and add the verbal phrase + modal auxiliary + "know." For example, "You must know. . . ." I have not come across in modern English any imperative sentence which begins with the verb "know."

Helicanus: No, Escanes, know this of me
Antiochus from incest lived not free
For which . . . (*Pericles*, II.iii.1-3)

I am aware that this is not a case of pure grammar, but of usage. Though "know" is a transitive verb, we do not begin an imperative sentence with that verb, probably because it sounds like the word "no."

Infinitive

Queen: The lion dying thrusteth forth his paw,
And wound the earth, if nothing else, with rage
To be overpowered; (*Richard II*, V.i.29-31)

The queen expresses her distress at King Richard's despair after he was deposed and imprisoned. She thought that her husband should not take things lying down and should fight back. In the image of the dying lion, he thrusts forth his paw in rage to wound the earth, if nothing else. He is outraged because he has been overpowered. But in the queen's language, the infinitive "to be overpowered" indicates an action that has not yet taken place. The action represented by the infinitive is actually the cause and not the result of the lion's rage. It is interesting to note that both the Oxford/Cambridge edition and the New Clarendon edition of the play have interpreted the infinitive as "at being overpowered." When I say that "he went there only to be insulted," what I mean is that the action of insult followed the action of going. But in the queen's speech, the rage of the lion is the result of the expectation or the future possibility of being overpowered.

Helena: That I should love a bright particular star
And think to wed it, he is so above me.
(*All's Well That Ends Well*, I.i.83-85)

The question that arises here is whether in modern English, we ever put the structure to + infinitive after the verb think. Do we say "think to wed it" or "think of wedding it"? To + infinitive is possible only after certain verbs. For example, "decide to wed" is quite possible. In the case of "think" of + gerund is grammatical but not to + infinitive. Shakespeare's English does not conform to this rule.

Lear: I loved her most, and though to set my rest
On her kind nursery, (*King Lear*, I.i.122-23)

We have another example of the same kind here.

Lennox: May it please your highness sit? (*Macbeth*, III.iv.38)

"Sit" in the sentence above is a bare infinitive, but today I think we prefer to + Infinitive. When the action of the finite verb precedes the action represented by the infinitive, the rule is to choose to + infinitive. For example, we say "I heard her sing," because the action of singing does not follow the action of hearing. On the other hand, singing had begun and I heard her. In the example "I asked her to sign the receipt," the action of asking is followed by the action of signing.

Modifier—Dangling Type

Ghost: Sleeping within the orchard,
My custom always of the afternoon,
Upon my secure hour thy uncle stole
With juice of cursed Hebona in a vial,
And in the porches of my ear did pour
The leprous distilment; (*Hamlet*, I.v.59-64)

Here is an instance of what is called an unattached participle or dangling modifier. Who is sleeping in the orchard? It is evident from the speech of the king who is now a ghost that he was sleeping and relaxing in the orchard. But as the sentence stands, the progressive participle refers to the uncle of Hamlet (thy uncle) as though he is the subject of the participle. The sentence should be rewritten beginning with the words "while I was sleeping within the orchard." Modern English grammar does not permit such a loose adjunct.

Noun Clause

King Richard: He is our cousin, cousin; but 'tis doubt,
When time shall call him home from banishment,
Whether our kinsman come to see his friends.
(*Richard II*, I.iv.20-22)

The third line begins with a noun clause; in other words, with a noun phrase which functions as a clause. It can be classified as a noun clause put in apposition to the pronoun "it." Every clause, according to a basic rule of grammar, must include a verb with a tense or what is called a finite verb. But here in the noun clause, "come" is the VP of the NP/Subject "our kinsman" which is singular in number. According to the concerned rule of modern English grammar, we should say "whether our kinsman comes." The verb in king Richard's speech is not limited by tense, number or person, though it has a singular NP/Subject. This is similar to the following sentence of Polonius in *Hamlet*.

> See you now
> Your bait of falsehood take the carp of truth; (II.i.62-63)

In his speech to Reynaldo, Polonius employs a clause which is the object of the verb, "see." But note that though the NP/Subject of the clause is singular, its verb "take" is not in the singular form. Another example is the speech by Player King:

> For 'tis a question left us yet to prove
> Whether love lead fortune or else fortune love. (III.ii.198-99)

Here in the noun clause, "love" is the NP/Subject, but its verb "lead" is not singular in number. In all the cases quoted above, the verb of the NP/Subject is in its basic form.

> Marshal: In God's name and the king's, say who thou art
> And why thou comest thus knightly clad in arms,
> Against what man thou comest, and what thy quarrel.

It is not difficult to see the oddity in the third line of the speech of Lord Marshal. There are, evidently, two clauses in the line, coordinated by the conjunction, "and." They are both objects of the verb "say" in the matrix clause. The first of these two clauses, "against what man thou comest" has both the two essential elements of a clause, namely, NP/Subject and finite verb. For example, "comest" is as we expect today singular in form. But the second, beginning with "what" does not have a finite verb at all. Its NP/Subject "thy quarrel" is not followed by a verbal phrase. It cannot, therefore, be called a clause at all, in which case the conjunction "and" will be co-ordinating two unlike structures. A clause must have both the Noun Phrase/subject and finite verb; the latter is absent in the second clause. The sentence is ungrammatical, according to the rules of modern English grammar. It can be made grammatical by adding the verb "is" at the end. This singular verb suits the number and person of its subject "thy quarrel."

Hamlet: Sir, my good friend. I'll change that name with you.
And what make you from Wittenburg, Horatio?
(*Hamlet*, I.ii.163-64)

The second sentence is a "who" question. There are two aspects of grammar here and both are at variance from the rules of modern English grammar. While the first is connected with the verb "make," the second concerns the absence of a non-finite verb which ought to be there. In modern English we are expected to say "what makes you to come from Wittenburg." The Oxford English Dictionary permits the deletion of such an infinitive for the sake of ellipsis. It means that this omission is not permitted by modern English grammar except as a stylistic device. Secondly it should be noted that when a clause beginning with "what " is the NP/Subject of a clause, the verb should be invariably singular. It is not singular here and that is the reason for replacing "make" with "makes" in modern English.

Not and No

Beatrice: I pray you is signior Mountanto returned from wars or no? (*Much Ado About Nothing*, I.i.28)

A negative statement, like a question, is a transformation and it is effected by introducing the adverb, "not" and not "no." The latter is used when we respond to a question with the choice of saying either "yes" or "no." "Has he returned or not" is the correct sentence and "no" is incorrect here. "No" as an adverb in the negative sentence in the sense of "not" is illustrated only from Old English and Middle English by even the Oxford English Dictionary. It is interesting to note that in the above question, a choice is implied by the conjunction "or. " This point is illustrated by a speech of Claudius in *Hamlet* also:

> Her father and myself—lawful espials—
> Will so bestow ourselves that, seeing unseen,
> We may of their encounter frankly judge,
> And gather by him, as he is behav'd,
> If it be th' affliction of love or no,
> That thus he suffers for. (III.i.132-36)

The last two lines illustrate the point I am making. Claudius is unfolding the plan to examine the affliction of Hamlet with the view to finding out whether Hamlet's odd behaviour has its origin in love. The choice involved is conveyed by the conjunction "if" which here means "whether." Here also we must replace "no" with "not." A negative sentence is a transformation and the T-negative requires "not." It is significant to note that in another part of the same play, the playwright uses "not," where "no" is preferable.

> Hamlet: (in a letter to Ophelia) O dear Ophelia, I am ill at these numbers. I have not art to reckon my groans; (II.ii.120-21)

Hamlet wants to say in his letter to Ophelia that he does not have the necessary skill to sum up his feelings in verse. In today's English the second sentence should be rewritten as either 'I have no art' or 'I haven't art.' "Have" is a peculiar verb which can be both a verb and an auxiliary. The kernel sentence which is also positive is "I have art." This can be transformed into "I have not art," "I do not have art" or "I haven't art." Shakespeare's sentence "I have not art" is ungrammatical today. "Not" is permitted only when it combines with "have" in an elision or when "have" is an auxiliary followed by the verbal or what is called the main verb.

Need: Is It an Auxiliary?

> Timon: I must needs say you have a little fault; (*Timon of Athens*, V.i.87)

In many examples that can be cited, in addition to the above speech of Timon, "needs" is used as an adverb in the sense "necessarily" or "of necessity." "Need" is an auxiliary according to modern grammar. But "needs" is not. The very fact that it follows the auxiliary "must" in the above speech of Timon shows that it cannot also be an auxiliary. In Shakespeare's plays "needs" is always used with the auxiliary "must." Here Timon says that he must necessarily say that the painter has a little fault. In modern English, this combination of "must" and "needs" is rare and it appears quaint and archaic. Other examples are *Troilus and Cressida*, I.i.16-17, *All's Well That Ends Well*, I.iii.26-28 and *King Lear*, II.iv.285-86. The word is employed as an adverb for the subject of First, Second and Third Persons.

Number

Brabantio: Is there not charms
By which the property of youth and maidenhood
May be abused? (*Othello*, I.i.172-74)

The reader can easily see the absence of concord between the number of the verb and the number of its subject in the first of the three lines above. The verb is singular, though the subject "charms" is plural. The speech is, no doubt, a question which is a transformation. But we can notice in the plays of Shakespeare the absence of agreement even in the indicative sentences and exclamations.

Helena: Yet these fixed evils sit so fit in him
That they take place when virtue's steely bones
Looks bleak i' th' cold wind;
(*All's Well That Ends Well*, I.i.100-2)

This is Helena's comment on Parolles, a follower of Bertram with whom she is in love. In the adverbial clause of time, the NP/Subject is "virtue's steely bones," but Shakespeare uses the singular verb "looks." It is evident that the playwright does not adhere to the rules of concord in number between the NP/Subject and its verb.

Apemantus: O you gods, what a number of men eats Timon, and
he sees 'em not! (*Timon of Athens*, I.ii.38-39)

The example is an exclamation and there is a brazen disagreement between the number of the subject and the number of the verb "eats." Apemantus is commenting on the flatterers and parasites of Timon.

Fluellen: It is the greatest admiration in the universal world, when the true and aunchient prerogatives and laws of the world is not kept: (*Henry V*, V.i.66-68)

The speaker is an army officer and we notice that the verb is singular while the NP/Subject is clearly plural. There is an example in *Hamlet* also in which the the verb is singular while the subject is plural.

Hamlet: There's letters seal'd; (III.iv.204)

Macbeth also provides an example where the subject is plural, while the subject is singular. In *Antony and Cleopatra*, the singular verb "affects" is the predicate for the subject "thou"! The Arden edition explains it by saying that "affects" means "choosest." All these examples may give us the impression that Shakespeare prefers the verbs of singular number even if it means the violation of grammar.

Berowne: Now, in thy likeness, one more fool appear!
(*Love's Labour's Lost*, IV.iii.46)

Berowne is not expressing any wish or uttering any prayer. The sentence is in the indicative mood, though it is an expression of happy surprise. We notice that while the verb "appear" is plural, the NP/Subject "one more fool" is singular. It is evident, therefore, that during the time of Shakespeare, grammar did not enforce any hard and fast rule concerning the need for concord between the number of the subject and the number of the verb.

Preposition

King Richard: We thank you both: yet one but flatters us,
As well appeareth by the cause you come;
(*Richard II*, I.i.25-26)

A grammatical oddity can be found at the end of the second line. The preposition "for" is missing. The prepositional phrase should be "by the cause you come for." What king Richard means is that one of them is only flattering him as is evident from the cause for which he has come to the king. In fact, the Oxford and Cambridge edition of *Richard II* interpret the word "come" as "come for" in its notes. Shakespeare's plays are known for dropping what we today regard as an essential preposition. The above example of king Richard addressing Bolingbroke and Mowbray is not the only one of its kind.

Bolingbroke: By this time, had the king permitted us,
One of our souls had wander'd in the air,
Banish'd this frail sepulchre of our flesh,
As now our flesh, is banish'd from this land;
(*Richard II*, II.ii.194-97)

It is clear that the preposition "from" should be placed according to the rules of grammar between the participle, "banished" and the noun phrase, "this frail sepulchre of our flesh." Indeed the Oxford and Cambridge edition of the play explains the meaning of the passage by adding the preposition "from" in its notes. Lord Bolingbroke says that if the king had permitted the combat between him and Mowbray, the soul of one of them would have been banished from his body just as the bodies of both of them are banished from England, their land. "Banished" is not the past tense of the verb "banish" here, but its participial form. Some other examples of dropping the preposition are: *Othello*, II.i.44-45 and *All's Well That Ends Well*. III.v.98-99. We can find similar examples in *Romeo and Juliet* and *Love's Labour's Lost*.

King Richard: Should dying men flatter with those that live?
(*Richard II*, II.i.8)

Here is an example of a preposition which we do not use with the verb "flatter." King Richard asks John of Gaunt, the Duke of Lancaster, whether dying men flatter those that are living. Notice the preposition "with" between the verb "flatter" and the noun phrase, "those that live." In modern English, the verb "flatter" is followed immediately by the NP which is its object without the intervention of the preposition "with." In other words, "flatter" is not a part of any phrasal verb.

First Lord: Here was he merry, hearing of song.
(*As You Like It*, II.vii.4)

In modern English, we do not say "hearing of a song" if the context is the same as above. The first lord is referring to Jaques, the cynic, when he tells the duke that he had seen Jaques just a while earlier and that the latter was listening to a song. Today we do not place the preposition "of" after the participle "hearing" and before its object. Only "listen" is followed by a preposition and even that is only "to." It is the first part of a phrasal verb.

King: He's lov'd of the distracted multitude
Who like not in their judgment, but their eyes;
(*Hamlet*, IV.iii.4-5)

King Claudius describes the mob psychology in the background of the killing of Polonius by Hamlet who, he is afraid, is loved by the crowd. Today we prefer the preposition "by," but Shakespeare uses the preposition "of." Another example of this kind is *King Lear*, V.iii.34 where the Duke of Albany speaks of the "great things of us forgot." Shakespeare writes the preposition "of" in the contexts in which we do not write it today. This can be illustrated also from the play, *Pericles*, IV.i.84-85.

Bertrand: My lord, this is a fond and desp'rate creature
Whom sometimes I have laugh'd with. Let your highness
Lay a more noble thought upon mine honour
Than for to think that I would sink it here.
(*All's Well That Ends Well*, V.iii.177-80)

This is a speech of Bertrand in a compromising situation. Today we do not add the preposition "for" after the conjunction "than" and before the particle "to" of the infinitive.

Caesar: This common body
Like to a vagabond flag upon the stream,

Goes to, and back, lackeying the varying tide.
(*Antony and Cleopatra*, I.iv.44-46)

Octavius Caesar's comment on the loss of his own popular favour and support is understandable. Shakespeare had no regard for the irrational crowds, but what is interesting here is the oddity in Shakespeare's English in adding the preposition "to" after "like" which is also a preposition in this sentence. In modern English, when "like" is a preposition, it is immediately followed by a noun phrase in the objective case. The preposition "to" is not placed in between them. There are many examples of this kind in Shakespeare's plays and one more example can be cited.

King Henry: Therefore to our best mercy give yourselves;
Or like to men proud of destruction
Defy us to our worst. (*Henry V*, III.ii.3-5)

This is the warrior king calling upon the governor of Harfleur and its citizens to give up resistance and surrender, for he would offer them best terms. The alternative is their destruction and as in the previous example, the preposition "like" begins the comparison. Notice the addition of "to." In Shakespeare's English, the combination "like to" is common but modern English does not permit it.

Parts of Speech

King Richard: He is our cousin, cousin; but 'tis doubt,
When time shall call him home from banishment.
Whether our kinsman come to his friends.
(*Richard II*, I.iv.20-22)

King Richard has some moments of anxiety at the growing popularity of Bolingbroke whom he has banished. In his talk with Aumerle, he expresses his fears and anxieties. He says it is doubtful whether his cousin will come to see his friends back in England at the end of his banishment. But instead of the adjective "doubtful," he uses the noun "doubt." All the editions of *Richard II* explain the meaning of the word "doubt" as doubtful. Frequently, various parts of speech in Shakespeare's English exchange their roles. In the above example, a noun is put in the place of an adjective. Today we prefer the word "doubtful."

Bushy: Old John of Gaunt is grievous sick, my lord,
Suddenly taken; (*Richard II*, I.iv.54-55)

Bushy reports to the king that the old Duke of Lancaster is seriously ill. Notice the word "grievous" in the phrase "grievous sick." The second word in this phrase is "sick," an adjective. It cannot be modified by another adjective which "grievous" is. Only an adverb can modify an adjective. That is why various editions of *Richard II* explain the meaning of this word as "grievously" which is the adverbial form of the word. For another example, we can turn to *Hamlet*. In the opening scene, Francisco, a night guard, greets Bernardo, his comrade, and then remarks that it is "bitter cold." We notice in this phrase the presence of "bitter," an adjective, while the word, "cold," which it modifies, is also an adjective. According to the rules of grammar, one adjective cannot modify or intensify the meaning of another adjective. Evidently, the word "bitter" is used by Shakespeare as an adverb. The OED states that "bitter" as an adverb is archaic, poetical and dialectical. We can come across the phrase "bitter chill," similar to the one used by Shakespeare, in a poem of John Keats.

King Richard: Mowbray, impartial are our eyes and ears;
Were he my brother, nay, my kingdom's heir
As he is but my father's brother's son,
Now by my sceptre's awe, I make a vow,
Such neighbour nearness to our sacred blood
Should nothing privilege him. . . .
(*Richard II*, I.i.115-20)

In the previous example, an adjective was made to qualify another adjective and in the present example, a noun is made to qualify another noun! According to the rules of modern English grammar, only an adjective can qualify a noun and the adjectival form of the word we want is "neighbourly."

Duchess of York: I will not peace. What is the matter, Aumerle?
(*Richard II*, V.ii.81)

The Duchess of York expresses her concern for the safety of her son even as his father, the Duke of York, prepares to inform the new king of the involvement of his son in a conspiracy against the king. The duke asks his wife to keep quiet. "Peace, foolish woman" is his order and it is her response to this order that has been cited as an example of a noun used as a verb. The word "peace" in the speech of the duchess is used as an intransitive verb and according to the OED, this usage is found only in Shakespeare's plays.

Bolingbroke: You have misled the prince, a royal king
A happy gentleman in blood and lineaments;
By you unhappied and disfigured clean!
(*Richard II*, III.i.8-10)

Bolingbroke assumes the role of the king's advocate while at the same time he rebels against the king. Unlike his father, the time-honoured Lancaster, he is ambitious, clever and diplomatic. In his charge against Bushy and Green whom he sentences to death, he uses the adjective "unhappy" as a verb. The OED notes that the word "happy" was employed as a verb, till the early seventeenth century and its meaning, no doubt, is related to the meaning of fortune. If "happy" could be used as a verb, why not "unhappy" which is its negative form only? But the use of these words as verbs was extremely rare even in the days of Shakespeare.

King Richard: I towards the north
Where shivering cold sickness pines the clime;
(*Richard II*, V.i.76-77)

All the editions of *Richard II* including Oxford and Cambridge and Clarendon Press interpret the verb "pine" as "cause to pine." That means the verb is used in the causative sense. Accordingly, King Richard means that in the northern regions, shivering cold and sickness cause the climate to pine. But as written, the verb "pine" is used as a transitive verb, though it is intransitive.

King Richard: Now, by my sceptre's awe, I make a vow
Such neighbour nearness to our sacred blood
Should nothing privilege him, nor partialize

The unstooping firmness of our upright soul;
(*Richard II*, I.i.119-22)

The word "privilege" is used in the speech of King Richard as a transitive verb. The king assures the Duke of Mowbray that Bolingbroke's close relation to the king will not bestow any special rights on him or license him to say or do things which are not authorised for others. Today the word "privilege" is not used as a Transitive verb. It is only a part of its passive form which invariably follows a form of "be," very much like the word "born."

John of Gaunt: Lascivious metres, to whose venom sound
The open ear of youth doth always listen;
(*Richard II*, II.i.19-20)

In the phrase "venom sound," the first word is a noun, but like an adjective it qualifies the noun, "sound." Various editions of *Richard II* equate the noun "venom" with the adjective "venomous" in their notes. We have here the case of a noun used as an adjective. In modern English, the phrase "venom sound" sounds extremely odd.

Nathaniel: Marvellous well for the pen.
(*Love's Labour's Lost*, IV.ii.143)

The phrase with which the sentence begins comprises two words, "marvellous" and "well." The first word is an adjective and the second is an adverb. Can adjective modify an adverb? No, it cannot, according to the rules of modern English grammar. The sentence spoken above is in response to the question "Did they please, you Sir, Nathaniel?" Evidently, "well" is an adverb of manner. "Marvellous" is only an adjective and it cannot modify the adverb "well." In modern English we need the adverbial form "marvellously."

Juliet: Well, thou hast comforted me marvellous much.
(*Romeo and Juliet*, III.v.232)

In this sarcastic response of Juliet who is speaking to her nurse, we notice another example of Adjective + Adverb. "Much" in this sentence is not a noun, but an adverb and it is modified by an adjective. This is not possible according to modern English grammar.

King: We doubt it nothing, heartily farewell. (*Hamlet*, I.ii.41)

This is the response of Claudius to the assurance given by Cornelius and Voltemand that they would perform their duties strictly when they are sent to Norway as Denmark's messengers. The king has no doubt about it. In this speech of the king we notice the use of the noun, "nothing," as an adverb in the sense of "not at all." In fact, this is how the word "nothing" is explained by the Collins edition of *Hamlet*. According to the OED, the use of "nothing," a noun, in the adverbial sense is archaic.

King: Meantime we thank you for your well-took labour.
Go to your rest; at night we'll feast together.
(*Hamlet*, II.ii.83-84)

This is Claudius thanking Voltemand and Cornelius who have just returned from Norway. Their mission has been successful and the king thanks them. But notice the oddity in the phrase "well-took labour." Here the participial modifier has the form of past tense in "well-took." Today, we require the participial or the "en" form, "well-taken."

Lepidus: 'tis noble spoken. (*Antony and Cleopatra*, II.ii.99)

Lepidus accepts the explanation, if not regrets, offered by Mark Antony and he expresses his appreciation diplomatically. But note how the participle is modified by the adjective "noble." Today's rules of grammar require "nobly." This is not the only example of this kind.

Guildenstern: Is, in his retirement, marvellous distemper'd.
(*Hamlet*, III.ii.293)

Here again, the participle "distempered" is modified by an adjective. Today we are required to say "marvellously" which is an adverb. "Distemper'd" is a participle and not a gerund! Guildenstern says that the king has retired to his room in a bad temper. An adjective like "marvellous" cannot modify a participle.

Demetrius: I am full sorry
That he approves the common liar, who
Thus speaks of him at Rome;
(*Antony and Cleopatra*, I.i.59-61)

This is Demetrius regretting the change he notices in Antony. In his speech, "full" is an adjective which modifies "sorry" which is also an adjective. This is regarded as ungrammatical in modern English grammer. What is needed is a suitable adverb like "very" or "extremely" in the place of "full."

Egyptian: A poor Egyptian yet; The queen my mistress
Confin'd in all she has, her monument
Of thy intents desires instruction,
That she preparedly may frame herself
To the way she is forc'd to.
(*Antony and Cleopatra*, V.i.52-56)

Antony and Cleopatra face defeat at the hands of Caesar and the Egyptian queen sends a message to the Roman ruler to get to know his intentions so that she may prepare herself to the conditions to be set down by him. Notice how the verb "prepare" is first turned into its participial or past tense form and then the morpheme "ly" is added to it in order to make it an adverb, This is Shakespeare's way of converting one part of speech into another. Verb → participle → adverb.

Helena: this fated sky
Gives us free scope; only doth backward pull
Our slow designs when we ourselves are dull.
(*All's Well That Ends Well*, I.i.13-15)

Helena asserts Shakespeare's favourite view that for our problems the remedy lies in ourselves. By "fated sky," Helena means the sky to which we attribute the powers of fate. In other words, "fated sky" means "fateful sky" as the various editions of the play explain. As it is, "fated" is a participle which gives a slightly different meaning. In fact, it means the sky which is subjected to fate as when we describe an accident and talk of the ill-fated vehicle. But in Shakespeare's play, the phrase means "fateful sky."

2nd lord: Away, unpeacable dog; or I'll spurn thee hence.
(*Timon of Athens*, I.i.271)

This is what the lord says to a cynical and churlish philosopher. We can notice how Shakespeare derives an adjective from the noun, "peace." This adjective is not current in modern English. We do not describe a man who is troubling us as unpeacable. Such a derivation is not permitted today.

Timon: I'll example you with thievery.
(*Timon of Athens*, IV.iii.437)

Here is another example of using one part of speech as another. Timon says cynically that he will give the bandits many examples to show that all are thieves. We can see how the noun "example" is employed as a verb, whereas in the previous example a noun is turned into an adjective.

Countess: Therefore, tell me true.
(*All's Well That Ends Well*, I.iii.170)

It is obvious that according to the rules of grammar, the adjective "true" should be replaced by truly, an adverb of manner. It is quite interesting to note that the same countess concludes her exhortation to Diana by employing the adverb of manner, "truly."

howev'r I charge thee,
As heaven shall work in me for thine avail,
To tell me truly.

The same character uses both the adjective and the adverb of manner in the same sentence pattern. We know that the sentence which has the formula NP1 + VT + NP2 cannot be followed by an adjective, but can be followed by an adverbial of manner.

Montano: And 'tis great pity that the noble moor
Should hazard such a place as his own second
With one of an ingraft infirmity: (*Othello*, II.iii.138-40)

Montano comments on the appointment of Cassio who, in his opinion, is not free from an ingrafted infirmity. But we can notice an oddity in the grammar of this sentence. "Ingraft" which means the same thing as "engraft" is a verb and Shakespeare forces it to function as a participle and modify the noun, "infirmity." A verb is employed as a participial adjective.

Edmund: Thou unpossessing bastard, does thou think,
If I would stand against thee, would the reposal
Of any trust, virtue, or worth in thee
Make thy words faithed? (*King Lear*, II.i.67-70)

What we notice here is the employment of a noun as a verb. Today "faith" is termed a noun and it is not used as a verb as Shakespeare has done in this speech. Many more examples can be given for his use of a noun as a verb. Here, of course, "faithed" should be taken to mean "believed." In the same play the noun, "threat," is used as a non-finite verb in the infinitive to "threat" in II.iv.57-58.

1st murderer: Then stand with us.
The west yet glimmers with some streaks of grey;
Now spurs the lated traveller apace
To gain the lengthy inn; (*Macbeth*, III.iii.4-7)

Even the murderer speaks a poetic language in *Macbeth*. But what interests us here is the use made of the word "late" which is either an adjective or an adverb. Shakespeare adds a participial morpheme to it and makes it "lated" which serves as a modifier for the noun "traveller." In modern English, writers prefer the word "belated."

Marina: The more my fault,
To escape his hands where I was like to die.
(*Pericles*, IV.ii.71-72)

Marina's regret here is that death would have been better for her than escaping alive. In any case, death was a probability and that is why she utters the word "like." But note that today we are required to use the adverb "likely" and not the adjective "like."

Simonides: Your presence glads our days: (*Pericles*, II.iii.21)

We are back in *Pericles*. The adjective "glad" is used as a verb by adding the singular morpheme "s" to it. Today, the rules of grammar do not permit this usage.

Longaville: and dainty bits make rich the ribs, but bankrupts the wits. (*Love's Labour's Lost*, I.i.26-27)

Accepting the king's proposal, Longaville adds the foot note that dainty dishes lead to the bankruptcy of wits. Notice how the adjective "bankrupt"—it can also be a noun—is employed as a transitive verb here.

King Henry: Five hundred poor I have in yearly pay,
Who twice a day their wither'd hands hold up
Toward heaven, to pardon blood;
(*Henry V*, IV.i.318-20)

During the battles in France, King Henry prays to God to forgive the sin of his father and not to visit His wrath on his son, since he has shed tears of remorse and employed poor people to pray for forgiveness. Note the word "poor" which is an adjective. Shakespeare employs it as a noun in the sense of poor people. Today "poor" can be used as noun only when we add the Definite Article "the," but then no modifier can be spoken or written before it.

Helena: But this exceeding posting day and night
Must wear your spirit low.
(*All's Well That Ends Well*, V.i.1-2)

This is Helena talking to Diana and the widow who had co-operated with her. The oddity that we notice in this speech is that an "ing" form of verb follows another "ing" form of verb. "Exceeding posting" here means excessive travel. The second word "posting" is a noun, a gerund, strictly speaking. Obviously, the first word "exceeding" is a participial modifier. This is the case of a participle modifying a gerund, both ending with "ing." That is why it looks very odd. Such a construction should be avoided, though it is not ungrammatical.

Phrasal Verb

Caesar: Sit.
Antony: Sit, Sir. (*Antony and Cleopatra*, II.i.26-27)

In this exchange of cold courtesies, between Octavius Caesar and Mark Antony, we should not fail to notice the absence of the adverbial particle, "down." In modern English, "sit" is a part of a phrasal verb in which the other word is an adverbial particle.

Touchstone: By my troth, well met, come, sit, sit, and a song.
(*As You Like It*, V.iii.10)

Touchstone who is in a happy mood with Audrey, a country wench, persuades the two pages to sing. He utters the verb "sit" not once, but twice in a row without any adverbial particle! Here the most suitable particle to be used is "down." In the play *Pericles*, V.i.63-64 we notice the same verb "sit," again without the company of the particle. Evidently, Shakespeare's English does not insist upon the phrasal construction. But today the verb "sit" without an adverbial in the situations described above looks odd and ungrammatical.

Lewis: Your grace shall pardon me, I will not back;
(*King John*, V.ii.78)

This example will show that it is not "sit" alone that is used by Shakespeare without a particle. Here it is the verb "back." Lewis, the prince of France, brims with confidence when he is about to attack the British army. He assures Pandulph, the Papal legate, that he will not back out. But the adverbial particle "out" is dropped, with the result the verb sounds like a transitive verb without its object.

Dogberry: an' there be any matter of weight chances, call up me:
(*Much Ado About Nothing*, III.iii.80-81)

This speech is quoted from the well-known comic scene of Dogberry and Verges. The structure of the main clause spoken by Dogberry is NP (deleted) + VT + Adverbial Particle + Personal Pronoun. This is not permitted by modern English grammar. Rules today demand the placing of Personal Pronoun before the particle "up" and, therefore, we say "call me up." The Personal Pronoun should have precedence over the particle.

Pronoun: Personal

Horatio: yet once methought
It lifted up it head and did address
Itself to motion, like as it would speak;
(*Hamlet*, I.ii.215-17)

The personal pronoun "it" should interest us here. It is quite evident that the word is equivalent to "its," a genitive form. In fact, the Collins edition (Alexander Shakespeare) explains its meaning as "its" in its notes. The playwright often writes "it" in the place of its genitive form. Another example can be found in *King Lear*.

Fool: For you know, uncle,
The hedge-sparrow fed the cuckoo so long
That it had it head bit off by it young.
(*King Lear*, I.iv.215-17)

In this scene full of the elements of the absurd theatre, the fool refers to some folk-lore, if not bird-lore. Notice the word "it" which appears three times in the third line. Only the first of them is in the nominative case; the second and third are in the genitive case. Today such a genitive case would be regarded ungrammatical. The New Shakespeare edition of Cambridge University Press explains its meaning as "its" and goes on to add that "it" is the "old genitive."

Relative Pronoun

Mowbray: 'Tis not the trial of a woman's war,
The bitter clamour of two eager tongues,

Can arbitrate this cause betwixt us twain;
(*Richard II*, I.i.48-50)

This is Mowbray's reply to Bolingbroke's accusations against him. Notice the absence of the Relative Pronoun "that" or "which." When a clause is in the position of a Noun Phrase/Subject, the Relative Pronoun which functions as a subordinator cannot be dispensed with. While it is grammatical, for example, to say "I am the person you are seeking," it is not grammatical to say "I am the person can resolve the dispute." In the former sentence, the clause is in the position of an NP/Object. But the latter has a clause which is in the position of an NP/Subject. If we rewrite Mowbray's sentence today, we must add either "which" or "that" in the third line before the word "can." Shakespeare's grammar is confirmed by the following example from his play, *Othello*.

Cassio: If the gentle woman that attends the general's wife be stirring, tell her there's one Cassio entreats her for a little favour of speech: (III.i.24-26)

In this speech of Cassio, the pronoun "who" should be written between the word "Cassio" and the word "entreats." Cassio's instruction to the clown is what is called transformation in grammar and while the clause "there's . . ." is the NP/Object of the verb "tell," there is also the Relative Clause "who entreats her" which is the NP/Subject of the verb "entreats." It should be noted that in the above two examples, the VP consists of verbals, "arbitrate" and "entreat." If either of these verbs had followed a form of "be" in the VP, it would have made a lot of difference.

Hamlet: Was it Hamlet wronged Laertes? Never Hamlet:
(*Hamlet*, V.ii.321)

This is Hamlet's explanation of his action to Laertes. Notice the absence of the Relative Pronoun "that" or "who" after the NP/Subject "Hamlet." In this example also, the VP of the clause which is in the position of the NP/Subject—rather, a part of the NP/S—consists of a verbal, that is, a form of verb other than "be" or auxiliary. As it is, the sentence will be treated ungrammatical today; a Relative Pronoun is essential.

Green: Now for the rebels which stand out in Ireland;
Expedient manage must be made, my liege,
Ere further leisure yield them further means
For their advantage and your highness' loss.
(*Richard II*, I.iv.38-41)

Here Green, described in the play as a servant of Richard II, tenders advice about managing the Irish rebels. Evidently, the people whom he is referring to are human beings, men or women or both. But the Relative Pronoun used for replacing this noun is "which." The rebels cannot be treated as neuter gender which alone can justify this Relative Pronoun. What we need in a situation like this today is the word "who" which can have a noun of masculine or feminine gender as its antecedent.

First Lord: A servant only, and a gentleman which I have some-time known. (*All's Well That Ends Well*, III.i.84)

The first lord tells the countess in reply to her query that Bertram, her son has gone to Florence to fight in a war and that he is accompanied by a servant and a gentleman whom he has known for some time. The Relative Pronoun is "which" though its antecedent, the noun phrase which it replaces, is masculine gender. Such a thing is not permitted in modern English.

Cleon: This Tarsus, o'er which I have the government
A city on whom plenty held full hand,
For riches strew'd herself even in the streets;
(*Pericles*, I.iv.21-23)

Cleon describes the former glory of Tarsus of which he is the governor. What is odd here is the Relative Pronoun "whom" related to the word "city" which is a neuter noun. But the playwright uses the objective form of "who" which is intended only for nouns of masculine or feminine gender. Today we put the Relative Pronoun "which" in the place of "whom."

Lodovico: Is this the noble moor whom our full senate
Call all-in-all sufficient? Is this the noble nature

Whom passion could not shake? (*Othello*, IV.i.265-67)

Lodovico who has come from Venice notices a change in Othello's attitude towards Desdemona whom Othello insults in the presence of others. "Nature" in this example is evidently neuter gender, but the playwright uses the Relative Pronoun "whom" appropriate only for human beings. It is quite interesting to note that the same Relative Pronoun has "Othello" as its antecedent! There is no correlation between human gender and the Relative Pronoun which it replaces.

Dolabella: O! Sir, you are too sure an augurer;
That you did fear is done.
(*Antony and Cleopatra*, V.ii.334-35)

This is Dolabella's exclamation when Octavius Caesar arrives, only to see the dead body of Cleopatra who had taken her own life before he could meet her. We can see here the absence of any distinction between "what" and "that." The former is not a Relative Pronoun, because it does not replace any noun or noun phrase: in other words, it has no antecedent. When there is no antecedent, the Relative Pronoun "that" cannot be used. The sub-ordinator "what" should be written in its place. "What you did fear is done" is how we should rewrite it today.

Claudius: For all our thanks.
Now follows that you know; (*Hamlet*, III.ii.16-17)

Claudius quite tactfully and diplomatically refers to his decisions already made and to the future course of action concerning the state of Denmark. The grammatical oddity here is that the Relative Pronoun "that" does not have an antecedent, that is, a noun or noun phrase which it has replaced. But still the playwright uses it in the place of "what" which we use today. Another example can be seen in *All's Well That Ends Well*, III.i.208-12, in which Helena confesses her love before the formidable and unsympathetic countess.

Incidentally, we may add that when a clause is the NP/Subject of a complex sentence, the subject of the main clause should be singular in number. For example, the sentence "what he said are not correct" is surely ungrammatical. "Are" should be replaced by "is." But this rule was not observed by Shakespeare who in *Hamlet* uses the plural "are."

Iago: Good name in man or woman, dear lord,
Is the immediate jewel of their souls;
Who steals my purse steals trash; 'tis something, nothing;
(*Othello*, III.iii.158-60)

What is the oddity here? You find it in the last line. "Who" is a pronoun and it cannot introduce the Subject/Clause unless its antecedent is also present. That is why today we say "He who steals my purse." Here the Personal Pronoun "He" is the antecedent of the Relative Pronoun "who." What about "whoever"? This compound word is acceptable because the word means "anyone who." The antecedent is inherent in the word "whoever." The pronoun "who" cannot introduce the NP/Clause which is the subject of a sentence, though the sentence is a transformation.

Pericles: Who has a book of all that monarchs do,
He's more secure to keep it shut than shown;
(*Pericles*, I.i.94-95)

This example reinforces our view of Shakespeare's grammar. The Relative Pronoun "who" above lacks an antecedent and it cannot begin an NP/Clause which is in the position of the subject of a sentence. "Whoever" is acceptable for the reason explained above.

Parolles: Loss of virginity is rational increase, and there was never virgin got till virginity was first lost. That you were made of is mettle to make virgins.
(*All's Well That Ends Well*, I.i.125-27)

Parolles, a follower of Bertram, is engaged in a naughty battle of wits with Helena in much the same way as Iago who entertained Desdemona with his witty and naughty comments on women. According to Parolles, virgins will not be born unless women lose their virginity. But the second sentence above will be dismissed as plainly ungrammatical today. This sentence begins with a clause in the position of a noun phrase/subject. It begins with the Relative Pronoun "that," but it does not have an antecedent in the sentence.

We do not see any NP which it replaces. Therefore, to make the sentence grammatical, we should replace "that" with the pronoun "what" which does not require any antecedent. The sentence then will be "What you were made of is mettle to make virgins." Parolles says that a woman is made of the substance which makes virgins!

Boyet: Now, madam, summon up your dearest spirits;
Consider who the king your father sends,
To whom he sends, and what's his embassy.
(*Love's Labour's Lost*, I.i.1-3)

It is evident that "who" in the second line is the object of the transitive verb "sends." But the playwright prefers to write "who" which is in the Nominative Case, whereas according to the rules of modern English grammar, it should be "whom" which is in the Objective Case. Similar examples can be found in this play.

Lear: Who would'st thou serve? (*King Lear*, I.iv.24)

This is Lear's question when Kent in disguise appears for the first time before him. The sentence is a transformation and the pronoun "who" is the object of the transitive verb "serve." Evidently, according to the rules of modern English grammar, "who" which is in the Nominative case should be changed to "whom." There are many examples of this kind in the plays of Shakespeare. They include *Much Ado About Nothing*, V.i.216-17 and *Othello*, II.ii.14-15.

Reflexive Pronoun

Hero: There will she hide her
To listen to our purpose.
(*Much Ado About Nothing*, III.i.11-12)

Hero has her own plans for Beatrice, her cousin. She instructs Margaret, one of her two gentlewomen, to fetch Beatrice so that she would overhear Hero's conversation with Ursula, another gentlewoman. Notice the absence of the Reflexive Pronoun "herself" which we use today according to the rules of grammar. Shakespeare uses the plain "her." This is not a solitary example.

Claudius: Arm you, I pray you, to this speedy voyage;
(*Hamlet*, III.iii.24)

This is Claudius asking Rosencrantz and Guildenstern to equip themselves and get ready to escort Hamlet to England. It is an Imperative sentence and we notice again the clear absence of the Reflexive Pronoun "yourselves" after the verb "arm." Today we are required to replace "you" with "yourselves." Another example of the conspicuous absence of the Reflexive Pronoun is *King Lear*, II.ii.115-17.

Other Pronouns

Cassio: To who? (*Othello*, I.ii.54)

This is Cassio's response when Iago informs him that Othello was married. What interests us in this context, however, is the absence of the accusative pronoun "whom," Shakespeare has written "who" though it is governed by the preposition "to." One of the basic things we learn in English grammar is that a pronoun or noun should be in the Objective Case when it is governed by a preposition. The Personal Pronoun is, no doubt, inflected and whether it is Nominative Case or the Objective Case becomes immediately clear. The playwright has used the Nominative Case. Here are some more examples.

Edgar: To who, my lord? (*King Lear*, V.iii.47)

This is Edgar's response when Albany asks him to run immediately to save the life of Lear and Cordelia. "To who" is the exact repetition of the prepositional phrase which we saw above. Another example is Ross's question in *Macbeth* (IV.iii.170-71) which ends with "for who." Whether the preposition is "to" or "for," Shakespeare uses "who," the Nominative Case!

Leonato: He hath an uncle here in Messina will be very much glad of it. (*Much Ado About Nothing*, I.i.17)

There are two finite VPs in the sentence, but we see only one clause on the surface. There are really two clauses, one for each finite verb. The subject of the second finite verbal phrase "will be" is actually the Relative Pronoun "who" which is missing in the sentence. This is, evidently, in the Nominative Case. According to the rules, when the clause is the Subject/NP of the sentence, the Relative Pronoun which replaces it cannot be dropped. How can both the replaced thing and what replaces it be dropped? In this sentence, if we go by the rules of grammar, "who" should be written after the noun "Messina" with a comma preceding it, since its antecedent is "uncle" and not "Messina." A similar example can be seen in *King Lear* (IV.ii.92). In fact, there are quite a few examples of this kind scattered all over the plays of Shakespeare.

Angus: Who was the thane lives yet,
But under heavy judgement bears that life
Which he deserves to lose. (*Macbeth*, I.iii.109-11)

Angus says that Cawdor has been stripped of his title and is under sentence of death. Grammatically, this sentence is the opposite of the above example, because here it is the noun which is missing while the Relative Clause is very much present. To put it in a more conventional language, the Noun/Noun Phrase/Pronoun which it qualifies is absent, while the Relative Pronoun which stands for it is "who" with which the sentence begins. In this particular instance, this noun is "Cawdor," but the antecedent can even be the pronoun "he." According to the rules of grammar today, the sentence above must begin with one of these antecedents.

Subjunctive Sentences

Bolingbroke: Norfolk, so far as to mine enemy
By this time, had the king permitted us,
One of our souls had wander'd in the air,
Banish'd this frail sepulchre of our flesh,
As now our flesh is banish'd from this land:
(*Richard II*, I.iii.193-97)

The defiant tone of Bolingbroke is understandable, because one challenger is speaking to another. What interests us from the point of view of grammar is the verbal phrase "had wander'd" in the third line. Bolingbroke is not, however, describing what has already happened, notwithstanding the past tense form of the auxiliary "have." He is only describing what would have happened. Today, in the place of "had wander'd," we say "would have wandered." The duke's son is describing only a possibility, because the encounter between the two contenders was not permitted by the king at the last moment. Similar examples can be found in *Othello* and *Antony and Cleopatra*.

Clown: Truly, madam, if God have lent a man any manners
he may easily put it off at the court;
(*All's Well That Ends Well*, II.ii.8-9)

A satirical comment on royal court is not unusual in the plays of Shakespeare. Notice the oddity in the word "have." It is a plural auxiliary and the clown uses it, not because he has respect for God, but because that is the way Shakespeare writes what may be called the "if" clause. It means it has no tense: in other words, it is in its basic form. Today we use the singular form of the auxiliary "have": we replace "have" with "has."

Helena: O, were that all! (*All's Well That Ends Well*, I.i.75)

Helena expresses the wish that the effort to bring credit to her father was all that was expected. Today, we express the same meaning by saying "I wish that was all." Evidently, the subjunctive mood is going out of fashion.

Simonides: Knights,
To say you're welcome were superfluous.
(*Pericles*, II.iii.1-2)

Shakespeare uses "were," a plural form of "be," in the place of "would be." Simonides welcomes the knights at the banquet and he says that to say "you are welcome" would be superfluous. But the playwright uses the plural and past tense form of the verb "be." This is not what we say today.

Berowne: Is ebony like her? O, wood divine!

A wife of such wood were felicity.
(*Love's Labour's Lost*, IV.iii.24-25)

Berowne admits that he is ensnared by love. Grammatically, the example is similar to the previous one and reinforces our comment. Here "were" in the second line means "would be" which is what we say today. Another example can be found in *All's Well That Ends Well*, III.iv.43-46.

Rosalind: Dear Celia, I show more mirth than I am mistress of;
and would you yet I were merrier?
(*As You Like It*, I.ii.3-4)

This is Rosalind's response when Celia, her cousin and friend tries to cheer her up. What interests us here is the grammatical aspect of the word "would" which is the form of the past tense of the auxiliary "will." What Rosalind means is "Do you wish." As the sentence is a question, "do" makes its appearance. Otherwise, one can say that Shakespeare uses "would" where we use the verb "wish." Today, the sentence looks quaint, if not ungrammatical to say, for example, "I would I were born in ancient India."

Gratiano: Did he live now,
This sight would make him do a desperate turn,
Yea, curse his better angel from his side,
And fall to reprobance. (*Othello*, V.ii.209-12)

Gratiano who is lamenting the murder of Desdemona imagines the reaction of her father if he were alive now. Notice the word "did" which is a substitute for the modern subordinator, "if." What Gratiano says is "If he lived now" or "If he were alive now." But in Shakespeare's plays you find "did" doing the job of "if" when he writes the adverbial clause of condition. Another example can be found in *Henry V*, III.i.4-5. It is always the past tense form of "do," namely "did" and never "does."

Tense Bearer

Duke of York: Seek you to seize and gripe into your hands
The royalties and rights of banish'd Hereford?
(*Ricahrd II*, II.i.189-90)

York expresses his shock at King Richard's move to confiscate the property of John of Gaunt, the Duke of Lancaster. What we read here is a question of what is popularly called Yes/No type. In such a question, tense is carried by the word "do" which must be added to the transformation, if the verbal phrase does not include "be" or any auxiliary. The verb other than these two is called "verbal" in some modern English grammars, but it is the same thing as the main verb, if it is alone. When a basic sentence containing such a VP is transformed into a question of Yes/No type, "do" must be added to carry the tense which is the same as the tense of the basic sentence. According to the rules of modern English grammar, York's question should be rewritten as "Do you seek to seize." But Shakespeare reverses the NP/Subject and the verb. A large number of such usage are scattered all over his plays. Constraints of space compel me to quote only one example of each type.

Queen: The lady doth protest too much, methinks

(*Hamlet*, III.ii.226)

This is Gertrude's comment when she watches the play arranged by her son. Hamlet asks her whether she likes the play and this is her response. The sentence is affirmative and is in what is called Indicative Mood. In English, the tense of such a sentence is carried by the verbal, a form of "be" or the auxiliary as the case may be. In this particular sentence, the last two are absent and we find only the verbal, namely, "protest." According to the rules, tense should be added only to this word and, therefore, the morpheme "s" should be added to it, since the subject is singular. But Shakespeare prefers to add "do" which is a word by itself and then makes it singular by changing it into "doth"! In the previous example, the dummy "do" was required, but Shakespeare had no use for it; in the present case, "do" is not necessary but he uses it. Note that the word "doth" can make the sentence emphatic, but the clause "methinks" rules out such a possibility. In order to strengthen this point, let me give an example from the play, *King Lear*.

Albany: Where was his son when they did take his eyes?

IV.ii.89

This is Albany's question when he learns from a messenger that the Duke of Gloucester had been brutally blinded by Cornwall, with the full support of his wife. There are two transformations in this sentence, but the question does not belong to the Yes/No type. Moreover, "take" is a verbal and it should carry tense, past in this case. But instead of "took," we find only "did take." Albany is only seeking information and, therefore, there is no emphatic mood. There is no need for "do."

King Richard: Cousin, throw up your gage; do you begin.
(*Richard II*, I.i.186)

The second sentence looks like a question, but it is not. It is a simple Imperative sentence and that is the reason of the absence of a question mark. King Richard who tries, however clumsily, to arrange reconciliation between Bolingbroke and Mowbray, asks Bolingbroke to throw up his gage. We are concerned here with the needless presence of the word "do" in the second sentence while no emphasis is intended. The king instructs his cousin to throw up his gage, that is all. In modern English it should be written as "You begin." The presence of "do" in such an imperative sentence gives it the form of Yes/No type of question.

Marina: What means you? (*Pericles*, IV.i.68)

This is Marina's question to Leonine when the latter, a servant appointed to kill her, asks her to say her prayers. The young lady is shocked and she asks him "what means you" which is equivalent to "what do you mean" in modern English. In this case, we notice the presence of a verbal in its VP and, therefore, in this question which is a transformation, the presence of "do" is essential.

Transformation

Rosencrantz: No, indeed, are they not. (*Hamlet*, II.ii.336)

This is what Rosencrantz says in reply to Hamlet's question whether the visiting company of players continues to be held in high esteem. Notice the form of the sentence. It looks like a Yes/No type of question. Indeed it does look like the Transformation

Yes/No of the sentence "They are not." As the VP of the sentence is be + tense, its transformation into a question would produce the sentence "Are they not." But in the text, it is not a question that Rosencrantz utters. There is no question mark at the end and it is certainly an affirmative sentence. Such a sentence will be regarded quite ungrammatical today.

Servant: Madam, the guests are come, supper served up.
(*Romeo and Juliet*, I.iii.100)

This is what the servant tells the hostess, Lady Capulet. In its form the sentence appears to be in the passive voice. The two elements that turn Active voice into Passive voice are there in the VP following the NP/Subject: a form of "be" and a participle. But today, we are required to say "The guests have come" replacing "are" with "have." The other word, "served," is both past tense and participle. No doubt, the speech is attributed to a servant, but this kind of voice which is grammatically passive can be found in the speeches of educated and upper class characters also.

Celia: By this kind of chase, I should hate him, for my father
hated his father dearly; yet I hate not Orlando.
(*As You Like It*, I.iii.30-31)

Celia teases her cousin and companion, Rosalind, about her love of Orlando. Her logic includes a negative sentence. According to the rules of modern English grammar, the dummy "do" must be added and made to carry tense, when we transform an affirmative sentence into a negative one, if the former's Verbal Phrase is a verbal. Today Celia's sentence "I hate not Orlando" would be regarded ungrammatical and rewritten as "I do not hate Orlando."

King: The main consents are had, and here we'll stay
To see our widower's second marriage today.
(*All's Well That Ends Well*, V.iii.69-70)

The presence of "are," a form of "be," is the signal to indicate the presence of Passive Voice. This is reinforced by the absence of any "ing" form of a verb in the word that follows it. Evidently, the word "had" which is not an auxiliary, a present participle, adjective, noun or adverb of place must be, after this process of elimination, only a transitive verb in the past participial form. But strictly speaking, it is not. What the king here means is that the prior consent of all the main characters has been obtained. Evidently, "had" is employed as a synonym for "obtained," a transitive verb. This is a unique example of usage.

Cassio: O, behold
The riches of the ship is come on shore!
(*Othello*, II.i.83-84)

This is Cassio's chivalrous exclamation at the appearance of Desdemona who alights from the ship in a harbour of Cyprus. The Verbal Phrase of the sentence should interest here more than the Italian Senator's beautiful daughter. "Is come" is, evidently, equivalent to "has come." In an earlier example we saw the use of "are" in the place of "has." The sentence has the form of Passive Voice and it looks as if the verb "come" is used as a transitive verb! But it is clear that Shakespeare is not using Passive Voice and that he employs a form of "be" instead of a form of "has." There are also instances of the use of "be" before the verb "become" which does not undergo Passive Transformation. The Verbal Phrase "is become" can be found in the plays of Shakespeare. It is obvious that here also, a form of "be" is exactly equivalent to a form of "have."

King of France: This is most strange
That she whom even but now was your best object
. . . should in a trice of time
Commit a thing so monstrous to dismantle
So many folds of favour. (*King Lear*, I.i.213-18)

This example can be with equal appropriateness considered under the heading "conjunction" also. It is taken up here because the sentence is a transformation. As it happens, the playwright stops short of the adverbial clause of result and obtains the same effect by using an infinitive. Today the sentence would be treated as ungrammatical, because the word "as" is absent, though it is a part of the compound conjunction "so as." The word "as" should be placed after the adjective "monstrous" and before the infinitive "to dismantle."

Oswald: When he, compact, and flattering his displeasure
Tripped me behind, . . . got praises from the king
For him attempting who was himself subdued,
(*King Lear*, II.ii.105-9)

According to the explanation offered by Transformational Grammar, a Relative Clause is a part of the concerned Noun Phrase and, in any case, it should be written immediately after the Noun which is treated as its antecedent in the traditional grammar. In Oswald's petulant complaint to Cornwall, the antecedent is conspicuously absent. Attempting whom? The various editions of *King Lear* recognise the necessity of the presence of an antecedent. In fact, the Cambridge edition of the play explains the meaning of the last line as follows: "for attacking a man who offered no resistance." Evidently a "man" is the antecedent here. In a complex sentence which is a transformation, Shakespeare sometimes omits the Noun/Noun Phrase which is qualified or replaced by the Relative Clause. Another example is found in *Antony and Cleopatra*, II.v.84.

King: How do you, pretty lady? (*Hamlet*, IV.v.39)

This is Claudius greeting Ophelia who is now insane. This sentence is a transformation of a basic sentence: in fact, it is a double-base transformation. Its VP is a verbal, that is, a verb other than "be" and auxiliary. When such a sentence is turned into a wh-question, it is necessary to add "do" which is assigned the job of carrying the tense. Today, according to the rules of grammar, we say "How do you do"? Another example is *As You Like It*, III.ii.38.

Clown: Your son will not be killed as soon as I thought he would.
(*All's Well That Ends Well*, III.ii.36)

This is the clown's characteristic way of speaking, but he cannot be exempted from the rules of grammar. The adverbial clause of time which we find in his speech has a verbal phrase of Passive Voice. We know that a sentence of passive voice is a transformation and that it should carry all the grammatical relations found in the basic structure which is always in Active Voice. Therefore, the entire clause should have been "As soon as I thought he would be killed." The participle "killed" is, however, common to the insert clause and the matrix or the main clause. Rules of grammar permit the deletion of the word "killed" in the insert or the subordinate clause. But the auxiliary "be" which is an essential addition when the Passive transformation takes place cannot be deleted. It is not common to the matrix and the insert clause. That is why the truncated "would" cannot stand alone at the end of the sentence. Today we add "be" to the sentence at the end.

Unattached Participle
Verb

Player King: But orderly to end where I begun
Our wills and fates so contrary run
That our devices are still overthrown;
(*Hamlet*, III.ii.256-58)

This is the player king's comment after he hears the protestations of fidelity by the player queen in the play which Hamlet has arranged. In this formal language, we can notice an oddity in the last word of the first line. This word "begun" cannot be a participle because it is not preceded by an auxiliary, a form of "have" or "be." It is evidently, the past tense of "begin." The meaning of the speech also supports this view. But then the past tense of "begin" is "began." Shakespeare employs what is apparently the participial form.

King John: The tackle of my heart is crack'd and burn'd.
(*King John*, V.vii.52)

This is what King John says to Bastard who has come in a great hurry to comfort King John who is dying. Note the word "burn'd." The word following "is" should have the participial form "burnt." But the playwright uses what to us appears to be the past tense form.

Pembroke: He is more patient
Than when you left him: even now he sung.
(*King John*, V.vii.11-12)

This is what the Earl of Pembroke says to Prince Henry, son of King John, who was seriously ill after he was poisoned, according to some reports. "Sung" is regarded today as the participial form of the verb "sing," whereas "sang" is the past tense form of the verb. But Shakespeare uses "sung" as the past tense. James Thomson, a poet of the eighteenth century, uses the same expression in his well-known poem, "Rule, Britannia."

> If she be very well, what does she ail that she's not very well? (*All's Well That Ends Well*, II.iv.6)

This question shows Helena's impatience at the clown's witty gymnastics in describing her mother's condition. Today, we use the word "ail" only in the intransitive sense; that is what the OED says. Helena uses it, however, as a transitive verb in a wh-question. If what Helena says is reduced to the basic or kernel sentence, we may have to write "She + ails + NP" which is not permitted in modern English. We can only say, for example, that so and so is ailing for some time. Here the verb is purely intransitive, though it is a part of a phrasal verb. Poetry is different and the practice of writing "ails + pronoun or noun" continued till the time of John Keats who uses this structure in one of his famous lyrics.

Lady Macbeth: Feed, and regard him not. (*Macbeth*, III.ii.156)

Lady Macbeth tries desperately to control the damage caused by Macbeth's behaviour and utterances at the sight of Banquo's ghost. The verb "feed" is used here in a purely intransitive sense, whereas today we use it either as a transitive verb or with a particle as in "he feeds on."

Voice: Active and Passive

Duke Frederick: How now, daughter, and cousin! Are you crept hither to see the wrestling?
(*As You Like It*, I.ii.136)

Duke Frederick asks in an affectionate manner whether Celia and Rosalind have come to watch the wresting match. In appearance and form, it is an example of Passive Voice. But though the Verbal

Phrase has the structure be + participle, we cannot jump to the conclusion that Shakespeare has put it in the Passive Voice, an impossible structure in the present context. "Creep" cannot be regarded as a transitive verb without which there can be no Passive Transformation. The variation from modern English grammar is clear. We should regard "are" in the above sentence as equivalent to "have" which is also an auxiliary. There are many examples of this kind. One of them is *Love's Labour's Lost*, III.i.64.

Ist Senator: That's well spoke. (*Timon of Athens*, V.i.193)

The first senator expresses his appreciation of Timon's statement that he loves his country and that he does not want to see it wrecked, though he is not in a position to comply with the request of the senators. We can see the Passive Voice in this short sentence; the necessary "be" is there, preceding the main verb. What is odd, however, is that it is followed by the past tense and not the participle of the verb; "spoke" is there and not "spoken." This is at variance with the rules of modern English grammar which insists on the presence of the "en" form of the verb. There are many examples of this kind and one of them is *Richard II*, II.iii.38.

Word Order or Syntax

Timon: Go not you hence
Till I have thanked you. (*Timon of Athens*, I.i.245-46)

In this language of courtesy and hospitality, Timon speaks an imperative sentence. Today we do not like to include the Second Person "you" in a sentence spoken to make a request or appeal, unless there are overriding reasons for it. Here in this example, there is no reason for its inclusion since it is spoken in a normal situation. There are quite a few examples of this in the plays of Shakespeare.

First Lord: Are not acquainted with him? Knows he not thy voice?
(*All's Well That Ends Well*, IV.i.8)

This is exactly the opposite of the above example. The first French lord asks the soldier whether he is not acquainted with Parolles. Note the absence of the second person "you" in the first sentence.

Without it, the sentence has no Noun/Subject at all and such a sentence will be treated as ungrammatical today. The sentence should be "Art thou not" according to the rules of modern English grammar.

Celia: Alas, he is too young! Yet he looks successfully.
(*As You Like It*, I.ii.135)

The young Orlando in the wrestling has won the sympathy of both Rosalind and Celia and the above sentence is the latter's exclamation. The second sentence ends with the word "successfully," an adverbial of manner. But according to the rules of modern English grammar, some verbs cannot be followed by any adverbial of manner and "look" belongs to that class of verbs. "Seem" is another verb of this class to which only a small number of verbs belong. Another example of this kind is *The Tempest* (III.i.34). "Successful," an adjective, is permissible here.

Costard: It may be so; but if he say it is so, he is, in telling true, but so. (*Love's Labour's Lost*, I.ii.219)

In this comment by the clown when the king is reading a letter, we notice an oddity concerning the word order. "Telling" is the "ing" form of the verb "tell" which is transitive and it cannot be followed by an adjective which "true" is. In modern English, "telling the truth" is grammatical, but not "telling true."

Orlando: As I remember, Adam, it was upon this fashion—bequeathed me by will but poor a thousand crowns, and as thou sayest, charged my brother, on his blessing to breed me well; (*As You Like It*, I.i.1-4)

The play begins with these words and Orlando bitterly complains about his ill-treatment at the hands of his elder brother, Oliver. Let us take a look at the phrase "poor a thousand crowns." In this noun phrase there are three elements besides "crown," a noun which is also the head word in the phrase. Of these three, one is a numeral and together with the noun it forms a unit. But we also have an adjective and an article. Rules of grammar say that the article cannot be written after the adjective. Today it is incorrect to write adj + art. We had better say "a poor thousand crowns" which has the structure art + adj + num + noun.

Helena: I put you to
The use of your own virtues, for the which
I shall continue thankful.
(*All's Well That Ends Well*, V.i.15-17)

Helena comes to Marseilles and wants the help of a man to submit a petition to the king of France. For his services she will be grateful to him. She says "I shall continue thankful." The word "continue" is either a transitive or intransitive verb and we find it here followed by an adjective "thankful." This structure VT or VI + adj is not possible in modern English. An adverbial is possible if it is a VI and a noun phrase is possible if it is a VT, but not an adjective.

Duke: 'Tis certain then, for Cyprus
Marcus Luccicos, is not he in town?
(*Othello*, I.iii.43-44)

The duke asks the senators whether Marcus Luccicos is in town. The simple question belongs to the Yes/no type. Its VP is in the form of "be." According to the rules of grammar, the NP/Subject should be written before the adverb "not." But Shakespeare has done the opposite. In his sentence, "not" does not follow the subject, but precedes the subject.

Bawd: Yes, indeed shall you, and taste gentlemen of all fashions.
(*Pericles*, IV.ii.76)

The bawd speaks an affirmative sentence in this address to Marina. In any affirmative sentence, the NP/Subject comes first and the VP including the modal auxiliary comes next. But here contrary to the rules of modern English grammar, the word order is just the opposite.

Diana: Or perform my bidding or thou livest in woe;
Do it and happy; by my silver bow!
(*Pericles*, V.i.245-46)

This is Diana's advice to Pericles, the prince of Tyre. The second line is an example of a verbless clause. According to the rules of grammar, every clause should have a finite verb. The sentence "Do it and happy" is ungrammatical; there is need for a finite verb in that clause. We must add the verb "be" after the conjunction "and" so that the two clauses are rightly combined by the conjunction "and." "It" is a pronoun and "happy" is an adjective and they are unlike structures. When "be" is added, we have two clauses and the co-ordination between them is possible.

Bishop of Ely: But what prevention? (*Henry* V, I.i.21)

The archbishop of Canterbury and the Bishop of Ely are worried over a bill brought forward by the government which would deprive the church of its property by and large. The Archbishop remarks that it would drink cup and all. The bishop responds with the above question. It is evidently a verbless sentence and its meaning is "What is the prevention." The verb, a form of "be," is absent, though a verb with tense is essential for a sentence. There are quite a few examples of this kind in Shakespeare's plays.

Herald: So much was his pleasure should be proclaimed.
(*Othello*, II.ii.7)

A sentence which has a single clause cannot have two finite verbs unless they are co-ordinated by a conjunction. To make it grammatical, we must rewrite it as: "So much was his pleasure to be proclaimed." We have converted the second finite verb into an infinitive. The herald has read an announcement and says that so much was Othello's pleasure to get it proclaimed.

Dogberry: An there be any matter of weight chances, call up me
(*Much Ado About Nothing*, III.iii.80-81)

This is the constable's instruction to Verges, a headborough. The main clause consists of only three small words, but it is ungrammatical. The playwright has placed "up," an adverbial particle, before the word "me." But today, we follow the rule which says that if the object of the verb is a personal pronoun, the adverbial particle should be written after and not before the personal pronoun.

Caesar: Cleopatra, know
We will extenuate, rather than enforce;
(*Antony and Cleopatra*, V.ii.12)

Octavius Caesar diplomatically handles the defeat of Cleopatra and he assures her that he would rather extenuate than enforce. Note how the imperative sentence begins with the verb "know." Today we do not begin an imperative sentence so abruptly. The general practice is to preface it with some other words.

Cassius: Let go sir, or I'll knock you o'er the muzard.
(*Othello*, II.iii.150)

Cassio is not in his senses as a result of drinking too much and warns Montano against his intervention. The sentence has two clauses and in the first one, "let" is a transitive verb. Therefore, we should place its NP/Subject between "let" and the infinitive, "go." "Let me go" is the way the clause should be written. Shakespeare, however, has dropped the NP/Object.

Paris: Younger than she are happy mothers made.
(*Romeo and Juliet*, I.i.12)

The importunate young man pleads that age should not be a bar to Juliet's marriage and that women younger than Juliet have been happy mothers. Every sentence should have a noun phrase/Subject and a finite verb. But there is no subject in this sentence. We have to overstretch the rules of grammar to find it. What Paris means is "women younger than she." Strictly speaking, the sentence should be "NP + who are younger." The rules of grammar permit the deletion of the Relative Pronoun + tense + be. But they do not permit the deletion of the NP also. But Shakespeare has dropped it.

Conclusion

I have tried to make this study exhaustive, but I am aware of the possibility of overlooking some other aspects of the subject. My only comfort is the conviction that such cases are not many. Secondly, it is worthwhile emphasizing that all the differences of grammar cannot be regarded as stylistic devices. Only a few of them can be explained under that heading. When Antony says to Pompey,

> I have heard it, Pompey,
> And I am well studied for a liberal thanks
> Which I do owe you. (*Antony and Cleopatra*, II.vi.47-49)

the phrase "a liberal thanks" cannot be regarded as a stylistic feature. Renaissance English made a liberal use of articles, perhaps. It can be argued, no doubt, that a noun or noun phrase may be plural in form, but singular in meaning. Nevertheless, we do not utter or write the phrase "a liberal thanks" today. We would rather omit the Indefinite Article.

Some grammatical features can be accepted, of course, as matters of style. When Cleopatra says,

> I will not hurt him.
> These hands lack nobility, that they strike
> A meaner than myself. (*Antony and Cleopatra*, II.v.82-84)

we are sure that Shakespeare deliberately drops the antecedent and shortens the Relative Clause for the sake of elliptical style. What Cleopatra means is that her hands will only betray lack of nobility if they strike a "person who is meaner than herself."

To an Indian, English is a second language and he learns it from models of English prose written by great masters and from the rules of modern English grammar. Shakespeare's English cannot in every case be a model of English prose for him, if he looks at it from the point of view of grammar. A good student of English in India should be able to say that the sentence of Mowbray's speech

> Then, thus I turn me from my country's light
> To dwell in solemn shades of endless night.
> (*Richard II*, I.iii.176-77)

shows a very conspicuous absence of Reflective Pronoun in the first line and that it is very necessary. He should be able to say when he reads the following sentence spoken by a messenger:

Ay, my good lord; 'tis he informed against him.
(*King Lear*, IV.ii.92)

that the sentence lacks the Relative Pronoun "who" and that its absence, however regrettable today, can pass muster in Shakespeare's English in the name of elliptical style. A student to whom English is a second language should think twice before imitating this style of ellipsis.

Grammar is only one aspect of language. But it is better to concentrate one's attention on one aspect at a time, when discussing the language of Shakespeare's plays, because his linguistic resources were inexhaustible.

Not all the linguistic oddities pointed out and discussed in this study are exclusively either Shakespearean or for that matter Elizabethan. Some of them can be found in the works of the writers of the eighteenth century also which is as near to our times as to the Elizabethan Age. Study the following lines from the "Ode on the Distant Prospect of Eton College" written by Thomas Gray.

The tear forgot as soon as shed,
The sunshine of the breast: (Stanza V, ll.3-4)

Evidently the word "forgot" is not the past tense form of the verb "forget," but its participial form equivalent to the modern "forgotten."

Stylistic Features of *Richard II*

A close study of the style of the historical play, *Richard II* by William Shakespeare, reveals some interesting features. The most important among them is repetition. This is the generic, though a drab name, which we must give to a rhetorical device used by Shakespeare frequently in this historical play. Fortunately, repetition can be treated as only a generic name which covers a variety of stylistic sub-divisions. At one extreme, we have just a repetition of words in the same sense and at the other end of the spectrum, we can see the opposite swing of the word order which facilitates repetition. In between, we can see among other things not only pun, a patent of Shakespeare, but also the repetition of not only words, but also of phrase and even clause structures.

It should be conceded at the outset that repetition is not the only stylistic device in the play and that the play is also known for anaphora, unusual negative formations and stychomythia. But repetition is so frequently resorted to by the playwright that it dominates the attention of any careful and alert reader of the play. Shakespeare was familiar with the writings of Elizabethan rhetoricians; rhetoric was a part of classical education in the days of Shakespeare and it was a part of the curriculum of the schools.

The simplest form of repetition is, of course, to repeat the same word in the same sense. The least complex example of this figure of speech is to repeat the words with no difference of meaning, either literary or figurative. King Richard who is apprehensive of Bolingbroke's plans says to Aumerle,

He is our cousin, cousin; (I.iv.20)

Both Bolingbroke and Aumerle are his cousins. The first of the two words is a part of the Noun Phrase that follows the verb, "be" and it, evidently, refers to Bolingbroke in the Nominative Case.

The other word, cousin is a reference to Aumerle whom King Richard is addressing and it is, in a sense, in vocative case.

Next in the scale that spans plainness and complexity is the play on the word "care" which is uttered nine times in four lines spoken by Richard II. He is peevish and petulant when he has to hand over his crown against his will to Bolingbroke. His speech is characterised by not only fanciful conceits, but also by the repeated use of the word, "care." When Bolingbroke observes in a dignified manner that Richard was giving him part of his care with the crown, the deposed king replies:

> Your cares set up do not pluck my cares down,
> My care is loss of care, by old care done;
> Your care is gain of care, by old care won;
> The cares I give I have, though given away; (IV.i.195-98)

The word "care" is spoken nine times in this group of four lines and in the third line alone, it is spoken three times. Its grammatical function does not vary, for it is used as a noun phrase all the times. But there is certainly a little cleverness here and it borders on paradox. The meaning is plain and transparent enough in the first line. In the second line, we notice the paradox when Richard says "my care is loss of care, by old care done." By abdicating the crown, Richard is freed from care or worries. But it is precisely the loss of his crown that starts his worry now. The old care has ended, and the new care has begun. Bolingbroke is crowned now, and, therefore, his gain is the acquisition of worries. The reader can cleverly defend this repetition of the word "care," but there is more ingenuity than complexity in the figure of speech.

Next in the scale of complexity comes the utterance in which the words that are repeated are assigned different grammatical functions. Such a device is possible in English, because in this language quite a few words function both as nouns and as verbs. Even Bolingbroke who speaks in a business-like manner cannot help resorting to this device. In his speech in which he admonishes Bushy and Green, Bolingbroke looks for a reason for rebelling against the God's deputy, namely the enthroned king and what these nobles have done can be exploited by him effectively.

> Whilst you have fed upon my signories,

Dispark'd my parks, felled my forest woods, (III.i.22-23)

Bolingbroke accuses Bushy and Green of removing the enclosures of his inherited lands and converting them into commons. This is what he means when he says that they have disparked his parks. The morpheme "dis" is added and the word "park" is changed into a verb, while the second "park" continues to be a noun which it is. 'Disparked' is an unusual innovation of Shakespeare.

This is not the only instance of repetition of words with different grammatical functions. We find one such example again in the desperate speech of the Duchess of York who implores Bolingbroke who was considered by some to be an usurper. Hearing her voice outside the closed doors of the room, Bolingbroke wants to know who she is. The Duchess replies:

A woman and thy aunt, great king: 'tis I.
Speak with me, pity me, open the door:
A beggar begs that never begged before. (V.iii.76-78)

Here is another example of repetition. The word beg is repeated twice in the last line in some form or the other. In other words, it appears three times in one line alone. Each time, however, it has a different grammatical role. The first is a part of the noun phrase, beggar. The second is a verb in present tense and the third is also a verb but in past tense. Bolingbroke's aunt is appealing to him for the first time in her life for the sake of her son, Aumerle. Considering the status and dignity of this lady, the repetition of the word "beg" does not jar on our ears.

The most notorious example of repeating words and assigning them different grammatical functions can be seen in the speech of the Duke of York when he and Bolingbroke meet for the first time, after the latter's return to England. Bolingbroke is diplomatic and skilful in managing his affairs. He kneels before York whose support he wants and addresses him as his gracious uncle. The Duke of York who is wavering between loyalty to the king and sympathy for the rebel, replies:

Grace me no grace and uncle me no uncle: (III.ii.87)

The Duke means that Bolingbroke should not pretend to respect him by addressing him with honourable titles. But we can see how in this line of nine words, there are two instances of the repetition of the words, "grace" and "uncle." In each case, the first such word is used as a verb and then as a noun. The use of "uncle" as a verb is quite novel and unique to Shakespeare. The style is elliptical and the prepositions that are required are dispensed with.

Another example of this kind is more memorable, because it is aphoristic and packed with a general truth relevant to all ages. Lord Northumberland has joined the ranks of Bolingbroke and is keen on pleasing him, though the latter has returned to England as a rebel. He assures the rebel that Ross and Willoughby are also joining him and that they are already on their way to Bolingbroke's camp. Northumberland assures him that their journey will not be tedious, because it will be enlivened by the hope of experiencing the joy of meeting Bolingbroke. Northumberland who has already joined the rebels compares this hope with the realization of such a hope in his case.

> And hope to joy is little less in joy
> Than hope enjoy'd: (II.iii.15-16)

We notice here the repetition of the words "hope" and "joy" in just two lines. "Hope" is a part of a Noun Phrase in both the cases, but in the first instance, it is qualified by an Infinitive and in the second, by a participle. "Joy" is an Infinite verb in the first instance and when this word is repeated, it is a part of a prepositional phrase. In the third instance, joy is a part of a participle. The tightness of the meaning in this succinct statement reduces the tedium of repetition.

Shakespeare forged novel forms of verbs and participles to employ the figure of speech called "repetition." When the Duke of York visits the Duke of Lancaster, his brother, the latter expresses his disapproval of the omissions and commissions of King Richard and this he does just before the expected visit of King Richard takes place. York advises Gaunt against criticizing the king when the king is present, since his visit was imminent.

> The king is come: deal mildly with his youth:
> For young hot colts, being rag'd, do rage the more.
> (II.i.69-70)

It is interesting to note that the Oxford English Dictionary refers to the participle "rag'd" in the second line while pointing out the use of "rage" as a Transitive Verb and Past Participle. The plawright repeats the word "rage," first as a Transitive Verb in Passive Voice and then as an Intransitive Verb in present tense. This line also has the compactness and brevity to qualify as an aphorism.

Next in this scale stretching between simplicity and complexity, we notice the repetition of words, not performing different grammatical functions, but communicating different but appropriate meanings. Such meanings may be sarcastic, poignant or even plain but appropriate for the occasion. The third in this list, namely, plain meaning is illustrated in the speech of Richard's queen. She does not know the reason for her own grief, but she must indulge in it! One of the ladies-in-waiting suggests that they should dance for the sake of diversion. The sentimental queen replies:

> My legs can keep no measure in delight,
> When my poor heart no measure keeps in grief; (III.iv.7-8)

The first "measure" is spoken in the sense of rhythm and the second in the sense of limit.

The king himself speaks in different styles including the stately style which is illustrated in the very first speech in the play. He also indulges in fanciful, if not frivolous conceits. But he also employs pun and talks ironically about Bolingbroke's effort to win popularity which he might exploit in his move against the king. Richard remarks that he, Bushy and Bagot have observed

> What reverence he did throw away on slaves,
> Wooing poor craftsmen with the craft of smiles (I.iv.27-28)

The word "craft" conveys different meanings: the first the sense of artifice and the second the sense of cunning.

Pun is employed by the strong characters also. It is seen in a moment of the swift anger of York whose heart is on the side of the king, but brain on the side of Bolingbroke. Lord Northumberland has totally aligned himself with the rebel, and when he refers to King Richard without the title, king, the Duke becomes angry. Northumberland explains away this rudeness by saying that he only wanted to be brief. The Duke of York, however, reprimands him:

> Time has been,
> Would you have been so brief with him, he would
> Have been so brief with you, to shorten you,
> For taking so the head, your whole head's length.
> (III.iii.12-15)

The words "brief" and "head" convey different meanings when they are repeated. Northumberland wanted to be brief in speaking and, therefore, he dropped the title, king. There was a time when the king was so powerful that he would have shortened the lord's height by removing his head! Why? The reason is that Northumberland had taken away the head, namely, the title, king. There is a certain degree of grimness in this pun.

The speech of the Bishop of Carlisle is an illustration of the possibility of repeating a word in a different sense, even if you are a man of poise with a perfect sense of right and wrong. There is no cleverness or ingenuity in this pun, for these are words that refer both to character and class and this lexical fact can easily trigger irony. When Bolingbroke announces that he would become the king, the bishop is dismayed. His religious conviction is that Richard as king was anointed by God Himself and that he cannot be judged and deposed.

> Would God that any in this noble presence
> Were enough noble to be upright judge
> Of noble Richard; then true noblesse would
> Learn him forbearance for so foul a wrong, (IV.i.117-20)

The pun on the word "noble" is triggered by the Bishop's theological conviction that no man has a right to judge his fellowmen. The courtiers may be nobles in the sense that they belong to nobility, but there is none among them who is noble (morally great) enough to judge the noble Richard. That is how both the senses of class and character are found in this pun.

That repetition is not always employed for the sake of verbal gymnastics is amply illustrated by another warning by the Bishop of Carlisle. He prophesies that the deposition of the king who is anointed by God Himself and who is God's deputy-elect would plunge the country into a civil war in which kinsmen will kill kinsmen and Englishmen would kill Englishmen.

> Peace shall go sleep with Turks and infidels,
> And in this seat of peace tumultandus wars
> Shall kin with kin and kind with kind confound; (IV.i.139-41)

We notice the duplication of the words "kin" and "kind" in the last line. This repetition serves a rhetorical purpose, the bishop's emphasis is on the clear possibility of civil strife.

In a speech, a word can be duplicated and the duplicated words may have the same meaning and a different meaning too, while serving as a different class word or part of speech. These strands are woven together in the famous speech of John of Gaunt who utters the word "gaunt" seven times in a speech of eleven lines. Only one of them is employed as a noun and that is when the old duke describes himself as "old Gaunt," with capital G in the printed form. All other duplications of the word "gaunt" begin with the small letter g and these six words are adjectives in the speech. The duke is keeping vigil over sleeping England and, therefore, he is gaunt. He is starved of the looks of his son who is banished and this starvation makes him gaunt, that is, thin and haggard. It should also be noted that all the six times, the adjective is used predicatively and not attributively. The device of duplicating a word in the same sense and in different grammatical capacities overlaps with the device of using them in different senses in this speech of John of Gaunt who in reply to a question by the king defends this play upon words by saying that a miserable man is making sport to mock himself.

In the last speech of the drama, the playwright has woven together two strands—the device of repeating the word in the same sense and the device of assigning them different grammatical functions. When Bolingbroke is informed by Sexton that on Bolingbroke's order, he had assassinated King Richard, the usurper observes mournfully:

> They love not the poison that do poison need,
> Nor do I thee: though I did wish him dead,
> I hate the murderer, love him murdered. (V.vi.38-40)

The word murder is duplicated, though in different forms. Different morphemes are added to it, but the free morpheme "murder" is certainly repeated. It is used in the same sense in both the cases and there is no pun. However, in the first of the two words, it is a part of the noun: in the second, it is a part of the participle. Bolingbroke's utterance assumes complexity if we read ambiguity in it. When he says "I love him murdered," he either means "I love the dead man" or "I love the fact that he is dead." What we see here is not just a play on words, but repetition used for the sake of complexity and grimness of meaning.

Repetition as a figure of speech is a generic name and has a wide range of forms. It includes anaphora also which is defined at the beginning of different lines, clauses or sentences. *Richard II* has at least three examples of this figure of speech in the speeches of King Richard. It suits the mood of this weak king who constantly indulges in sentimental self-pity and self-dramatization. When the news comes that the king was deserted by his own men, he gives way to despair, and whines:

For God's sake, let us sit upon the ground
And tell sad stories of the death of kings:
How some have been deposed; some slain in war;
Some haunted by the ghosts they have deposed;
Some poison'd by their wives; some sleeping killed;
(III.ii.155-59)

King Richard, a sentimental and incompetent man, seeks consolation in the sad stories—real and imaginary—of murdered and deposed kings. He has no particular king in mind and hence, the common and general noun "some" is used by him repeatedly. We can see this common noun, "some" repeated at the beginning of not fewer than four phrases which in effect are shortened clauses.

The weak king is not only sentimental, but petulant also: he is no match for the practical and business-like Bolingbroke. He hands his crown to the rebel cousin but continues to complain. Bolingbroke is impatient and asks him bluntly whether he was not contented to resign the crown. The deposed king replies:

With mine own tears I wash away my balm,
With mine own hands I give away my crown,

With mine own tongue deny my sacred state
With mine own breath release all duty's rite: (IV.i.207-10)

The prepositional phrase "with mine own" is repeated four times in this peevish speech. The deposed king dwells repeatedly on what he is giving away—crown, oil of consecration, ceremonies and estates—rather monotonously, with the same words at the beginning of each line. When anaphora crosses the limit, monotony is the danger.

The king finds anaphora quite tempting. This is in tune with his character because Richard not only suffers and complains, he also develops a narcissus complex. At the time of abdication, he asks for a looking glass and looking at his own image, he indulges in self-admiration and self-pity.

Was this face the face
That every day under his household roof
Did keep ten thousand men? Was this the face
That, like the sun, did make beholders wink?
Was this the face that faced so many follies,
And was at last out-faced by Bolingbroke? (IV.i.281-86)

The word "face" is repeated five times. But what is relevant here is the duplication of the words "was this the face" at the beginning of two questions and virtually the same words at the beginning of another sentence. Anaphora, no doubt, is a feature of rhetoric, but it does not wear well in the speech of King Richard who is a feeble and petulant man fond of self-pity and self-admiration. After all, he is a victim of his own weakness. Incidentally, we may notice the echo of Dr. Faustus's famous speech in the tragedy of the same name by Christopher Marlowe who wrote his play some eight years before Shakespeare wrote *Richard II* (1597).

Repetition as a figure of speech may assume different forms for the sake of rhetorical effect and one such form in this play is the pairing of two small repeated words or similar-sounding words. They are made to chime with each other, as it were, by pairing and balancing them with a preposition or conjunction. One of the earliest speeches of King Richard abounds in them. When John of Gaunt presents before him the case of Bolingbroke and Mowbray, the king orders him to call both of them to his presence:

> Then call them to our presence; face to face
> And frowning from brow to brow, ourselves will hear
> The accuser and the accused freely speak: (I.i.15-17)

The king who is weak and irresolute compensates his weakness with an exhibition of firmness in words; each of the three lines here illustrates the feature of repetition. The king is going to hear the case face to face, frowning from brow to brow. He will let the accuser and the accused freely speak. Notice how the nouns in these three phrases are repeated and paired with either by a preposition or conjunction. These nouns chime, as it were, with each other in each case. Even Bolingbroke who is a matter-of-fact man has recourse to rhetorical devices and uses this figure of repetition or duplication in the midst of his speech. Bolingbroke and Mowbray challenge each other, and throwing down his glove, Bolingbroke dares Mowbray to pick it up.

> If guilty dread have left thee so much strength
> As to take up mine honour's pawn, then stoop;
> By that and all the rites of knighthood else,
> Will I make good against thee, arm to arm,
> What I have spoke or thou canst worse devise. (I.i.73-76)

"Arm to arm" is similar to what we have discussed above: words duplicated and paired by a particle and made, as it were, to chime with each other. They balance each other with a preposition or conjunction in between.

Shakespeare has added some variety to repetition as a figure of speech which would have been otherwise regarded as monotonous. This device of coupling of words that are repeated is extended by the playwright to words that alliterate and have similar meaning, but not literally the same. Bolingbroke who has no use for ornamental language and who can be blunt finds rhetorical speech useful on some occasions. He lists grave charges against the Duke of Mowbray and goes on to say:

> That all the treasons for these eighteen years
> Complotted and contrived in this land
> Fetch from false Mowbray their first head and spring.
> (I.i.96-97)

Notice the pairing of the words "complotted" and "contrived." These participles alliterate with each other and have related meanings. They may not be synonyms but they are very much related in meaning since they mean "plotted" and "devised." The cumulative effect: is not diluted but enriched. Bolingbroke's eloquence takes him to anaphora also when he says in the next line itself: "Further I say and further will maintain" in order to hammer the point that he can establish the charges he has made.

King Richard assures Mowbray that Bolingbroke's neighbour nearness to his blood (I.i.119) will not be allowed to come in the way of an impartial enquiry by him. This phrase is not only an example of alliteration, but also of near duplication of meaning, because the first of these two words is derived from a root which also means nearness. It must be conceded that these two words are not balanced by any particle.

Should duplication or repetition involve only words or grammatical structures only? A word is not the smallest unit in a language: certainly not in English. On the contrary, a phoneme is the smallest unit in the spoken language. If this view is taken, the device of pairing or coupling borders on the device of pairing of phonemes also. An example of this kind we notice in King Richard's speech when he advises Bolingbroke and Mowbray to "forget, forgive." (I.i.154) These paired words illustrate the repetition of the first syllables only and not of the whole words.

All is grist that comes to the linguistic mill of Shakespeare while writing *Richard II*. He cannot resist repeating the phonemes for the sake of rhetorical effect. Lord Northumberland resorts to this device when he exhorts Willoughby and Ross to join the ranks of the rebel duke:

> Imp out our drooping country's broken wing,
> Redeem from broking pawn the blemished crown,
> (II.i.292-93)

At first, the readers may think the words "broken" and "broking" are the different participial forms of the same verb. But they are not. The first is the "en" form of the verb, "break"; the second is the "ing" form of the verb, "broke," a different verb. Their meanings are different, because the second is related to the action of pledging an object for obtaining money. The first of these two words is the participial form of the verb, "break" and this point is of some significance, because in line 281 of the same scene, its past tense form, "broke" is used by the author when Lord Northumberland mentions the names of those who had ceased relations with the Duke of Exeter. In all the three cases, meanings may differ, but the first syllables are the same.

Repetition of the words of the same spelling and same pronunciation but with different meanings is another type of duplication. There are many scenes in this historical play in which charges are vehemently made and are denied with equal vehemence. In the presence of Bolingbroke, now a de facto king, Fitzwater accuses Aumerle of the murder of Gloucester. The Duke of Surrey who was present refutes this charge whereupon Fitzwater accuses Surrey of lying. The duke responds by denouncing Fitzwater.

> Dishonourable boy;
> That lie shall lie so heavy on my sword,
> That it shall render vengeance and revenge
> Till thou the lie-giver and that lie do lie
> In earth as quiet as thy father's skull: (IV.i.65-69)

The word lie is used five times in this passage of four lines. But while the spelling and the pronunciation are the same throughout, they do not always mean the same thing. The first, the third and the fourth words mean falsehood and the second besides the fifth word have the other meaning. This is an example of the repetition of a word which has more than one meaning, but there is less poetry and more cleverness in this repetition.

Shakespeare's linguistic resources are not, however, limited to the repetition of the above types only. There are two other kinds which must be discussed before this essay is closed.

Repetition may involve only grammatical structures. This device can be found in a speech of King Richard. Announcing that he is going to hear the case of Bolingbroke and Mowbray personally, the king adds:

> High-stomach'd are they both and full of ire,
> In rage deaf as the sea, hasty as fire. (I.i.8-19)

In this couplet, there is no repetition of words, though it must be said, that there is this device in the lines that precede this couplet. We see, on the contrary, the duplication of the grammatical structure, adjective + Preposition + Noun Phrase in the second line above. Another example of this linguistic device can be found in the same scene which witnesses charges and counter-charges in the presence of the king.

> Thou art a traitor and a miscreant,
> Too good to be so and too bad to live, (I.i.39-40)

The second line is another example of the repetition of the above kind. The structure Intensifier + Adjective + To + Infinitive is duplicated and the two structures are neatly balanced by the conjunction "and."

We must now consider a device which involves both repetition of words and linguistic structures. In this device, repetition of words is made possible by the transposition of word order involving NP/Subject, NP/Object and Nouns governed by Prepositions. This reversal resembles a swing in the opposite direction, because the action itself is reversed. King Richard who is brooding over his fate after he was deposed and imprisoned, says:

> I wasted time, and now time doth waste me; (V.v.49)

We can notice in this single line the repetition of the words "waste" and "time." This is made possible by the transposition of the word order. What the first clause says is reversed by the second clause in this compound sentence. The king wasted time in the past and now time is wasting him. No doubt, the king embarks from this point on an elaborate conceit which is not great poetry. But in this figure of speech, we find both repetition and reversal. In the first clause, I is the NP/Subject and time is the NP/Object: in the second, I the speaker, becomes the NP/Object and time becomes the NP/Subject. This transposition facilitates the repetition of the words, "time" and "waste."

Reversal or the reverse swing of the situation paves the way on more than one occasion in the play for the device which we have called repetition. When Richard is deposed, he faces Bolingbroke who has put on the mantle of the king, and this reversal of their positions provides another example worth quoting. Bolingbroke who was a subject and who has now become a king addresses Richard as 'my fair cousin' reminding King Richard that he is no longer a king, and the deposed king replies:

> 'Fair cousin'? I am greater than a king;
> For when I was a king, my flatterers
> Were then but subjects; being now a subject
> I have a king here to be my flatterer. (IV.i.306-9)

The note of sarcasm is easily discerned here. A subject has become the king, and he who was the king has become a subject. Is not the new king flattering his subject—normally it is the king who is flattered by his sycophantic subjects—by addressing him as 'fair cousin'? No wonder, the word king is mentioned three times: the words "subject" and "flatterer" are repeated twice each. This has been made possible by the reverse swing of the situation when the king and the subject have exchanged their places: the words, "king," "subject" and "flatterer" are common to both the situations. Repetition resulting from transposition or reverse swing can be found in the speech of Bolingbroke even when he was still a subject. The trial by combat at Coventry is called off by King Richard who wants to evade an unpleasant reality and in turn, banishes both the plaintiff and the defendant. Bolingbroke is severely disappointed and says to Mowbray:

> By this time, had the king permitted us,
> One of our souls had wander'd in the air,
> Banish'd this frail sepulchre of our flesh,
> As now our flesh is banish'd from this land: (I.iii.194-97)

The repetition of the words "flesh" and "banish'd" is facilitated by the reversal of the situation caused by King Richard's capricious decision to call off the trial by combat. If the combat had been permitted, Bolingbroke says, the soul of one of them would have been banished from flesh by the victorious man. But now the flesh itself stands banished. This is the third instance of reversal or the opposite swing of action. The home from which a soul would have been banished now itself stands banished. Flesh which is an object in the third line is the subject in the next line. We must presume the existence of the preposition from after the word "banished" in the third line.

The character of Bolingbroke differs as much from the character of King Richard as Gaunt's character differs from that of either of the other two. Bolingbroke is wily and efficient, whereas Richard is feeble, sentimental and capricious. Gaunt is sober and patriotic, almost the voice of England herself and his speech on his motherland remains unsurpassed till today. Gaunt's speech illustrates what can be called reversal of situation necessitating repetition. Being an elderly man, he rebukes King Richard, his nephew.

> O; had thy grandsire, with a prophet's eye,
> Seen how his son's son should destroy his sons,
> From forth thy reach he would have laid thy shame,
> Deposing thee before thou wert possess'd,
> Which art possess'd now to depose thyself. (II.i.104-8)

According to the Duke of Lancaster, what has now happened is the reverse of what would have happened if King Richard's grandfather had a prophet's eye. In the second case, Richard is deposing himself; in the first, that is the hyphothetical case, his grandsire would have deposed him. Thus Richard is the subject of the verb "depose" in the situation as it obtains now and would have been the object of the same verb in the hypothetical case. The word "possess" in the last but one line means "put in possession" of or "cause to possess." Hence in this line, King Richard is the real subject of the word "possess." In the last line, he is the object of the same verb. Now he is possessed by madness. In the hypothetical case, according to the dying duke, Richard would have been deposed even before he possessed the crown. That is why, words like "possess" and "depose" are repeated. The opposite swing from speculation to the present historical reality causes the repetition of words.

In all these examples what we have called return swing or reversal is marked by the exchange of places by the subject and the object in two different clauses of a sentence. This is a part of the central reversal or return swing of the play, namely, the king and his subject exchanging their places as a result of the latter's rebellion. King Richard II is forced to give up his crown and become a subject. His own subject, Bolingbroke wears the crown and becomes his king. Richard II had banished Bolingbroke: now Bolingbroke banishes the king and sends him to Pomfret castle. The king in the beginning was accused of complicity in the murder of Gloucester: now the king himself is murdered after deposition and Bolingbroke stands accused of complicity in that murder. King Richard himself is painfully aware of one such swing of fortune and he describes it himself in a far-fetched simile. He parts with his crown to his cousin unwillingly and starts complaining in a sentimental language.

> Now is this golden crown like a deep well
> That owes two buckets filling each other;
> The emptier ever dancing in the air,
> The other down, unseen and full of water:
> That bucket down and full of tears am I,
> Drinking my grief, whilst you mount on high. (IV.i.184-89)

One bucket is going down, full of tears and heavy. The other bucket is going up and it is Bolingbroke. Sentimentality, feebleness and elaborate conceit can be seen here. The play revolves around reversal and this is expressed in many ways including linguistic structures. Not only King Richard but the patriotic and sagacious Duke of Lancaster also resorts to this technique of reversal. Deploring the condition of England for which he holds the king responsible, Gaunt says:

> That England, that was wont to conquer others,
> Hath made a shameful conquest of itself. (II.i.65-66)

The conqueror is herself conquered and this reversal is brought about by the maladministration of King Richard. John of Gaunt has no vested interests and has faith in traditional values like loyalty and patriotism. The reversal of the situation which is deplorable prompts him to repeat the word "conquer" in its noun form. There is another instance of such a reversal in this dialogue between the king and John of Gaunt, in which, while the verb remains the same, the subject and the object are repeated, because they exchange places. Explaining the pun on his name, Gaunt the duke says that he mocked his own name to flatter the king. Richard asks him: "Should dying men flatter with those that live?" John of Gaunt replies:

No, No; men living flatter those that die. (II.i.88-89)

King Richard's actions can only lead to death; he is surrounded by men who serve their own interests by flattering him. Thus living men flatter those that die. Living men and dying men exchange their places. The subject "dying men" in King Richard's speech becomes the object in Gaunt's reply. Correspondingly, "living men" which is the object in King Richard's speech becomes the subject in Gaunt's cryptic reply. Hence the noun phrases and the verb "flatter" are virtually repeated. This dialogue between King Richard and his uncle is frequently marked by such repetitions through reversals: in fact, in the above context alone, six such examples can be cited. It will suffice to quote one more example with which we will conclude this part of the discussion. King Richard who is incompetent becomes hysterical at this admonition by his uncle and hits back in any angry and shrill voice:

Now, by my seat's right royal majesty,
Were thou not brother to great Edward's son,
This tongue that runs so roundly in thy head
Should run thy head from thy unreverent shoulders.
(II.i.120-23)

Note the duplication of the words "run" and "head." In the principal clause, the verb "run" is used transitively to give the meaning "cause you to lose your head." In the subordinate clause, the same verb "run" is used intransitively to give the meaning "speaks outspokenly." The word "head" which is also repeated is the NP/Object in the principal clause: in the subordinate clause, it is a part of the Adverbial phrase. This return swing or reversal of the word order is necessitated by King Richard's shrill warning that he would have reversed the situation if Gaunt were not his uncle. This warning shows, though disrespectfully, that King Richard does not always indulge in fanciful and silly conceits.

If we take the entire play into account, we can point out twelve instances of what may be called repetition caused by reversal or return swing which is in tune with the major political reversal which is the substance of this drama in which a subject who rebels becomes a king and the lawful king becomes his subject, after being deposed. It is not necessary to dwell on all the twelve such instances and I believe that the eight instances which I have discussed in this paper can illustrate the point that there is a wide range of repetition in this play of which repetition through reversal or transposition of word order as a stylistic feature is a manifestation of the theme of the play itself.

There are, it must be conceded, other stylistic features also which are too prominent to be ignored. For instance, contrary meaning is achieved by a rare form of negative. A noun is treated as a verb for which there is no precedent and then the negative verb is formed by adding the negative morpheme to it. "Unking," "undeaf," "unhappy"—these are verbs in this play. This is a significant feature in a play in which contrary things happen: the king is overthrown and in his place an usurper becomes the king; weeds are not cut off, but allowed to grow unchecked; Gaunt, a venerable old man who supports traditional values, is not respected, but insulted; the Duke of Lancaster hopes on his death-bed that while the young king did not heed his advice when he was alive, may yet consider his advice when he is breathing his last.

> Though Richard my life's counsel would not hear,
> My death's sad tale may yet undeaf his ear. (II.i.15-16)

The unusual word "undeaf" deserves to be noted. First of all, "deaf" as a verb is extremely rare and archaic even for Shakespeare and his contemporaries. On the top of it, Shakespeare gives it a negative form by adding to it the negative morpheme, "un."

Shakespeare goes to the extent of transforming an adjective into a verb and then making it a negative verb by adding the negative morpheme. The coining of this new lexical structure cannot by any standard be regarded as normal. Imagine the word "unhappy" as a verb. Gaunt uses the word "undeaf" as a verb and his son assigns the same grammatical function to the adjective "unhappy." The son is ambitious and diplomatic at the same time, and while rebelling against the king, he dons the mantle of the king's advocate as if he is more loyal than the king, and sentences Bushy and Green to death. This is his charge against Bushy and Green.

> You have misled the prince, a royal king,
> A happy gentleman, in blood and lineaments,
> By you unhappied and disfigured clean: (III.i.8-10)

The king is unhappied by Bush and Green. The OED has noted that the word "happy" was used as a verb also in the early seventeenth century and its meaning, no doubt, is related to the meaning of the word "fortune." *Richard II* was written before the turn of the seventeenth century and there is an entry for it in the Stationers' Register on August 29, 1597. It is quite probable that Shakespeare was the first writer to use the word "happy" or "unhappy" as a verb. In any case, its use as a verb must have been rare even in the days of Shakespeare.

There are two more examples of the formation of odd negative verbs. The word "curse" also undergoes the same negative transformation in Shakespeare's individual grammar. When King Richard curses Bushy and Green with two others among his supporters, whose fate he did not know, Sir Stephen Scroop pleads on behalf of their souls, since he was responsible for creating some serious misunderstanding by his ambiguous language.

> Sweet love, I see, changing his property,
> Turns to the sourest and most deadly hate.
> Again uncurse their souls; their peace is made
> With heads and not with hands: those whom you curse
> Have felt the worst of death's destroying wound
> And lie full low, grav'd in the hollow ground. (III.i.135-40)

Unlike "deaf" and "unhappy," "curse" is a common verb but its negative "uncurse" is a contribution of Shakespeare's grammar, though it is not as rare as the other two negative verbs discussed above.

We have seen the Duke of Lancaster, his son and Sir Stephen Scroop employing these unusual negative verbs. King Richard also speaks one such rare negative verb. Northumberland who was once a king's man has defected to the camp of Bolingbroke and brings to the deposed king the orders of the usurper. What has happened to his oath of loyalty? Pathetic and weak as Richard is, he can speak ironically at times. He says to Lord Northumberland

> Let me unkiss the oath 'twixt thee and me
> And yet not so, for with a kiss 'twas made. (V.i.74-75)

By any standard, "unkiss" is an unprecedented form of verb. It is not ungrammatical but the combination of the two morphemes is certainly rare and a departure from the norm. In the context mentioned above, it has a devastating effect.

The fifth example of unusual negatives is found in the speech of King Richard again. But there is a difference. In this final example, noun is used as adverb. This is illustrated by the ruminations of the deposed king who is imprisoned in a castle.

> And so I am: then crushing penury
> Persuades me I was better when a king;
> Then I am king'd again; and by and by
> Think that I am unking'd by Bolingbroke,
> And straight am nothing: (V.v.34-38)

The use of "king" as a verb is rare: and the use of its negative "unking" and its use as a verb are rarer still. Only Shakespeare can experiment with language like this. These five unusual contraries, "undeaf," "unhappy," "uncurse," "unkiss" and "unking" used as verbs are symbolic of the central or basic contrary in the play—the king forced to become a subject after a violent deposition and his subject ascending the throne.

We can say the same thing about another feature of the style of this play: the inversion of the normal word order. Consider the following line in the speech of the Bishop of Carlisle who is protesting against the decision of Bolingbroke to assume the kingship.

> Worst in this royal presence may I speak. (IV.i.115)

The sentence has the structure: Adjective + Prep Phrase + Tense + Modal + NP/Subject + Verb. Surely, this is an instance of the inversion of the normal word order. Almost all the characters in this play speak in this style. Here the bishop is saying that he is the humblest in the presence of the king and the nobles, and yet he must speak out. But he puts the Adjective first in the sentence followed by the Adverbial phrase, and the Noun Phrase/Subject comes almost at the end.

In some sentences, the adverbial comes first followed by the Noun Phrase/Object and finally the transitive verb as illustrated in the following speech.

To smooth his fault I should have been more mild:
A partial slander sought I to avoid,
And in the sentence my own life destroy'd. (I.iii.240-41)

The old Duke of Lancaster regrets the order to banish his son together with Mowbray. In the first line/clause, the adverbial adjunct is followed by NP/Subject. The second line has the structure, Noun Phrase/Object + Tense + VT + NP/Subject + Inf. The third line/clause has the structure Conj + Adverbial of Manner + NP/Object + Tense + VT. In none of the above the NP/Subject is placed at the beginning. There are quite a few examples of inversion in this play and most of them are not necessitated by the consideration of interrogative transformation or accent-based rhythm. We find inversion in the theme of the play also. But then, this figure of speech called inversion of normal word order can be found in many other plays of Shakespeare and, therefore, the relation between inversion as a stylistic device and the general theme of the play need not be taken as the intention of the author.

The play is also known for some rare figures of speech like Hendiadys, Zuegma and Stychomythia besides the more common figures of speech like Transferred Epithet. The very first speech of the play is known not only for the stately style befitting a monarch, but also for Hendiadys.

Old John of Gaunt, time-honour'd Lancaster,
Hast thou according to thy oath and band,
Brought hither Henry Hereford thy bold son,
Here to make good the boisterous late appeal,
Which then our leisure would not let us hear,,
Against the Duke of Norfolk, Thomas Mowbray? (I.i.1-6)

It is a speech of only one sentence but needs six lines and has forty-six words. Attributive adjectives for almost all Noun Phrases besides Adverbial phrases, Adjectival clauses and Noun Phrases in apposition contribute to the length and majesty of the very first utterance of the king. Let us note also the rare figure of speech, Hendiadys in the Noun Phrase, oath and band. This phrase is explained by the Oxford and Cambridge edition of the play as bond given under an oath. This meaning is condensed in the phrase "oath and bond" which consists of two nouns co-ordinated by the conjunction, "and." This is exactly the definition of Hendiadys.

Zeugma is another unusual figure of speech and it is found in a speech of King Richard. He assures the Duke of Norfolk that he can speak freely and fearlessly in his defence against the charges made by Bolingbroke, though the latter is his cousin.

> He is our subject, Mowbray; so art thou;
> Free speech and fearless I to thee allow. (I.i.122-23)

The second line here is not only an example of inversion of word order, but also of Zeugma. Let us take a look at the Direct Object of this sentence, "free speech and fearless." If it is read mechanically, it will be found ungrammatical, because while the word "free" is an Adjective which qualifies the Noun speech, it cannot qualify the other word, "fearless" which itself is an Adjective. What King Richard means is free and fearless speech. The author has, however, pushed "fearless" to the last place. The Adjective "free" is structurally in the position of a qualifier, but it cannot qualify both "speech and fearless." Zeugma is defined as a rhetorical figure in which a single word standing in relation to two others is correctly related to only one of them. It involves the failure of a single word to give meaning to one of the pair with which it is connected. Surely, what we read here in this play is a perfect example of Zeugma.

Common figures of speech like "transfer" epithet and such others need not detain us long.

> If guilty dread have left thee so much strength
> As to take up my honour's pawn, then stoop: (I.i.74-75)

This is Bolingbroke's challenge to Mowbray against whom he has made grave charges. Notice the phrase, "guilty dread." It means, of course, the dread or fear of a guilty man, not guilty fear. The epithet "guilty" is transferred to "dread."

The Duke of Lancaster also employs this figure of speech. Conceding that the king has caused the death of Gloucester, he declines to take up arms against the king.

> Let heaven revenge; for I may never lift
> An angry arm against his minister. (I.ii.40-41)

Evidently, "an angry arm" is an example of transferred epithet. The phrase means the arm of an angry man. The epithet "angry" is transferred from man to arm.

The Duke of Lancaster employs this figure again and again. His son is banished together with Mowbray: the plaintiff and the defendant are both banished. The old duke tries to comfort his son, though strictly speaking, he is a party to the king's order.

> The sullen passage of thy weary steps
> Esteem as foil wherein thou art to set
> The precious jewel of thy home return. (I.iii.265-67)

The first line has two examples of transferred epithet. Obviously, it is the exiled man who is sullen and it is he who is weary in his exile. We see how the adjective "sullen" and "weary" are transferred to "passage" and "steps," both inanimate things.

This essay on the style of *Richard II* cannot be concluded without a reference to stichomythia which is defined as a rapid dialogue in verse in which two characters dispute a point in alternate lines, each speaking a line/sentence only alternately. John of Gaunt is trying to comfort his son, Bolingbroke who is exiled by the king for six years.

Gaunt: Thy grief is but thy absence for a time.
Bolingbroke: Joy absent, grief is present for that time.
Gaunt: What is six winters? They are quickly gone.
Bolingbroke: To men in joy; but grief makes one hour ten.
Gaunt: Call it travel that thou takest for pleasure.
(I.iii.258-62)

This is a fine example of stichomythia, a figure of speech to which Shakespeare was attracted in the early phases of his dramatic career. Up to a limit, this figure of speech is tolerable and in this instance, it is engaged to show the contrast between illusion and reality. At the end of the play, the imprisoned king also tries to cultivate illusion and finds that reality cannot be dismissed.

Listing the figures of speech is not important. All of them are not related to the theme of the play. What is important is to point out the dominant feature of the style of the play and this is surely none other than repetition in its various forms as illustrated earlier.

Repetition manifests itself in thirteen different forms ranging from the simple repetition of the same word in the same sense to the more complex transposed word order. The numerous examples in the play prompt us to conclude that Shakespeare consciously employed this stylistic device in this play which he wrote in the early phase of his dramatic and poetic career. Perhaps, Shakespeare was familiar with the writings of the Elizabethan rhetoricians from which he might have learnt these stylistic devices.

Shakespeare's Plays: Fancy and Imagination

L'Allegro in the well-known poem of John Milton enjoys all the good things of life including the plays of "sweetest Shakespeare, Fancy's child" who warbles "his native wood-notes wild." Is this all that Milton has to say about Shakespeare whom his friend and fellow playwright, Ben Jonson, placed in the ranks of Aeschylus, Sophocles and Euripides? Shakespeare is fancy's child in the eyes of the author of *Paradise Lost*. Is Milton paying a left-handed compliment to Shakespeare?

The editors of Milton's verses equate "fancy" with imagination in their notes and they see in the lines of Milton the image of Shakespeare as the author of romantic comedies enriched by imagination and freshness. It is not clear from the poem whether Milton regarded imagination as a synonym for fancy. Nowadays these two words are charged with distinct meanings and the critics have, by and large, accepted the meanings which Coleridge has asigned to them. The romantic poet's note on fancy and imagination is a milestone in the history of literary criticism. In the pre-romantic era, these two words were used almost as synonyms and the former word was used a little more frequently than the latter. However, one must be cautious in making this statement, because the relative dignity of one or the other word went on fluctuating in the midst of the general tendency to bestow a more sober and serious meaning on the word "imagination." When they were regarded as synonyms, the tendency to prefer the shorter word is understandable.

When we pass from the poetry of William Shakespeare to that of William Blake, we notice that the poets themselves did not mind using one as a vague synonym for the other. In a section of Blake's enigmatic masterpiece, *The Marriage of Heaven and Hell*, the poet holds discussions in a simple and unassuming manner with Isiah and Ezekiel, the Hebrew prophets who uphold the religion of the jews, which, they believe, is based on poetic genius. Blake asks Isiah whether he really saw God and spoke to Him and in reply, the Old Testament prophet says that he neither saw God nor spoke to Him in the organic sense, but adds that his senses discovered the infinite in anything and that honest imagination is the voice of God. Then he is confronted with the question whether his persuasion that a thing is so really makes it so. The prophet is ready with the answer: "All poets believe that it does, and in the ages of imagination this firm persuasion removed mountains; but many are not capable of a firm persuasion of anything." This passage describes a vision which bridges the age of William Blake and the age of the Old Testament prophets. The subject is faith which can move mountains, according to the prophet, but as it happens, miracles are assigned to the past which cannot be probed. In any case, the vision and the faith in miracles lend a certain degree of seriousness to this subject of the religion of Israel based on poetic genius. That is why the word "imagination" is used by the poet. What Isiah says is not fanciful, but what is interesting, the entire section of the poem is given the heading "A memorable fancy." This example reinforces the view that within a single poetic work, "fancy" and "imagination" were treated as vaguely synonymous.

When we turn to some other poets of the seventeenth and eighteenth century, we find the word "fancy" applied to what was elegant, pretty and pleasing to the eye. William Blake himself has used the word "imagination" in connection with supernatural events in another poem which he calls "The Everlasting Gospel." He imagines Sir Isaac Newton refuting the supernatural aspect of religion and the concepts of Personal God and Incarnation.

> For this the Gospel Sir Isaac confutes:
> God can be known by His attributes;
> And as for the dwelling of the Holy Ghost,
> Or of Christ and his Father, it's all a boast
> And pride, and vanity of the imagination,
> That disdains to follow the world's fashion.

It is worth noting in this context that the poet does not use the word "fancy" here, since preaching doubt and scepticism is not a matter of fancy. In the poet's eyes, such a thing is vanity because the sceptic thinks that he knows a lot, more than enough to question the factual basis of the Christian faith. To question what the whole world believes is nothing but a form of pride and disdain. As it is a serious and grave issue, the word "imagination" is preferred to "fancy." We can, therefore, draw the tentative conclusion that these words are related not only to creativity and inventiveness, but also to the contents of images: in other words, to meaning also. What is light, pretty and elegant in the creation or invention goes with fancy. What is dignified, grave and weighty goes with imagination which also, of course, involves creativity. Does not William Blake find any use for fancy at all? He does.

The readers can expect to find the word "fancy" in the short lyrics of Blake called *Songs of Innocence* and *Songs of Experience* and strangely enough, it is in the latter they find it. In the poem, "The Little Girl Found" we can find the phrase "fancied image" though the context is charged with pity and pathos, the characteristic emotions of Blake's lyrics.

> Pale, thro pathless ways
> The fancied image strays
> Famish'd, weeping, weak
> With hollow piteous shriek.

The parents who have been searching their missing child are desperate and grief-stricken and see in their dream the image of a famished, weak and tearful child. This image is "fancied" in their dream. Evidently, the word "fancy" is employed as a verb here and it means "portrayed in the mind." The word "fancy" is used in the context of what is tragic and serious. This fact strengthens our view that throughout the seventeenth and eighteenth century, there were no clear-cut definitions to distinguish "fancy" and "imagination" from each other.

Even Thomas Gray, the melancholy and elegiac poet of the eighteenth century, has use for the word "fancy." He recalls his happy time when he played and disported on the green bank of the open space near Eton College and wonders who is playing there now. The new generation of children must be enjoying themselves, unaware that their own days of innocence and freedom from care would end soon.

> Gay hope is theirs by fancy fed,

Less pleasing when possest;
The tear forgot as soon as shed,
The sunshine of the breast:

The poet talks of the tiny tots playing on the green banks of Thames and in this context of their innocence and lack of experience, with worldliness still far away, their gay hopes are fed by fancy. The word goes well with the context for, after all, it means pretty, elegant and pleasing things invented by the mind. A more sober word like "imagination" would be unsuitable here.

Another poet of the same age has employed the word "fancy" in the same sense. In a philosophical and meditative poem on death, G. Swell describes what he calls "fancied green."

Thy narrow pride, thy fancied green
(for vanity's in little seen)
All must be left when death appears,
In spite of wishes, groans and tears.

Fancy is always seen in the mental invention, cultivation or creation of what is elegant and small. The poet uses the word "little" in this philosophical and other-worldly view. The greenery which the gardener is cultivating is spatially little and the cultivation of the little patch of greenery is his fancy, but all is vanity according to the poet. The context itself is religious in the sense that the poet sees in the gardener's devotion to his earthly garden an attachment to what is ephemeral. The poet sees only vanity, narrowness and pride in his devotion to gardening. Futility and fancy are strange bed-fellows here. But as in William Blake's poem above, we notice the collocation of vanity and pride with fancy, the only difference being the presence of fancy in the place of imagination.

Let us go back to the Age of William Shakespeare and study the sense in which he employs the words, "fancy" and "imagination." Like many other poets, Shakespeare uses the word "fancy" a little more frequently than "imagination" and in some plays the two words appear synonymous. It is interesting to study the meanings of these two words as they reveal themselves in his plays and compare them with the meanings attributed to them by Wordsworth, Coleridge and William Taylor.

Florizel: I am: and by my fancy. If my reason
Will thereto be obedient, I have reason;
If not, my senses, better pleased with madness,
Do bid it welcome. (*The Winter's Tale*, IV.iv.483-86)

Florizel asserts that he would be advised by his fancy and not by restraint and cautiousness, though his father, the king of Bohemia is flatly opposed to his love for Perdita. If reason also supports his action, well and good. But if it does not, he would rather say farewell to it and be guided by his senses and fancy. It is evident that the word "fancy" here means amorous inclination to love. The Arden edition of the play also supports more or less the same view, when it says that "fancy is a fascinating word which seems to mean true love." True or not, it means amorous inclination or love. The other meanings of the word "fancy" are not suitable here: neither the taste for what is elegant or pretty nor an arbitrary notion nor imagination. There is variety in its meaning and the same word occurs again in another sense in the same play.

Paulina: No longer shall you gaze, lest your fancy
May think anon it moves. (I.iii.60-61)

The last scene of the play is also the scene of reconciliation brilliantly executed by Paulina. She unveils the life-like statue of Hermione, the queen supposed to be dead and the king is naturally overwhelmed by feelings. He asks Paulina not to draw the curtains and Paulina says in response that he should not continue to gaze at it lest his fancy should make him think that it moves. What does fancy mean here? Obviously, it does not mean what it means in Florizel's language. Hermione is alive, breathing: no wonder, the king thinks that it is moving though he is sure that he is watching only a statue. Paulina's disclosure of the statue is superbly timed and she herself drops the hint that the statue is a living person. How does she do it? She advises the king against gazing too long because his arbitrary and subjective imagination will make him think that the statue is moving. That is what the word "fancy" means here: arbitrary, subjective but not creative imagination. It is related to a particular person at a particular place and time. That the word "fancy" implies what is subjective and arbitrary is fairly well indicated by the request of king Leontes when Paulina tries to veil the statue again.

> No settle senses of the world can match
> The pleasure of that madness, Let't alone. (V.iii.72-73)

The king knows that it is madness to think that the statue lives, but he prefers that madness. It is evident that fancy and madness go together, because any personal and arbitrary notion can always be described as madness in the metaphorical language, particularly if it leads to some action. An almost similar meaning of the word "fancy" can be seen in one of the speeches of the play, *Much Ado About Nothing.*

> Ursula: I pray you, be not angry with me, madam,
> Speaking my fancy, signior Benedick,
> For shape, for learning, argument and valour,
> Goes foremost in report in Italy. (IV.i.94-97)

Ursula's speech is a part of the game conceived by Hero, daughter of Leonato, to checkmate Beatrice and Benedick and bring about their marriage, since they had vowed that they were above love and would not marry. Here the gentlewoman's part is to praise Benedick within the hearing of Beatrice. The commendation of his various merits is prefaced by the admission that it is her fancy. It is clear that in this context, fancy means a personal and individual notion or judgement.

The word "fancy" is employed again in the same play in the speech of Don Pedro. Curiously enough, the word is spoken four times, but has different meanings each tine.

> There is no appearance of fancy in him, unless it be a fancy that he hath for strange disguises; as, to be a Dutchman today, a Frenchman tomorrow or in the shape of two countries at once, as a German from the waist downward, all slops, and a Spaniard from the hip upward, no doublet. Unless he have a fancy for this foolery, as it happens he hath, he is no fool for fancy, as you would have it appear he is. (III.ii.29-36)

This speech is Don Pedro's response to Claudio's remark that Benedick is in love. The very fact that Don Pedro contradicts him in the very first sentence is clear proof that word "fancy" in it means the amorous inclination to love. Don Pedro dismisses Claudio's theory saying that there is no appearance of fancy in him. The only fancy in Benedick, according to Don Pedro, is his frivolous choice of different national costumes which he wears together, one waist downward and another waist upward. Evidently, this type of dress is what we call nowadays as fancy dress. There is no difficulty, therefore, in concluding that fancy in this part of the speech means only whimsical taste or judgement in matters of elegance. The word means the same thing when Pedro employs it the third time, but when he utters the word for the fourth time, he returns to the meaning of amorous inclination to love. This is the meaning when Pedro says in conclusion that Benedick is no fool for fancy. Obviously, the word "fancy" which is regarded as fascinating by the Arden edition of a Shakespearean play yields a variety of meanings which include 1) amorous inclination to love 2) personal or individual judgement and 3) capricious taste or display of elegance. Another possible meaning is imagination which is the hypothesis with which we started this essay. This meaning we can discover in some other plays of Shakespeare in which also the word "fancy" is uttered frequently. Let us now turn to *The Merchant of Venice*.

> Tell me where is fancy bred—
> Or in the heart, or in the head?
> How begot, how nourished?
>   Reply, reply.
> It is engendered in the eyes,
> With gazing fed, and fancy dies
> In the cradle where it lies,
> Let us all ring Fancy's knell.
> I'll begin it—ding dong bell
>   Ding, dong, bell. (III.i.63-72)

If in *Much Ado About Nothing*, the word "fancy" makes its appearance four times in a single speech, we have here a song in which it appears twice. Here the meanings do not vary. The text is sung at the time of the choice of the casket by Bassanio whom Portia loves and she does not want him to make a mistake by being guided by what is only materially and, therefore, superficially attractive. "Fancy" is used by the singer in the sense of what is elegant on the surface only. It is closely related to the third meaning listed above, but it is not exactly the same.

Does not "fancy" have the meaning of delusive imagination? It has and it is illustrated by the following passage in the play, *Macbeth*. The usurper has lost his peace of mind and is keeping to himself after the murder of Duncan. Lady Macbeth asks him:

> How now, my lord? Why do you keep alone,
> Of sorriest fancies your companions making,
> Using those thoughts which should indeed have died
> With them they think on? (II.iii.8-11)

Lady Macbeth who is herself cheerless tries to cheer up Macbeth who is in an unhappy and tragic state of mind. She is aware that Macbeth had said ruefully that he heard voices which said that Macbeth had murdered sleep and that Macbeth should sleep no more. These voices, she is certain, are the creation of Macbeth's mind, disturbed by anxieties and fears. These are considered by her as miserable fancies by which she means delusive imagination. Long before Fancy and Imagination were assigned different meanings by literary critics, the former overlapped with the latter, but here it is not creative imagination, but delusion created by fears and worries. No doubt they were mental creations, but they were not creations of a normal and healthy mind.

The word "fancy" is repeated in the concluding Act of the play and is charged with the same meaning.

> Not so sick, my lord,
> As she is troubled with thick-coming fancies
> That keep her from rest. (V.iv.38-40)

This is the doctor's reply to Macbeth's enquiry concerning Lady Macbeth's condition. His reply suggests that she is not physically ill, but mentally troubled. The doctor had heard what to him were incoherent utterances of his patient and he had not known that Lady Macbeth was recounting what she had said to Macbeth before and after the murder in a psychological sense. The doctor who is unaware of the complicity of Lady Macbeth in the murder is only puzzled by what he hears and sees. In the absence of any other data, the doctor cannot help thinking that Lady Macbeth is a victim of delusory imagination. A delusion is also an act of imagination, but it is neither positive nor creative. It is a sign of morbidity. It can be cured.

In *Othello*, the word is used in the sense of whim or whimsical notion.

> Emilia, come, Be as your fancies teach you;
> Whatev'r you be, I am obedient. (III.iii.89-90)

The second part of the first line and the entire second line are addressed to Othello. Desdemona is insulted by Othello, but being a great lady, she does not create a scene. She withdraws from the place and assures the moor that even if he acts according to his fancies, she will be obedient. Othello is tormented by jealousy and naturally, when there is no basis for it, Desdemona believes that he is acting according to his fancies. The word "fancy" means here a whimsical notion which has, of course, no objective basis. The moor's conduct is only guided, Desdemona thinks, by a capricious humour. This word is employed once again in the same sense by the same character.

> What horrible fancy's this? (IV.ii.26)

Desdemona is not aware of the cause of Othello's jealousy and when he starts examining her eyes, his behaviour appears very odd to her. It is clear, therefore, that Desdemona uses the word "fancy" again in the sense of caprice or whim and it is farthest from the meaning of the word "imagination."

Othello also has the occasion to speak the word "fancy," but in a different sense. We find this word in his famous disclosure of the significance of the charmed handkerchief. It had come into his possession from his mother to whom an Egyptian had given it.

> He told her, while she kept it
> 'Twould make her amiable and subdue her father
> Entirely to her love; but if she lost it
> Or made a gift of it, my father's eye
> Should hold her loathed and his spirits should hunt
> After new fancies. (III.iv.61-66)

The story of the handkerchief lends an element of mystery and suspense to the tragedy and it is charged with an ominous note. The meaning of the word "fancy" is qualified by the adjective "new" at the end of the speech and the word is used in the context of love. The phrase "new fancies" clearly means new loves. The husband will go in search of new loves, if the lady to whom the handkerchief was given as a present loses it or makes a gift of it to someone. We have already seen the use of this word "fancy" in the sense of amorous inclination to love.

The word appears several times in the drama, *All's Well That Ends Well*. We find it in the speeches of Helena, Bertrand and a lord and its meanings vary from speech to speech. Helena who is experiencing a sense of desolation after the departure of Bertrand was used to finding happiness in the sight of Bertram when he was in Rossillion.

> But now he's gone, and my idolatrous fancy,
> Must sanctify his relics. (I.i.95-96)

Helena was in the habit of drawing the figure of Bertrand on the table of her heart and this figure remains in her memory. Now that he is gone, she can only worship the relic, though the worship of relic is idolatry. Her love, therefore, is idolatrous and she cannot help it, though her religious faith does not approve of sanctifying a relic. The word "fancy" here does not mean worship, but love, because she says that her love has become idolatrous with the compulsion to behold only the relic and hold it as sacred in the absence of Bertrand who had departed for the distant royal court.

The hero of the play also has use for that word when the king persuades him to marry Helena whom he really did not want to marry because she was beneath him in social rank. The king virtually forces him to marry Helena by threatening him, besides conferring a social honour on Helena so that in social status she will be equal to him.

> Pardon, my gracious lord, for I submit
> My fancy to your eyes. (III.iii.167-68)

As the Methuen edition of the play explains, the word does not mean judgement here. Bertrand had declined to take Helena's hand in marriage as she was only a physician's daughter and did not belong to aristocracy. This class consciousness is strong in him and only in the face of strong persuasion and threat, he submits but unwillingly. We cannot, therefore, conclude that "fancy" in his speech is his notion of social rank. This notion cannot be a subjective whim. Earlier, Bertram had asserted that he cannot love Helena. It is logical hence to conclude that by fancy he means amorous inclination or love.

When we come to the word in the speech of one of the lords, it reveals a different meaning.

> He must think us some band of strangers i' th' adversary's entertainment. Now he hath a smack of all neighbouring languages: therefore we must everyone be a man of his own fancy, not to know what we speak one to another.
>
> (IV.i.14-18)

The lords are plotting against Parolle who has come to take part in the war in Florence. He is, like them, a Frenchman and a follower of Bertram. They have no respect for him and want to play a trick on him. They pretend that they do not know either his language or any of the languages of the neighbourhood. The first lord suggests that each one of them should invent some gibberish to give the impression that they do not know even the languages they themselves speak. In this babel which they will create, "fancy" means, obviously, some unintelligible gibberish which they create according to their own whims.

Bertram again utters this word as an equivalent of amorous inclination to love. He is cornered by the good-natured king and tries to explain what he regards as his affair with Diana:

> Certain it is I lik'd her
> And boarded her i' th' wanton way of youth,
> She knew her distance and did angle for me,
> Madding my eagerness with her restraint,
> As all impediments in fancy's course
> Are motives of more fancy. (V.iii.209-14)

The association of the phrases and words, "wanton way of youth," "eagerness" and "boarded" indicate that the word "fancy" does not mean romantic or exalted love which we see in Shakespeare's romantic comedies and romances. That he had sex, not with Diana but his own wedded wife is a different matter.

Does the meaning of the word "fancy" not ever overlap with that of "imagination" in Shakespeare's plays? It does, for example, in *Henry V*. The following speech of the chorus raises this question and also answers it:

> Thus with imagined wing our swift scene flies
> In motion of no less celerity
> Than that of thought. Suppose that you have seen
> The well-appointed king at Hampton pier
> Embark his royalty; and his brave fleet
> With silken streamers the young Phoebus fanning;
> Play with your fancies, and in them behold
> Upon the hempen tackle the ship boys climbing;
> Hear the shrill whistle which doth order give
> To sounds confused; behold the threaden sails
> Borne with the invisible and creeping wind,
> Draw the huge bottoms through the furrow'd sea,
> Breasting the lofty surge; O, do but think
> You stand upon the rivage and behold
> A city on the inconstant billows dancing; (III, 1-15)

Here, Shakespeare uses the words "imagine," "think" and "fancy" in the same context for reasons that are identical. First, through the chorus, the playwright invites the spectators to "imagine" the swift change of scene because the king has moved away from the council chamber to the Hampton Pier, the water front at the harbour. Next, what is described is vast and it is related to the naval expedition which is fraught with grave consequences. The king himself in full equipment is embarking; the huge battleships have started their voyage encountering the lofty waves; the silver steamers are fanned by powerful winds; the ship boys are climbing the tall masts and whistles are blown amidst a babble of commands. Surely, the audience has to imagine such a vast and majestic war preparation; it cannot be presented on the stage. Shakespeare calls upon the audience to see this naval expedition by playing with their fancies. In other words, here "fancy" means "imagination."

Fancy has a totally different meaning in the example taken from *The Tempest*:

> Spirits, which mine art
> I have from their confines call'd to enact
> My present fancies. (IV.i.96-98)

This is Prospero's response when Ferdinand expresses his admiration for the entertainment arranged by Prospero. The young man had called this entertainment a majestic vision and Prospero replies that it is an enactment of his "fancies." The word "enact" is also significant here because what is enacted is Prospero's idea or concept of entertainment.

The same word in Act V has an altogether different meaning when Prospero as yet invisible rebukes his enemies, Alonso, Antonio, Sebastian and others.

> A solemn air, and the best comforter
> To an unsettled fancy, cure thy brains,
> Now useless, boil'd within thy skull. (V.i.58-60)

The word "fancy" is complicated by being attached to the participial adjective "unsettled" and by Prospero's assurance that the solemn music which his magical powers had provided would be its best comforter. The brains of his enemies are boiling pots in which amazement, wonder, fear and anxiety are brewing. This state of mind is the "unsettled fancy." Fancy means here just mental faculty.

Antony and Cleopatra is the tragedy of not only Antony, but also of Cleopatra who knew the importance of displaying her beauty and charm. During the memorable description of Cleopatra's first appearance in the full view of Mark Antony, Enobarbus says that Cleopatra surpassed the famous painting of Venus in which fancy surpasses Nature:

> For her own person
> It beggar'd all description: she did lie
> In her pavillion—cloth of gold, of tissue—
> O'er-picturing that Venus where we see
> The fancy outwork nature. (II.ii.197-201)

In the context of the contrasted pair, "fancy" here means art.

Cleopatra uses the same analogy when she describes Antony.

> Nature wants stuff
> To vie strange forms with fancy, yet to imagine
> An Antony were Nature's piece, 'gainst fancy,
> Condemning shadows quite. (V.ii.97-100)

In a highly condensed speech, both fancy and imagination are used with both positive and negative sides. The Egyptian queen describes Antony in almost ideal and cosmic proportions, presenting him as a figure larger than life and asks Dolabella whether there can be such a man as she has dreamt of. Dolabella's negative reply infuriates the queen who admits that if there is such a man, he is past the 'size' of dreaming: Nature lacks substance to compete with the strange and fantastic forms which fancy can create. In the previous quotation, fancy had surpassed Nature in the portrait of Venus, but in this speech of Cleopatra, Nature surpasses fancy. Fancy is understood in the sense of artistic imagination, but it can only create insubstantial forms compared to the imagined form of Antony who is real. This is an involved description in which there is an inherent admission that art can be beaten only by an imagined and ideal person.

In *Hamlet* also, the word is used in two different senses. Polonius, a worldly and practical man, gives advice to his son who is leaving for France.

> Costly thy habit as thy purse can buy,
> But not express'd in fancy, rich, not gaudy. (I.i.70-71)

He is no idealist preaching plain living and high thinking and he knows the importance of dress. Laertes is advised to spend money on dress according to his capacity to pay, but the dress, however rich, should not be expressed in fancy. The word only means what is decorative and showy.

Again, while paying a tribute to Yorrick, Hamlet exclaims:

> Alas, poor Yorrick! I knew him, Horatio; a fellow of infinite jest, of most excellent fancy; he had borne me on his back a thousand times. (V.i.176-79)

The Alexander Shakespeare published by Collins equates the word with imagination and wit in its notes. Hamlet talks about Yorrick's jests and pleasantries to entertain him when he was a child. In this context, the word "fancy" can be interpreted as inventiveness or aptitude for invention of witty and practical amusement.

The word is used in a similar sense in the play, *Love's Labour's Lost*. The king of Navarre commends the talents of Armado whose services he has engaged to entertain a group of courtiers besides the king himself.

> A man of complements, whom right and wrong
> Have chose as umpire of their mutiny:
> This child of fancy, that Armado hight;
> For interim to our studies, shall relate
> In high-born words, the words of many a knight
> From Tawny Spain, lost in the world's debate (I.i.166-71)

The group comprising the king, Demain, Biron and Longaville are expected to spend three years in seclusion, shunning all pleasures and seeking only intellectual activity. But even these people need some diversion. Don Adriano De Armado is engaged to keep them amused since he can with his gift of the gab spin words and relate witty and humorous stories. He is, therefore, called a child of fancy. Obviously, the word "fancy" here means the capacity for inventing entertaining stories and jokes.

Often in Shakespeare's romantic comedies, the word "fancy" means amorous inclination to love. In *As You Like It*, Rosalind, a tall, beautiful and resourceful girl, calls Orlando a fancy-monger:

> There is a man haunts the forest, that abuse our young plants with carving 'Rosalind' on their barks; hangs odes upon hawthorns, and elegies on brambles; all, forsooth, deifying the name of Rosalind; if I could meet that fancy-monger, I would give him some good counsel, for he seems to have the quotidian of love upon him. (III.ii.328-34)

The Pitt Press Shakespeare edited by A.H. Verity explains the word "fancy-monger" as dealer in love. Rosalind who is in disguise is talking to Orlando himself and describes his activity of writing odes and elegies and hanging them on bushes. It is obvious that Orlando is not just a lover, but an imaginative one. His imagination is characterized by an elegance. The word "fancy" is rich in its connotation here and embraces imagination, love and elegance.

There is at least one thing which is meant by fancy and not by imagination in Shakespeare's plays and that is love, but only in collocation with imagination and elegance. Consider, for example, the following passage in *As You Like It*.

> O dear Phoebe,
> If ever—as that ever may be now—
> You meet in some fresh cheek the power of fancy,
> Then shall you know that wounds invisible
> That love's keen arrows make. (III.v.28-32)

It is in this passage that the meaning of fancy is nearest to love. Silvius complains that Phoebe is not responding to his overtures. He goes on to say that only when she meets the power of fancy in some fresh young cheek, she will realize the anguish caused by the keen arrows of Cupid!

Phoebe, a girl of the working class, also uses the word "fancy" in the sense described above. At the end of the play, every lad gets his lass and those of the working class are no exceptions.

> I will not eat my word, now that art mine;
> The faith my fancy to thee doth combine. (V.iv.145-46)

Silvius's love is also requited at the end when the truth about Rosalind is revealed.

Fancy, of course, does not always means love. It also means presenting what is not present to the senses of the body like seeing, touching and the like. No doubt, this activity looks similar to imagination, but it is not as exalted as the latter.

> Be attent,
> And time that is so briefly spent
> With your fine fancies quaintly ache:
> What's dumb in show I'll plain with speech.
> (*Pericles*, Prologue, III.11-14)

After Pericles has married Thais, the princess of Pentapolis and

Gower, the Chorus describes the nuptial night. The chorus wants the audience to supply with their imagination what is not enacted and assures them that he on his part would describe in speech what would be enacted shortly in a dumb show. The activities of the night which he describes are banal and trivial and he wants the audience to supplement them with their fancies. The word "fancy" here means imagination in the limited sense of presenting what is not present to the senses of the body.

Before classifying the meanings of the word "fancy" in the plays of Shakespeare and drawing conclusions, we must study the meanings of the word "imagination" also in his plays, since in some respects the meanings of these two words overlap. In this study we are on exalted grounds. Aesthetics and creativity are called into play. Let us begin with a well known passage from *A Midsummer Night's Dream*:

> Lovers and madmen have such seething brains,
> Such shaping fantasies, that apprehend
> More than cool reason ever comprehends.
> The lunatic, the lover and the poet,
> Are of imagination all compact.
> One sees more devils than the vast hell can hold;
> That is the mad man. The lover, all frantic,
> Sees Helen's beauty in a brow of Egypt:
> The poet's eye, in a fine frenzy rolling,
> Doth glance from heaven to earth, from earth to heaven;
> And as imagination bodies forth
> The forms of things unknown, the poet's pen
> Turns them to shapes, and gives to airy nothing
> A local habitation and a name.
> Such tricks hath strong imagination
> That, if it would but apprehend some joy,
> It comprehends some bringer of that joy,
> Or in the night, imagining some fear,
> How easy is a bush supposed a bear. (V.i.3-22)

The word "imagination" is used four times in this passage. The order in which the lunatic, the lover and the poet are arranged is quite meaningful. The lunatic and the lover do see what is not present to the senses. The former sees, however, what is delusory and what he sees is purely involuntary. He cannot help seeing delusions and hallucinations which is a sign of ill health. The poet sees like a lunatic what is not presented to the senses of the body like the eyes, but what he does see is not a sign of ill health. He sees what is elevating and beautiful, but what he sees is, nevertheless, purely subjective. The poet is on a higher step, though he also sees what is not presented to the senses. This activity is voluntary: there is consistency, logic and reality in what he sees. What the poet sees is what is mentally created by him and it pleases the readers with its aptness and not just with its sensuous contents. Imagination, therefore, is not only the activity of presenting what is not presented to the senses of the body, but also a sign of creativity. Secondly, the poet gives expression to it in the form of words.

In this play, Hippolyta, the duke's fiance, compares the moon to a silver bow new bent in heaven. A bow made of silver is seen by the mind's eye and it is consistent with the waning moon, because its brightness is that of silver and its crescent shape is that of the bow which is newly bent. The comparison is consistent and therefore, apt. It is not a delusion, but sign of creative imagination.

The word occurs again in the same long scene in the speech of Duke Theseus, one of the wisest characters in the plays of Shakespeare.

Theseus: The best in this kind are but shadows; the worst are no worse, if imagination amend them.
Hippolyta: It must be your imagination and not theirs.
Theseus: If we imagine no worse of them than they of themselves, they may pass for excellent men. (V.i. 219-23)

The duke is quite kind in appreciating the dramatic entertainment put up by the Athenian craftsmen who had neither the talent nor the stage equipment to make it a success. In fact, it looked ridiculous to the newly married duchess. The duke amends what she says by pointing out that the acting of these artisans should be supplemented by the imagination of the audience.

The word is more complex in the tragedy of Macbeth.

I am thane of Cawdor.
If good, why do I yield to that suggestion
Whose horrid image doth unfix my hair,

And make my seated heart knock at my ribs
Against the uses of nature? Present fears
Are less than horrible imaginings;
My thought whose murder yet is but fantastical,
Shake so my single state of man that function
Is smothered in surmise, and nothing is
But what is not. (I.iii.133-42)

Macbeth is extremely agitated by the fulfilment of the prophecy that he would be the thane of Cawdor. His mind is in a state of turmoil, because it would make it logical that he would also become the king. The witches seem to have had a glimpse into his mind which was contemplating the assassination of King Duncan. This murder is still imaginary, but he, a man with conscience, is shaken by it, leading to the unfixing of his hair. Macbeth imagines a future event, the event of robbing Duncan of his life and with it, his crown. Here the word "imagination" means the activity of mentally visualizing a future event. When Macbeth speaks of murder whose thought is but fantastical yet, he means murder which is yet only imaginary. It is interesting to note that "imaginary" and "fantastical" are used as synonyms. The word "fancy" itself is derived from the word "fantasy."

The word "imagination" makes its appearance thrice in *King Lear*, the bleakest and most pessimistic of the tragedies of Shakespeare. Once it is spoken by Lear and once by Gloucester who are victims of conspiracies. It is a commonplace of literary criticism that there are flashes of sense and wisdom in the harangues of Lear after he has become mad. In Dover, the Duke of Gloucester now blinded meets Lear whom he recognises by his voice. One has no sight and another no sense. Gloucester is a loyal and good-natured courtier who still regards Lear as his king. Unable to recognise him by sight, he recognises him by his voice and asks him whether he is not the king. Hearing the word "king" and seeing the duke, Lear begins a harangue that runs over twenty lines. The crisscross of Lear's memories and judgements in this tirade begins with kingship and dispensation of justice, passes on to the theme of adultery—there is before him Gloucester who had committed adultery and had not concealed the fact—and ends with the question of punishment in Hell. Fiend and hell remind him of darkness and sulphurous pit in which the sinners are punished. Therefore, he asks for a perfume thinking that Gloucester is an apothecary.

> Give me one ounce of civet; good apothecary, sweeten
> My imagination; there's money for thee. (V.vi.130-31)

Lear sees an adulterer, an adulteress and hell with its boiling sulphurous pit which are not physically present before his eyes. He forms a mental concept of things. His fulmination has a grave moral and a word like "fancy" cannot take the place of "imagination" here. This activity involves the integration of other faculties of man, because Lear sees the irony of what he believes to be the bastard son's kindness to his father, the universal weakness for sex and the hypocrisy of those who are virtuous in their pose but adulterous in reality.

In Shakespeare's plays, imagination is never a negative state of mind: it is always positive and creative. That is why when Gloucester expresses his wish that he were distract, he equates it with wrong imagination:

> Better I were distract:
> So should my thought be severed from my griefs,
> And woes by wrong imagination lose
> The knowledge of themselves. (IV.vi.278-81)

Gloucester's sufferings are made more acute after he sees the total madness of Lear. He wishes that his mind were also deranged and he equates the derangement with what he calls wrong imagination. The adjective "wrong" is important here. The right or normal imagination is an attribute of an able poet, but wrong "imagination" can be the attribute of only a deranged mind. An insane man—we can recall here what Duke Theseus says in *A Midsummer Night's Dream*—sees what does not exist and is affected by it, but a poet sees not only what does not exist before his eyes, but is able to integrate it with social and human situations. He sees in this integration the beauty and the ugliness, the tragedy and comedy of human life.

Imagination finds a place even in *All's Well That Ends Well*, one of the problem plays of Shakespeare. Helena is a romanticist in the world of realistic characters and is in love with Bertram who believes that her social status is inferior and that his marriage with her is for that reason quite unthinkable. But Helena does not give up her hope.

> What was he like?
> I have forgotten him: my imagination
> Carries no favour in't but Bertram's. (I.i.79-81)

The young lady is not thinking of her late father, but of the young man, the son of her guardian. Unabashedly she says that she has forgotten her father and that her mind does not carry his picture. Her mind carries no favour in it but that of Bertram. Helena is desperately in love with Bertram who has departed in order to be in the royal court of the king of France. She knows that in social status, she is far beneath Bertram. She also knows that he is not reciprocating. This is a gloomy situation, too gloomy for the use of the word "fancy." Only "imagination" can be apt here, and she is aware that her imagination is carrying the picture, not of her father, but of Bertram whom she used to see almost every day when he was with his mother. Naturally, imagination here means the formation of the picture in her mind, corresponding to the actual features of the man. This activity is not creative, but imitative: she has seen him earlier and the picture she forms is faithful to the original.

It is not possible to overemphasise the importance of the word "imagination" in a historical play presenting naval expeditions. *Henry V* has much use for that word.

> And let us, ciphers to this great accompt
> On your imaginary forces work. (V.i.18-19)

In the opening scene, the chorus is apologetic because events of epic proportions including heroic battles fought by kings and armies are presented before the audience, while the stage itself is nothing more than a scaffold or cockpit. The chorus wants the imagination of the audience to make good what cannot be physically and adequately shown on the stage. The word "imagination" means the activity of mentally inventing and thus creating sights and sounds that are not presented to the senses, especially the eyes. What needs to be invented or created is august and mighty, and "fancy" cannot do this job.

The activity of imagination goes with consistency and reality and without them, it would be mere fancy. Consider the following example from the same chorus.

Suppose, within the girdles of these walls
Are now confined two mighty monarchies
Whose high, upreared and abutting fronts
The perilous narrow ocean parts asunder;
Piece out our imperfections with your thoughts;
Into a thousand parts divide one man,
And make imaginary puissance;
Think when we talk of horses, that you see them
Printing their proud hoofs i' the receiving earth. (I.i.19-27)

In addition to the vastness of the scale, the details are also important. The formidable waterfronts of England and France, the narrow and dangerous English channel separating them, the scale of representing a thousand men by one man, the proud horses printing their hoofs in the earth that receive their impressions—all these details are not only vivid, but also consistent and real. All these can be imagined and not fancied. The consistency, the realism and vastness are beyond the range of fancy.

The word is employed four times by the chorus. The reason is clear. In addition to the vastness of the military operations, the change of scene from port to port and from country to country can only be imagined and not literally seen by the audience in the Globe Theatre. The chorus calls upon the audience to fly with the king and his army on "imaginary wings" (III.i.1-3) and to imagine the return of the triumphant king to England (V.16,17). There is a dynamism and mobility in the activity of imagination and it is not static.

The word is also used in *Romeo and Juliet* written at the early stage of Shakespeare's career. Romeo has arranged his secret marriage with Juliet which would be solemnised by Father Lawrence.

Ah Juliet, if the measure of thy joy
Be heap'd like mine, and that thy skill be more
To blazon it, then sweeter with thy breath
This neighbour air and let rich music's tongue
Unfold the imagin'd happiness that both

> Receive in either by this rich encounter. (II.vi.24-29)

Romeo and Juliet are on the brink of what promises to be their permissible happiness, since they are about to be married. They are, as it were, at the gates of paradise and each can only imagine the joy that results from their wedding. This is a mood of exaltation and the joy that is imagined is intense.

In *The Tempest*, the word is spoken by a person in love talking to the person who is loved. Ferdinand is the only male youth whom Miranda has seen and she is in love with him. Her love borders on devotion and she does not want any other male companion.

> I would not wish
> Any companion in the world but you;
> Nor can imagination form a shape
> Besides yourself, to like of. (III.i.54-57)

The speech is a part of the log-bearing scene in which Ferdinand performs the ordeal prescribed by Prospero. Miranda declares her love and she says that though she has not seen any man except her father and Ferdinand, she does not wish any companion but Ferdinand and that her imagination cannot form a shape besides him.

The word "imagination" is similarly used by Antonio who tries to persuade Sebastian to murder his brother, King Alphonso, and usurp his kingdom.

> What might,
> Worthy Sebastian,—O what might?—no more;—
> And yet methinks I see it in thy face,
> What thou shouldst be: the occasion speaks thee,
> And my strong imagination sees a crown
> Dropping upon thy head. (II.i.7-12)

Antonio, the younger brother of Prospero whom he has deposed, skilfully suggests to Sebastian that he should get rid of him and become the king himself, since circumstances are quite favourable. They have been cast away on a distant island and Sebastian is tempted by Antonio's suggestion. But the same island had both Ariel and Prospero, a fact which the usurper had not reckoned. Antonio is careful and after stating that he sees in Sebastian's face what he should be, adds that his strong imagination sees a crown dropping on his head. Here "strong" may be taken to mean "vivid." "Imagination" means here the activity of mentally visualizing a certain action which is not taking place in the purely material sense.

The word is used differently in *Timon of Athens.*

> Admirable. How this grace
> Speaks his own standing! What a mental power
> This eye shoots forth! how big imagination
> Moves in this lip! to the dumbness of gesture
> One might interpret. (I.i.34-38)

This is the remark made by the poet while he compliments the painter who, like the poet, the merchant and the jeweller, has come to meet Timon. All have come with gifts to meet the Athenian noble. The poet remarks that the gracefulness of the portrait of Timon painted by the artist represents faithfully the standing of the poet. Here imagination means the activity of interpreting the person or event, with its emotions, feelings and thoughts. Therefore, it is organic.

In *Hamlet*, Shakespeare employs the word "imagination" thrice, twice in the speeches of Hamlet and once in the speech of Horatio. It is very difficult to ascribe a clear meaning to its first occurrence in the play.

> He waxes desperate with imagination. (I.iv.87)

The Collins edition in the series, The Alexander Shakespeare, says in its notes: "Horatio says anxiously that Hamlet is going out of his mind." The remark of Horatio is his immediate reaction when the prince shakes off Horatio and Marcellus who had tried to prevent him physically from following the ghost which, they are afraid, can be a devil in disguise. They are astounded by Hamlet's fury. Marcellus, a night guard expresses the fear that it is not fit to obey him. The word "desperate" should be seen in the proper context. Horatio is a staid and balanced person and earlier, he had tried to dissuade the prince from going to the ghost. His caution is understandable.

What if it tempt you toward the flood, my lord, . . .
And draw you into madness? (I.iv.69,74)

Hamlet, according to Horatio, is driven by unreality, by what is not real. The prince is not to be obeyed in his own interest, because he is not in his senses. Imagination means here unreality.

The great discussion on the distinction between the meanings of fancy and imagination that took place in the Romantic Age appears to have been anticipated by Shakespeare. In *Antony and Cleopatra*, a sentence includes both the words, but with different meanings.

You lie up to the hearing of the gods.
But if there be, or ever one such,
It's past the size of dreaming; nature wants stuff
To vie strange forms with fancy, yet to imagine
An Antony were Nature's piece, 'gainst fancy,
Condemning shadows quite. (V.ii.95-100)

In this involved sentence, Cleopatra involuntarily distinguishes the meanings of fancy and imagination. Ignoring Dolabella, the Egyptian queen describes her dream in which Mark Antony appears as a hero of cosmic proportions and asks Dolabella whether any such man ever existed or will ever exist. When Dolabella replies in the negative, the unpredictable Cleopatra becomes furious and accuses him of telling a lie that would be heard even by the gods. She goes on to add that if Nature had indeed produced such a man he would be beyond even dreams. No dream can match that reality. Nature lacks stuff to compete with fancy in the creation of fantastic forms. But if one imagines Antony as a really existing person, it would be Nature's masterpiece before which fancy's insubstantial forms will pale into insignificance. Here fancy and imagination are juxtaposed: imagination is associated with what is vast, august, majestic or serious, whereas fancy does not create anything more than what is insubstantial.

Fancy and imagination are on less exalted grounds in Hamlet's exclamations in Elsinore's cemetery.

Let me see. (Takes the skull) Alas, poor Yorrick! I knew him, Horatio, a fellow of infinite jest, of most excellent fancy; he hath borne me on his back a thousand times. And now how

> abhored in my imagination it is! My gorge rises at it.
> (V.i.176-86)

Hamlet recalls the guips and pleasantries with which the court jester entertained him when he was a small boy. Yorrick, according to him, was a genius. Originality and inventiveness were called into play when he amused the boy and hence fancy which Hamlet attributes to him can be taken to mean inventiveness which characterises wit. When the prince comes to the present symbolised by the skull, the word "fancy" gives way to imagination. Hamlet is disgusted and horrified at the thought that Yorrick's head had been reduced to a skull after passing through several stages of transformation. Imagination here means the mental visualization of the macabre change leading to the grinning and socketless skull.

Hamlet, a sensitive youth, talks like a poet and philosopher with the skull in his hands after it has been thrown away by the gravedigger.

> To what base uses we may return, Horatio! Why may not imagination trace the noble dust of Alexander till 'a find it stopping a bung-hole. (V.i.195-97)

Unlike fancy, imagination is creative and organic: it faces the challenge of grave and pensive moods. We require creative imagination to trace the various stages of the long course of the transformation of the body of Alexander into dust and loam which in turn can be changed into a stopper for casks.

In *As You Like It,* Rosalind employs the word "imagination":

> Yes, one; and in this manner. He was to imagine me his love, his mistress; and I sent him everyday to woo me.
> (III.ii.371-72)

Rosalind is not only beautiful, but also resourceful and witty. She is in disguise and claims that she can cure a man of love which she describes as mere madness. Her tongue-in-the-cheek comments disguise her love for him very much as her garments disguise her appearance. The method she adopted according to her was to ask the man first to imagine that he loves her (him), though she was in disguise as a man. Here the word "imagine" means "mentally consider what is physically not in existence."

The use of the word "imagination" in *Pericles* reminds us of the purpose served by that word in *Henry V*:

> In your imagination hold
> This stage the ship, upon whose deck
> The sea-tost Pericles appears to speak. (Prologue, III.58-60)

Gower who speaks the prologue asks the audience to imagine a scene which cannot be physically presented on the stage. He expects them to regard the stage as the ship upon the deck of which Pericles will appear in the ensuing scene. The king is virtuous and the queen pregnant. The ship in which they are travelling is tossed on the stormy sea with unfortunate consequences. The scene is charged with grave foreboding and that is the reason for preferring imagination to fancy which always carries the implication of what is elegant and pleasing. The ship, the deck, the wind-lashed waves—all these collocations constitute the scene and hence imagination is organic also.

Imagination is given a less challenging task when Gower speaks the prologue at the beginning of the next Act. As in *The Winter's Tale*, a female child grows up and blossoms into a young woman in *Pericles*. There is frequent shifting of the scene of action from town to town and shore to shore. The play employs a prologue to ask the audience to bridge time and space with the help of their imagination.

> Thus time we waste, and longest leagues make short;
> Sail seas in cockles, have and wish but for it;
> Making—to take your imagination—
> From bourn to bourn, region to region (IV.iv.1-4)

Vast distances and passage of time spanning several years are visualized by imagination.

The twenty seven examples of fancy and twenty examples of imagination from sixteen plays of Shakespeare belonging to the different phases of his career, ranging from apprenticeship of maturity, bring forth the following meanings.

FANCY: 1. Amorous inclination 2. Personal and individual/subjective judgement 3. Whimsical and capricious taste for elegance 4. What is pretty and elegant on the surface only 5. Delusive imagination 6. Inclination to like what is superficially pleasing and attractive 7. Delusion 8. Whim or caprious humour 9. Imagination 10. Concept of elegant and pleasing entertainment 11. Mental faculty 12. Art 13. Creative faculty: but creates only insubstantial and strange forms 14. What is decorative and showy 15. Aptitude for wit and pleasantry 16. Aptitude for inventing jokes and entertaining stories 17. Imagination pertaining to love and elegance, but on the lighter side 18. Imagination on a limited scale, excluding what is vast or majestic or august.

IMAGINATION: 1. Mental concept of what is not presented to the eyes and other senses of the body: consistent and real in an ideal sense, that is, in the non-material sense 2. Mentally visualizing a future event or possibility. 3. Synonymous with fantastical form or fantasy from which the word "fancy" is derived 4. A vivid mental concept of what is not presented to the senses, but what is august, majestic, grave or vast 5. Mentally forming a scene with consistency and reality 6. Dynamism and mobility present in imagination but not in fancy 7. Imagination creates not only what is not presented to the eyes and other senses, but also emotions and feelings; hence it is organic and creative 8. Unreality, illusion, near madness 9. Mentally creating what is vast and august 10. Mentally visualizing a change which is not presented to the eyes, including all its parts. Hence it is organic and creative 11. Mentally conceiving what is vast, deep and inspiring in space and time.

The two words "fancy" and "imagination" were treated as vaguely synonymous in the sixteenth and the seventeenth century. If any effort was made to distinguish them, from each other, it was imagination that emerged with greater honours. It was associated with what was more sober, responsible and evocative than what was suggested by fancy. But no systematic study of the distinction between the two words was made till the beginning of the nineteenth century. William Taylor (1765-1836), a contemporary of the romantic poets and a friend of Robert Southey, must be credited with the first analytical study of the literary, philosophical and psychological aspects of the words "fancy" and "imagination." William Wordsworth quotes William Taylor's comments in detail in his preface to his 1815 edition of poems in order to refute what the latter has written:

> A man has imagination in proportion as he can distinctly copy in idea the impression of sense: it is the faculty which images within the mind the phenomena of sensation. A man has those internal images (*phantazein* is to cause to appear) so as to complete ideal representation of absent objects. Imagination is the power of depicting, and fancy of evoking and combining. The imagination is formed by patient observation, the fancy by a voluntary activity of shifting the scenery of the mind. The more accurate the imagination, the more safely a painter, or a poet, undertake a delineation, or a description, without the presence of the objects to be characterized. The more versatile the fancy, the more original and striking will be the decoration produced. (*The Complete Works of Wordsworth*)

William Taylor has given more elevated place to fancy than to imagination. He was guided by the light thrown on the two words by their etymology. That is why Wordsworth mocks him, saying that Taylor had looked at the foundation and mistaken it for the superstructure. The poet of the Lake District elaborates what he means with illustrations not only from the works of other poets like Shakespeare and Virgil, but also from his own works! He sees in imagination a certain metaphorical meaning conferred upon imagery, by the poet's mind. Secondly, he asserts that imagination "shapes" and "creates." The figurative meaning which the poet associates with the object is called modification by him and he goes on to say that in fancy there is little or no modification. "Fancy does not require that the materials which she makes use of should be susceptible of change in their constitution by her touch and where they admit of modification, it is enough for her purpose if it be slight, limited and evanescent."

Wordsworth also speaks of the effects of the law under which fancy's processes are carried as capricious and amusing, playful and tender. In his analysis, even conceit comes under the definition of fancy. Wordsworth places the faculty of imagination on a higher pedestal by saying that imagination supports the eternal. In the plays of Shakespeare also, imagination is endowed with an august meaning, elevating it to a higher pedestal.

In Coleridge's view, fancy is "mechanical and logical" and it has aggregative and associative power. Imagination is responsible and is "organic and curative." A great Shakespearean play, comedy or tragedy, is not a work of fancy, but of imagination.

Within a single speech, Shakespeare can employ both fancy and imagination. Othello on the brink of suicide wants the world to speak

> of one whose hand
> Like the base Indian, threw a pearl away
> Richer than all his tribe: of one whose subdued eyes
> Albeit unused to melting mood,
> Drop tears as fast as the Arabian trees
> Their medicinal gum. (*Othello*, V.ii.345-50)

The first image in the above quotation is an example of imagination: the second of fancy. We have in the first the images of an ignorant aborigine, a precious pearl richer than his tribe, the action of his throwing it away—all these correspond to their counterparts in Othello's tragic situation. They constitute a perfect whole without the rattle of rhetoric.

Othello speaks of his tears dropping from his eyes as fast as the medicinal gum dropping from the Arabian trees. This image does not enhance the tragic seriousness of the situation: the image of the fast dropping tears and that of gum-shedding trees do not fit into the whole because the latter is a lifeless thing and the only thing common is their fastness. The image is only aggregative, that is, the eyes of Othello and the Arbaian trees discharging medicinal gum are just put together mechanically. This image is an example of fancy.

Rawlinson Collection:
An American's Discovery

In the year 1985, on the 14th of November, to be precise, Garry Taylor, an American scholar borrowed for reference a manuscript anthology of poems in the famous Bodleian Library of Oxford University and found in it a poem attributed to William Shakespeare. This discovery fascinated him because he found that the world would be reading it for the first time in two hundred years, if it was published. A few others had seen it before and these readers included even E.K. Chambers, but nobody had taken it seriously. But Garry Taylor pursued the matter further very earnestly and after studying both external and internal evidence, came to the conclusion that this love lyric of ninety lines was authored by William Shakespeare, Garry Taylor is the joint editor of *The Complete Works of Shakespeare*, which is now being compiled and edited by Oxford University Press and the editors of the OUP propose to include this poem in Shakespeare's complete works. This fact is testimony to the confidence with which Garry Taylor asserts that the unpublished poem was written by Shakespeare.

The manuscript anthology contains, besides the untitled poem, a few other hand-written poems and they are attributed to John Donne and George Herbert among others. This manuscript known as Rawlinson Collection had been gifted by Richard Rawlinson (1689-1755) to Oxford University, a year after his death. The poems attributed to Donne and Herbert are found to be authentic, but till now, barring Garry Taylor and one or two others, no one has considered the poem attributed to Shakespeare as genuine. At present, the manuscript is its only source and it has not found general acceptance in the academic circles. However, Garry Taylor has expressed the following opinion: "Its vocabulary, imagery, style—everything scholarly jargon lumps together as internal evidence—

are at least compatible with Shakespeare's authorship, and if one gives them the most weight they will bear, they suggest that it could hardly have been written by any other known poet." He draws our attention to what he calls "verbal parallels." They are words, images, phrases, and stylistic features which are seen both in the published works and in the unpublished poem. Garry Taylor's advocacy rests on the following points.

1. The proportion of these parallels in the poems and plays of Shakespeare is much greater than in the poems of Spenser.
2. The parallels are more striking in the case of Shakespeare.
3. Neologism, that is, either new words or the new grammatical features of old words used for the first time in the manuscript poem.

Garry Taylor concludes his arguments by stating that the poem has merits and defects, and that unless there is proof to the contrary, the unpublished piece should be taken as Shakespeare's poem. For neologism, he cites the gerund "admiring" and the adjective "scanty" which, according to him, were employed for the first time by William Shakespeare. Taylor's conclusion does not, of course, rest entirely on the originality in the use of words and not repeating them elsewhere. As the American scholar says: "Everything he wrote contained words he didn't use anywhere else. Paradoxically, the appearance in the poem of words that don't appear anywhere else in Shakespeare is good evidence that the poem could be by Shakespeare." This inference is drawn by Taylor on the basis of the generally held view that Shakespeare had a penchant for coining new words. But this originality is by itself not adequate proof that Shakespeare wrote the poem attributed to him.

English language is rich in vocabulary and the playwright might have turned to synonyms while writing his other poems and plays. He thought probably that it was better to use "admiration" as a noun, instead of the gerund, "admiring" which is, when compared to the former, awkward because it can be mistaken for a participle. In the unpublished poem itself, the bard perhaps needed words that would rhyme and the poem is notorious for its innumerable internal rhymes. If he had used "admiration," it would not have rhymed with "desire," a noun or "desiring," a gerund. The best way out for the poet was the use of "ing" forms of both the words and hence emerged the word "admiring." But to be fair to Garry Taylor, we must grant that his conclusions are based on the cumulative force of verbal parallels and neologisms.

In this paper I propose to depart from the approach adopted by Garry Taylor and concentrate on (1) the unique grammatical features (2) images and (3) collocations and not just words to which we find parallels in the other works of Shakespeare. Single words alone are not important. Words like "blot," "plot," "treasure," "lips" and the like are found again and again in Shakespeare's works, but this verbal frequency might be due to choice of theme. The frequent use of a romantic theme by the poet may be responsible for the frequent occurrence of the words like "lips," "beauty," "treasure," "stars" and "fair." Garry Taylor has made a list of ninety verbal parallels which include even such phrasal verbs as "keep out" which, he says, appears three times in Shakespeare's works. I consider this phrasal verb and its frequency as non-significant. In contrast, Garry Taylor points out the fact that the Noun Phrase "all the world" occurs fifty six times in the dramatist's works. The phrase is striking and equally striking is the frequency of its occurence. But in his exhaustive list, Garry Taylor includes even a phrase like "fair love." That is why in my approach, I would like to emphasize the presence of only (1) the grammatical features (2) collocations and (3) images.

At the outset, I must draw the attention of the readers to the sentence "Oh, admiring desiring breeds" in lines 9 and 10 of the 6th stanza of the manuscript poem. In this short sentence of three words—here, the interjection "Oh" may be left aside—both the subject and the object of the Verb are gerunds, that is, the "ing"-form of the Verbs. The poet could have used the regular nouns like "admiration" and "desire." But, instead, he prefers the "ing"-forms of the verbs. A look at one of the sonnets of Shakespeare written during the initial stages of his career reveals the exactly same tendency. The first six lines of sonnet 87 are dominated by gerunds. Addressing the youth, the poet says

> Farewell! thou art too dear for my *possessing*,
> And like enough thou know'st thy estimate,
> The charter of thy worth gives thee *releasing*:
> My bonds in thee are all determinate.
> For how do I hold thee but by thy *granting*.

> And for that riches where is my *deserving*?

There are four gerunds in the above six lines and there are five more in the next eight lines. But I have mentioned only those for which alternatives in the form of suitable nouns derived from the same verbs were available to the poet. Nouns like "possession" and "release" were available to Shakespeare, but he preferred a string of gerunds indicating a fancy for the "ing"-form of verbs.

The use of the word "compare" as a noun has been traced by Oxford English Dictionary to earlier writers and the farthest it has gone is the year 1621. Even granting that this does not necessarily mean that its presence in Shakespeare's works was unknown to OED, we cannot ignore the significance of finding it not only in *Romeo and Juliet*, but also in the unpublished poem. Not only the contexts are the same, but even the prepositions in the noun phrase are the same. Describing the girl, the poet of the manuscript piece, says

> A pretty bare, past compare,
> Parts those plots which besots
> still asunder. (stanza 8, ll. 1-3)

The poet who is evidently very young employs a sensous language. But in *Romeo and Juliet* also the context is the same, though the language is sober. The old nurse describes Romeo's figure to Juliet and she says

> Romeo! no, not he: though his face be better than any man's, yet his leg excels all men's; and for a hand, and a foot, and a body, though they be not to be talked on, yet they are *past compare*!

We must notice here that the contexts in both the works are the same: the description of human figure. Secondly, the same verb "compare" is used as a noun. Thirdly, it is preceded by the same preposition, "past." These three common points constitute compelling evidence unless the phrase was a cliche even during the days of Shakespeare, for which there is no evidence so far. The word "compare" is used as a noun by Christopher Marlowe in Act 5, sc. 1, l. 30 of his play *Dr. Faustus* written in 1588 or 1589. But there, it is not part of a prepositional phrase. It is just a noun phrase, object of the verb, "passeth." The context too is different. It is just a general reference to Helen's beauty in the words of a scholar, when Helen appears before the scholars on the order of Dr. Faustus.

When a poet repeats not only the grammatical feature, but also chooses the same context for its use, the reader is alerted and he wonders whether the same poet wrote both. One such striking grammatical feature is the participial phrase "being set." In the unpublished poem, the poet speaks directly:

> Being set, lips met,
> Arms twined, and did bind my heart's treasure.
> (stanza 4, ll.9-10)

The participial phrase lacks the Noun/Subject to which it must be related. The meaning of the phrase is fairly clear; it is something equivalent to "after settling down in the proper course." In any case, the same structure occurs again in Shakespeare's *Venus and Adonis* written around the same time.

> Here come and sit, where never serpent hisses;
> And *being set*, I'll smother thee with kisses;
> (Stanza 3, ll. 17-18)

We notice here not only the same phrase but also the same context: the rendezvous of lovers, the meeting of the young man and the young woman who are now seated on the grass. In the unpublished poem, it is the young man who takes the initiative and in *Venus and Adonis* it is the young goddess who persuades the reluctant Adonis. The same participial phrase is repeated in another earlier poem of Shakespeare.

> But as the earth doth weep, the sun being set,
> Each flower moisten'd like a melting eye;
> (*Rape of Lucrece*, ll. 1225-26)

One interesting thing here is that unlike the phrase in the manuscript poem and *Venus and Adonis*, the participial phrase "being set" is related to the Noun/Subject, namely, the sun. The context too is different: it is the situation following the night when Lucrece was raped by prince Torquin. The poet has described the return of the sunlight in the previous stanzas. The sun is the nominative absolute here and the phrase means the sun being placed in the proper course.

I must now refer to the use of the "ing" form of the verb "content." Ordinarily, we find only its passive form, namely, "contented." But Shakespeare finds use even for the gerundial form of the verb "content" by turning it into "contenting." In the unpublished poem, the lover expresses his confidence that he would make love to the girl.

> Therefore I will try
> To compass my heart's chief *contenting* (stanza 9, ll. 7-8)

Shakespeare's use of the "ing" form of the verb "content" can be seen in the long poem, *Venus and Adonis*. Venus urges the reluctant Adonis to respond to her urge and when he doesn't, she complains;

> Fie, lifeless picture, cold and lifeless stone,
> Well-painted idol, image dull and dead,
> Status *contenting* but eye alone, (ll. 211-13)

Though the context is the same, the longer poem employs the participial form of the verb and not its gerundial form. However, the "ing" form of the verb is very unusual, whether it is Venus who speaks or the lover. Another grammatical feature that attracts our attention is the use of the verb "annoy" as a noun which no other writer had used before. This originality can be seen not only in the unpublished poem, but also in *Venus and Adonis* which Shakespeare wrote at the beginning of his writing career. The lover in the manuscript poem says to himself;

> Therefore, try! Her reply
> Gives thee joy or *annoy*, (Stanza 8, ll. 4-5)

The situation is marked by youthful love and desire. In *Venus and Adonis*, the reluctant Adonis kisses Venus who has fainted at his indifference. This act leads to her ecstatic joy, though the kiss was intended only as a first aid to revive her. Venus exclaims:

'O where am I' quoth she, 'in earth or heaven,
Or in the ocean drench'd, or in the fire? . . .
Do I delight to die, or life desire?
But now I liv'd and life was death's annoy.' (ll. 493-96)

The same verb used as a noun is found in *Rape of Lucrece*:

The little birds that tune their morning's joy
Make her moans mad with their sweet melody;
For mirth doth search the bottom of *annoy*;
Sad souls are slain in merry company; (ll. 1107-10)

Here, of course, the context is different. What we notice here is the bitterness of Lucrece after the nightmarish experience of the previous night. Innocent of the crime committed by the prince, the birds have started singing in the morning and their melody is contrasted with the annoy and anguish of the general's wife. The word "annoy" as a noun is used more than once in this long poem.

The presence of the noun "mishap" is also significant in the manuscript lyric. The earliest example of its use in literature is found in Shakespeare's poetry as recorded by Oxford English Dictionary.

It is meet naught but sweet
Should come near that so rare
'tis a wonder
No *mishap*, no scape
Inferior to Nature's perfection; (Stanza 8, ll. 5-9)

The word "mishap" is also employed in the poem *Venus and Adonis*. In the unpublished poem, the lover describes the girl whom he loves, in *Venus and Adonis*, the context is the same, that is, love's appreciation. Adonis does not respond to the overtures of Venus, even though he falls on the body of the goddess when she pulls him down.

Even as poor birds, deceived with painted grapes
Do surfeit by the eye and pine the maw,
Even so she languisheth in her *mishaps*, (ll. 601-3)

Let us now consider some significant collocations which will serve as evidence of Shakespeare's authorship of the manuscript lyric. They are much more significant than mere single words, because it is very unlikely that the minds of two different writers will bring together words of the same set in the same context at the cost of originality and betray a lack of imagination. Let us take a look at the following collocation. In the unpublished lyric, the youth describes the hair of the girl that has attracted him.

> Gentle *wind sport* did find
> *Wantonly* to make fly
> her gold tresses,
> As they shook, I did look
> But her fair hair did impair
> all my senses. (Stanza 5, ll. 1-5)

The key words that collocate with each other here are "wind," "wanton," "gold," tress" and "fair." The image is quite natural when the young man is describing the copious blond hair of the girl, particularly when he and the girl are walking on the meadows and in the midst of the trees through which the winds blow. Compare this image with what Bassanio says in *The Merchant of Venice*:

> So are those crisped snaky *golden locks*
> Which make such *wanton gambols* with the wind,
> Upon supposed fairness . . . (III, 92-94)

Here Bassanio is expatiating upon the artificial beauties among which he includes wigs worn by women. Even though the theme is outer appearance, the vision of a young woman's hair releases a stream of images which had already embodied a similar vision in the unpublished poem written much earlier. Five images cluster together starting from the same source. They are "gold locks" ("tresses"), "wanton," "gambol" ("sport") and "fair." One passage expresses admiration and the other is explicitly sarcastic, but the visions are the same. The collocations are also the same, though in one or two cases synonyms are used.

There are quite a few examples to be noted so far as collocations are concerned. Recording his admiration of the woman's beauty, the lover in the manuscript poem says:

> Next her head, *forehead* fair
> Fresh and high next doth lie,
> Without a wrinkle. (Stanza 6, ll. 1-3)

We note here the association of forehead with the adjective "high." This must be contrasted with the phrase "forehead fair" where the need for alliteration might have led the writer to the frequently used adjective "fair." What we see here is a visual observation. In *Romeo and Juliet*, a play written during the years which saw the composition of the unpublished poem and the long poems, we have the following image.

> I conjure thee by Rosaline's bright eyes,
> By her *high forehead* and scarlet lip,
> By her fine foot, straight leg and quivering thigh (II.i.17-19)

This is a part of the speech of Mercutio who is looking for Romeo, Mercutio can speak an obscene language, but in spite of it, the association of forehead with the qualifier, "high" persists. Mercutio who is explicitly describing female anatomy has in his description room for a non-erotic zone like forehead and employs the same adjective "high" to describe it.

Another collocation leads us from the manuscript lyric to the same romantic tragedy. The description of beauty in the lyric includes the following image.

> Her fair brows under those
> *Star-like eyes* win love's prize
> When they *twinkle*. (Stanza 6, ll. 4-6)

I am not referring to the adjective "fair," which Shakespeare employs number of times not only in the unpublished poem but also in the other poems and plays. But its association with other images which are common to the manuscript poem and *Romeo and Juliet* is important enough to be noted here. In the romantic tragedy, we read the following description in Romeo's tribute to Juliet's beauty.

> Two of the fairest stars in all heaven,

Having some business, do entreat her eyes
To *twinkle* in their spheres till they return. (II.ii.15-17)

The contexts are the same: the young man is admiring the beauty of his love. When the minds are the same and what is to be described is the same—here, the eyes of the young woman—the same images return one after another, since at the first vision, these images had embedded themselves in the mind of the poet with great clarity. Here it is not only the stars and their twinkle, but the adjective "fair" also which returns, though in one image it is the brows that are qualified and in another case, it is the stars.

We must now turn our attention to imagery which is a part of the cumulative force of our argument that the poem could have been written by William Shakespeare. Sometimes, variations of the same image may be resorted to by the poet to suit his needs like rhymes, rhythm, alliteration and the particular situation. In the manuscript poem we have the youth saying

In her cheeks who seeks
Shall find there *displayed beauty's banner*; (Stanza 6, ll. 7-8)

In the poem *Rape of Lucrece*, two of these three words return to create an image, the image of displayed banner. The cheeks that are at the top of a person's figure remind the poet of the banner that always flies at the top of the pole and it becomes beauty's banner. The beauty of the cheeks is evidently conspicuous like a banner. But in *Lucrece*, it is the image of only displayed banner with no mention of beauty. In this longer poem, Torquin, the Roman prince, advances towards the defenceless Lucrece, and he debates the point whether to proceed or not. The image of displayed banner is used ingeniously. Once the banner is displayed by the captain, the soldier has no alternative but to fight,

Affection is my captain and he leadeth;
And when his gaudy *banner* is *displayed*;
The coward fights and will not be dismay'd, (ll. 271-73)

The interesting point here is that "display" and "banner" go together again after the author wrote the unpublished poem. When the bard of Avon wrote *Romeo and Juliet*, the association of cheeks with beauty's banner takes place again. A little before the tragic conclusion of the lives of Romeo and his love, the young man looks at Juliet's cheeks and exclaims:

> . . . *beauty*'s *ensign* yet
> Crimson in thy lips and in thy *cheeks*. (V.iii.94-95)

In the play, the word "ensign" replaces the word "banner" of the manuscript poem, but the two words mean the same thing. The images of "beauty," "cheeks" and "banner"/"ensign" cluster together again in a context similar to that in the unpublished poem.

Let us now study the stylistic features of the manuscript poem and try to find out whether the poet repeats them. The young author of the manuscript poem speaks of the lovers' arms twining.

> Being set, lips met
> *Arms twined*, and did bind my heart's treasure.
> (Stanza 4, ll. 9-10)

In *Venus and Adonis*, the lovers have their meeting, but while Venus is passionate, Adonis is unwilling. In the unpublished lyric, the youth is passionate, but we do not know the response of the young woman. Just as the youth liked to draw her into his arms, Venus in the longer poem has drawn Adonis into her arms. The similarity of the situations is quite significant.

> Her words are done, her woes the more increasing;
> The time is spent, her object will away,
> And from *arms twined* doth urge releasing; (ll. 254-56)

The same two words are found together in comparable context: in the first case, they constitute a clause and in the second a noun phrase. But the two words are used in exactly the same order and the image is the same also.

Now we must pay attention to some single words. The word "proceeding" appears to be the most important of all these single words. The word sounds so formal, but the poet uses it in more than one poem in the sense of lover's advance. In both the manuscript poem and *Venus and Adonis*, one of the two parties makes an advance towards his or her goal; in both the cases, the poet denotes it with the word "proceed." The unpublished poem is a monologue and the youth asks the question:

> Shall I sue, and not rue
> My *proceeding*? (Stanza 1, ll. 5-6)

In *Venus and Adonis*, it is the male god who is reluctant and the goddess has to teach him the approach. Showing him his own horse which is trying to mate with a mare, the persuasive and impatient Venus says to Adonis:

> Let me excuse thy courser, gentle boy;
> And learn of him, I heartily beseech thee,
> To take advantage on present joy;
> Though I were dumb, yet his *proceedings* teach thee.
> (ll. 403-6)

Venus hopes that the proceedings of the stallion will teach Adonis the approach to fair sex! What is important, however, is that the poet uses the same word to denote the male's advance. Shakespeare is known for using the images and jargon of diverse professions including those considered to be humdrum and dry as dust. "Proceeding" is one such example.

We should not fail to see the significance of the re-occurrence of key phrases and clusters of key words since it is the sign that they have proceeded from the same mind when a certain theme is handled on more than one occasion. The girl in the unpublished lyric is beauty's queen (Stanza 8, l. 10) and so is Cytherea in *The Passionate Pilgrim* (Stanza IV, l. 4) written by Shakespeare. What is equally important, the key words, lover's "bait," "admiration," "of parts," "commendation" and "wonder" of the manuscript poem reappear in the stanzas 4 and 5 of the poem *The Passionate Pilgrim*. In essence, the contexts are similar.

The frequent use of the adjective "fair"—at least four times in the unpublished poem—is matched by numerous instances of its occurrence in the play *The Midsummer Night's Dream*. The realization of tense by the use of the word "do" is another example. In fact, within a span of four lines in stanza 4 of the manuscript poem, the poet avoids the tense morphemes and uses the word "do." For example, when the poet writes the line "In a dream, it did seem" (Stanza 4, l. 1) the reader suspects that the poet does so for the sake of internal rhyme which is found in plenty in this lyric of ninety lines. Words are forced into this rhyming pattern by this device of using "do" to carry the tense while leaving the verb in the uninflected form. Correspondingly, even in the play *The Midsummer Night's Dream* written during the same period, there are numerous examples for the use of "do" as a tense carrier. The most famous example, of course, is the line *The course of true love never did run smooth.* (I.i.134) Some thirty lines earlier, Lysander who speaks the above line says to Demetrius "Do you marry him." It is not a question, though the sentence begins with the word "do." It is an imperative sentence, but again "do" and the uninflected form of the verb are seen here. These numerous examples indicate that the employment of "do" for the sake of tense is not due always to the need to make the words rhyme. It is a stylistic feature.

So far I have pointed out the stylistic features of the manuscript poem shared by the authentic works of Shakespeare. But there are also other stylistic devices that are not typical of this writer. Firstly, the unpublished poem is dominated by internal rhymes. There are nearly forty five internal rhymes including eye rhymes in this short poem of ninety lines. The first stanza alone—it has ten lines like the other stanzas—accounts for eight internal rhymes. This cannot be considered as a great stylistic feature, neither is it a characteristic feature of William Shakespeare.

The second stylistic device we notice is the tendency to end a sentence with a participle at the cost of placing its object first. For example, the third line of the first stanza ends with a participle taking precedence over its object.

> Shall I die? Shall I fly
> Lovers' baits and deceits
> *Sorrow breeding*?

Similarly, the sixth line of the second stanza places the object first and the participle next.

> If she smiles, she exiles
> All my moan; if she frown
> All my *hopes deceiving*—

This device has nothing to do with the compulsion of rhyme. Thirdly, I am not able to make out the meaning of the second part of the last line of the third stanza. It is not clear, because the group of words beginning with the word "wronging" gives the impression that they constitute a phrase, a participial phrase, but in reality they constitute a sentence, because it has a finite verb. If wronging is a participle, where is the noun/subject which can be related to it? In other words, who is wronging whom? What is the antecedent of the pronoun "whom"? The presence of the finite verb "doth" justifies our considering the structure "wronging doth her duty" as a sentence. Then why does it begin after a comma, as though it is a participial phrase? Who is "him" again?

Finally, a word or two about the unique phrase, "beauty's inflection" in the last line of stanza five. I do not find the word "inflection" in any other work of William Shakespeare. Many collocations, grammatical features and clusters of images found in the manuscript poem can be found again in one or the other authentic works of Shakespeare, but not this remarkable phrase. The Oxford English Dictionary (Volume 5, pp. 268-69) traces the word "inflection" to the year 1537 in the works of Sir Thomas Elyot, a great humanist and prose writer who lived between 1490 and 1546. The word is used by him in the literal sense of bending. Its earliest figurative use is traced by the OED to the works of Richard Hooker (1554-1600) published in 1597. Richard Hooker was a theologian and prose writer and both he and Elyot were contemporaries of the bard of Avon. But the OED does not trace the word to Shakespeare whose richness of vocabulary had no parallel during his age. Evidently, the OED had not considered at the time of its publication the manuscript poem lying neglected in the library of Oxford University library, now the focus of the attention of the Shakespearean scholars.

Shakespearean scholars can never be dogmatic in their assertion that the unpublished poem was or was not authored by the sweet swan of Avon. But it is certainly amateurish and adolescent in its style and substance and it does not contain a single memorable line, while even *Venus and Adonis* and the sonnets do.